The Taming of Eagles

Imogen Edwards-Jones

The Taming of Eagles

····························

Exploring the New Russia

····························

Photographs by Joth Shakerley

WEIDENFELD & NICOLSON
London

First published in 1993 by
Weidenfeld & Nicolson
Orion House
5 Upper St Martin's Lane
London WC2H 9EA

Map by Swanston Graphics Limited

A CIP catalogue record for this book is available from
the British Library

ISBN 0 297 83206 9

Photoset in Great Britain by Selwood Systems, Midsomer Norton, Avon
Printed and bound in Great Britain by Butler & Tanner Ltd, Frome, Somerset

To Gabriel

Contents

. . . .

Contents

Acknowledgements

With special thanks to: Kolya, Peter, Anka, Leo, Milana, Katya, Alice, Atalanta, Marcus, Leonie, Toby, Verity, Ivo, Ruth, Ivor, Jo, everyone we stayed with on our journey, or who helped us in any way and, of course, Stewart Steven, who put us up to the whole idea.

I.E.-J.

With special thanks to: Ken Ashby of Safelight Zone for his printing skills and guidance, and also to Nick, my brother.

J.S.

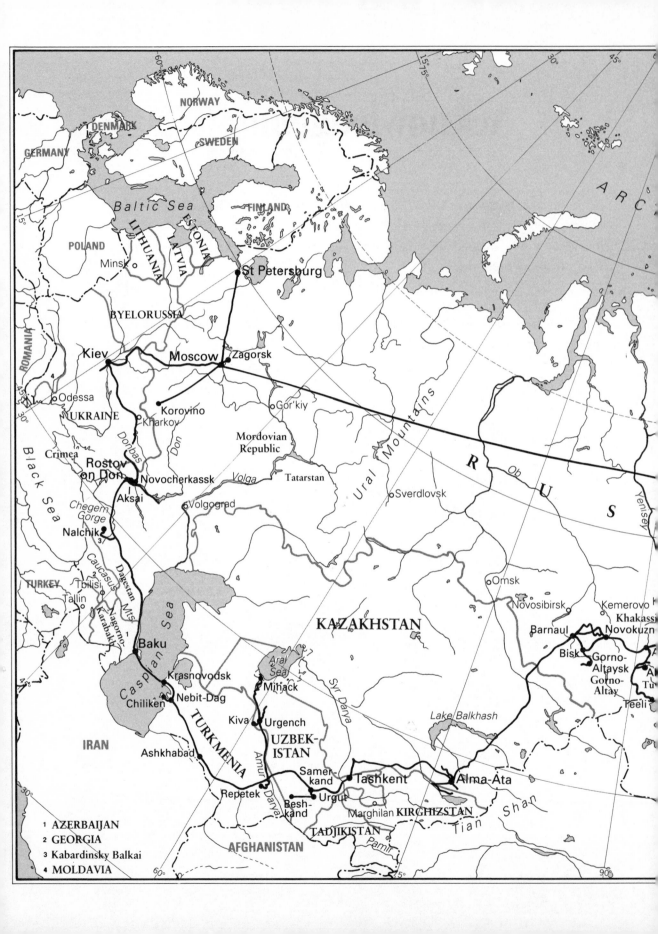

NORWAY

DENMARK

GERMANY

Baltic Sea

SWEDEN

FINLAND

POLAND

LITHUANIA

ESTONIA

LATVIA

Minsk

St Petersburg

BYELORUSSIA

ROMANIA

Kiev

Moscow

Zagorsk

Odessa

UKRAINE

Kharkov

Korovino

Gor'kiy

Don

Mordovian
Republic

R U S

Ural Mountains

Ob

Yenisey

Crimea

Donbas

Rostov
on Don

Novocherkassk

Volga

Tatarstan

Sverdlovsk

Black Sea

*Chegem
Gorge*

Aksai

Volgograd

Nalchik

Omsk

TURKEY

Tbilisi

Tallin

Caucasus Mts

Dagestan Mts

*Nagorno-
Karabakh*

Caspian Sea

Baku

KAZAKHSTAN

Novosibirsk

Kemerovo

Khakassi

Barnaul

Novokuzn

Bisk

Gorno-
Altaysk

Gorno-
Altay

A
Tu

Teeli

Krasnovodsk

Nebit-Dag

Chiliken

*Aral
Sea*

Mihack

Syr Darya

Kiva

Urgench

Lake Balkhash

IRAN

TURKMENIA

Ashkhabad

UZBEK-
ISTAN

Amu Darya

Repetek

Samer-
kand

Urgut

Tashkent

Alma-Ata

Besh-
kand

Marghilan

KIRGHIZSTAN

Tian Shan

TADJIKISTAN

Pamir

AFGHANISTAN

1 AZERBAIJAN
2 GEORGIA
3 Kabardinsky Balkai
4 MOLDAVIA

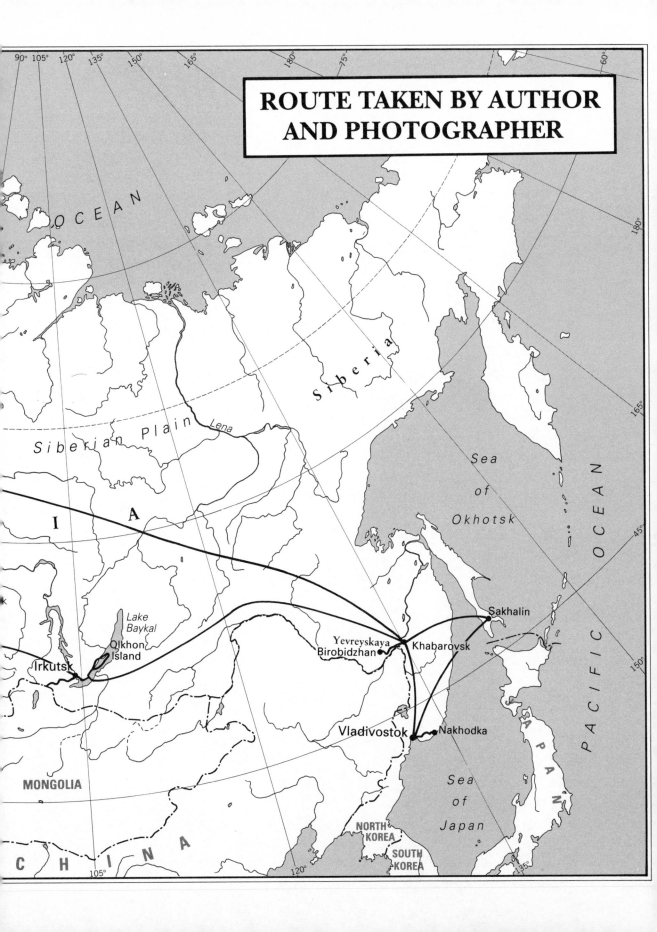

Prologue
. . . .

Where would your good be if there were no evil
and what would the world look like without shadow?

The Master and Margarita, Mikhail Bulgakov

When Stewart Steven, then Editor of the *Mail on Sunday*, commissioned me to write this book, he asked me to 'travel within the borders of the old Soviet Union' and witness the end of an empire and the collapse of a political ideology through the eyes of its people. From its furthermost edges, the former Union stretches 13,000 kilometres west to east and 5,000 kilometres north to south; it spans a longitude of 170°, or nearly half the planet. Starting in the last hours of 1991, I had 100 days to travel as far as I could. I had less than ten days in which to prepare for the journey and, apart from friends in Kiev, where I had studied at the university, I had only one Moscow telephone number.

I arrived with little idea of what to expect, although I suspected there to be some truth to the general descriptions banded about in the West and was prepared to find a way of life built around food shortages and long queues, interminable bureaucracy and drinking bouts. But nothing prepared me for people's generosity: I never anticipated being so warmly welcomed into the homes and lives, or being allowed to share the candid thoughts and hopes, of people who had learnt not to trust anyone. Perhaps being foreign helped, for foreigners are still a rarity and, coming from a country about which people knew little, there was a mutual fascination.

The result is a glimpse into the lives of people who have lived through war, famine and purges; who very often have virtually nothing and yet are prepared to give everything. There were occasions when I knew that, on leaving the flats and houses of people I had just met, I had exhausted carefully stored supplies and had drunk the last, dusty bottle of vodka.

I do not profess to have fathomed this vast empire and its people. I have simply described what I saw and heard as I travelled through. I have tried to let people, whom we would not normally hear, have their say.

I have not used the surnames of most of those whose stories are told here because of the continuing political uncertainty – many of them had no idea what would happen to them the next day, let alone in three years' time. Some of those to whom I talked were frightened to speak; others were desperate to give their opinions, saying that the only advantage of *perestroika* was that they could now voice what they felt.

During the 100-day journey across the Caucasus, through the Southern States, across Siberia and on to the Pacific, one line was repeated over and over. People would clasp my hands in theirs and, looking into my eyes, would say: 'Write the truth, write the truth. That's all we ask.' It never occurred to me that I should lie, but then, it never occurred to them that I would not.

Russia

· · · · · · · · · · ·

DAY 2: New Year's Eve

Running through the snow, we headed for Red Square. It was a quarter to midnight and almost 1992. The hammer and sickle had already come down over the golden, illuminated domes of the Kremlin. The Soviet Union was no more. Thousands of people were trying to barge their way to Lenin's mausoleum at the front of the square; thousands more just stood in long coats and fur hats, champagne bottles in hand. There was madness in the air.

Suddenly the Kremlin bells announced the New Year, the crowd let off a deafening cheer and plastic champagne corks flew into the sky. I stood alone, staring up at the new red, white and blue flag that fluttered above the Kremlin, a fine mist of champagne spray covering my face. All around, people were laughing and grabbing hold of one other. Yet their exuberance and ostentatious happiness had a certain urgency and while mouths smiled, eyes remained cold. Most of the crowd was already drunk. Lacking all coordination, they threw themselves at one another wildly, shouting 'Happy New Year' as they grabbed each other around the neck.

The first fireworks ever seen at New Year in Red Square launched into the sky. Everyone looked up, their mouths hanging open, their eyes fixed. Then, as circles of light exploded over the Kremlin, everyone cheered once more. I began to cry, seeing nothing but grey faces with red rimmed eyes, a false and desperate happiness. A man next to me started to chant. 'Yeltsin! Yeltsin! Long live Yeltsin and the new Russia,' he yelled, punching the air with his fist. His call was not taken up by the crowd. He tried again and a few people joined in, but soon lost interest.

As the last embers of the fireworks died in the sky, the crowds began to disperse. Groups of soldiers hugged groups of soldiers in an expansive display of camaraderie. An old man with icicles hanging off his beard, his eyes glazed with drink, stood in the middle of the square, leaning on an old musket with an apple stuffed on the end. Through an intoxicated smile he mumbled 'Happy New Year', over and over, to anyone who would listen. A group of Cossacks, their red trousers hanging over their boots, strode through the crowd, their arms around each other's shoulders. They shouted out their joy.

Two boys grabbed hold of me and, singing Paul McCartney songs, danced me round in a circle before running off, giggling, into the crowd. Dima from the Ukraine gave me a slug of pink and white champagne and a sloppy kiss on the lips. A Latvian chatted up a couple of girls, asking them to come back with him to his country. Then a group of hardliners marched through the centre of the festivities. Waving their red flags, they called for the restoration of the Soviet Union. The crowd made way, but ignored their protest.

Soon, only the rowdy minority were left. They began to throw bottles, tossing them over their shoulders and whooping with laughter as the glass smashed on the ground. A man ran towards me, blood pouring down his face and leaving a trail in the snow. Swaying and stumbling on the broken glass, he cut himself over and over again before he finally collapsed. No one came to help him.

DAY 3: New Year's Day

We had been in Moscow two days and already our plans had fallen apart. We were to have been met at the airport and taken somewhere to stay, but no one met us, nor were we given accommodation. Instead, we ended up spending our first night in the extortionately expensive Intourist hotel and wandering the cold, dark streets of Moscow in search of food. I had one telephone number, of an English friend, Leo, who worked in Moscow exporting honey. I knew he was back in England, but rang anyway. Milana answered and immediately asked us to come and stay.

She seemed in a terrible hurry when she arrived to collect us from the hotel lobby, but I soon came to realize that this was her normal state. Uttering a tirade of obscenities, she drove us through the centre of Moscow and dropped us at Leo's flat. Throwing us the keys and telling us the entry code, she left us standing in the snow, surrounded by our bags. We had no idea where we were but, dumping our things in the flat, we set out once more to look for food.

Drawing a map of our route as we went, we searched for the nearest shop. The first one we found was full of nothing but old women in white overalls, chatting – the shelves were empty except for large glass jars of apple juice with a thick layer of sediment at the bottom. Moving on, and still marking our route, we came across a small shop on a corner. Commercial rather than state-run, it was covered in flashing lights and a sound system blared out 'Money, Money, Money' by Abba. Through the greasy windows I could see produce that we had heard was un-obtainable – red caviar, tinned prawns and sausage. A crowd of Russians had gathered round, their faces pressed against the glass. They could not afford to buy; they were merely staring at those who could. We bought an odd selection of prawns and sausage, but once back at the flat, discovered that there was nothing to eat them with. We sat with the tins on our knees, shovelling the food back in silence.

Milana returned, still in a frantic rush. A television producer for World Television News, she had gone straight into journalism from school, starting work on an in-house, monthly factory paper. With only the editor to help her, she reported the latest company news for the 7,000 readers. 'Can you imagine?' she laughed. 'We had to fill the paper without using any names, ages, dates or any place names. I mean, what could we say? The editor and I would laugh and say, "How are we going to fill this thing?" '

'This country's crazy. I'd rather not think about it. The only time I should think about it is when I'm alone, but when I'm alone, I'm so tired I can't be bothered. Everyone has their theories but no one knows what will happen. How much more can our people take? They've taken so much. No other people would have taken so much. I'm just sitting here waiting for them to crack. All they need is a powerful leader who can round up all this unhappiness and then there'll be blood on the streets of Moscow, just as in Tbilisi. Some labour party or something – something that the workers will believe in.'

DAY 4

Russia became a capitalist country and the prices rose tenfold. In driving snow and a wind that cut through to the bone, we wandered through the streets of Moscow. An old woman stood at a road junction, clearing the tram lines. Stooping over a small tin of salt at her side she flicked the snow out with a stick and filled the crevice with salt. Then she shuffled on a few paces and started again.

At a flower market next to a metro station, bright tulips stood tall and snug in glass cases while their sellers, shoulders hunched against the cold, blew on their hands. Amongst the flowers were low tables, each with a three-pack pyramid of rough Russian cigarettes. There was no attempt at hard sell. If you needed them, then you would buy; no one was going to entice you with any banter.

We found the Irish House, an Irish/Russian joint venture where anything from cheese-and-onion crisps to nappies can be bought for dollars. Next door was a state-run supermarket, which had food for the first time in three months. Industrial-sized blocks of bland cheese, chickens, eggs and some meat packed the shelves. Around 500 people were queueing for cheese. Having ordered huge hunks, they re-queued at another counter to pay, and queued again to collect their purchase, showing their receipt. They had come prepared with books and newspapers and would spend all morning waiting for cheese before moving on to queue for something else in the afternoon. Beer, which was being sold at the next counter, could only be bought if you had your own empty bottles. An old man with a plastic bag of empties soon found a queue had gathered round him. He could not believe his luck.

An old woman in a flowered head scarf and with holes in her ginger tights wandered around the shop. I followed her as she shuffled up to the egg counter. Yesterday they had cost 90 kopecks; today they were 12 roubles. '12 roubles,' she muttered to herself in disbelief. '12 roubles! Who can afford that?' She walked up to every counter, checked the prices and walked away again, shaking her head. No one queued at the tinned-fish counter: it was too expensive.

Leaving the supermarket, we came across what looked like a petrol tanker. A crowd was slowly gathering around the siphon, holding their empty jam jar or milk bottle, waiting to be served with a thick, dark brown wine from Azerbaijan. Excited, they all jumped around, shouting 'Happy New Year' between heavy swigs. One man to my left rushed up and tried to sell me a Bible. 'Now is the time to believe in God,' he said, looking over his shoulder at the vat of wine. 'You must buy a Bible immediately.' I smiled. 'It's amazing how useful God can be,' I said. 'Shut up,' he replied. 'Someone has to buy it, I'm desperate for a drink.'

In another state-run shop, the queue stretched right out into the street. There was sugar here, and people were leaving with carrier bags of it under their arms.

With Milana's help, we went with a WTN film crew to a higher education military academy on the outskirts of Moscow. In the courtyard surrounded by huge, red-brick buildings, children were sliding around in the snow on home-made skis. Inside, at the top of a dark stairwell, was a long and equally dark corridor. Sixteen families lived here. Four or five people to a room, they slept stacked up on bunk beds. There was one bathroom and one kitchen.

This was the accommodation given to soldiers while they trained to become officers. Aged between twenty-five and thirty, most of them had young families, whom they had to support on 600 roubles, or $6, a month. Their wages had not increased with the price rises. 'We shall have to wait and hope that the government will give us some money. No one knows what will happen. All we can do is wait and hope,' said a young soldier as he waited for the kettle to boil on the greasy stove.

Leaning against the corridor wall was a white-haired man. Nicholai was fifty-four and had come from the country to stay with his daughter for Christmas. He was sleeping on the floor in the family's room as all the bunks were full. A woman stood in the doorway of her room, clutching a child to her hip. 'There's nothing to buy,' she said as she wiped the child's nose. 'We have no money. I don't know how we'll survive the winter. We have no future.'

The corridor stank of urine. As we walked along, many people slammed the doors in our faces. Small children ran around in dark woolly tights; they had neither shoes nor trousers. As soon as one of the camera men turned on a light to film, the children ran towards it, squinting and bathing in its strength. 'What a beautiful big light,' said one little boy, standing on tiptoe, his hand raised towards the camera.

That evening we met Viola. As a tour guide, she had travelled all over the country and was going to help us plan our route. But, while we sat eating hard-boiled eggs, she became bored of travel and wanted to talk about the present situation. 'Life will get very hard now,' she said as she peeled an egg. 'People have been buying stocks of food, ready for the price rises. Those who have fridges have large supplies, which will run out about the end of January. Then who knows what will happen. It's the old who will have the hardest time. They've lived through the purges, the Second World War, the Cold War and now they have this. *Perestroika* is for the young, who can understand business and are resilient. The old don't know what's happening. Even for me, it's hard,' she said. 'We have to queue for everything. I forgot our Christmas tree, so went to look for one in the market. But they were all so small and expensive that I fetched some branches from the forest instead. No one can even buy flowers any more. Before, you'd buy them even if you weren't going to visit someone; now they're too expensive.' She said that everything was rationed all over the country, except in Moscow, where it was only wine, tobacco and sugar. 'The most essential things,' she said with a smile.

DAY 5

We went with a different WTN crew to a cardiac hospital in Moscow. Alexei, one of the young producers, was nervous. 'I hate hospitals,' he said. 'You leave more ill than when you went in. My wife is about to have a baby and I'm not letting her go anywhere near a hospital. They use dirty needles, old equipment and no drugs, and you're only looked after properly if you bribe people.'

The hospital was a warren of bleak corridors. Three men sat in their slippers on broken, plastic chairs, watching a black-and-white television and arguing over the channels. Wrapped in blankets and scarves to protect them from the cold, other patients shuffled by. The head sister would not let us go into any of the rooms until she had made the beds and instead we were shown an operating theatre, where a selection of used needles sat in a bowl of water next to a rusty basin with a dripping tap. 'Come and see our computer,' said the head doctor, leading us into his office. He proudly sat at his desk, posing for the cameras, and then asked his assistant to show him how to turn the machine on. 'We have just got it, you see,' he said, embarrassed. 'It does accounts and everything.'

He admitted that the hospital was having difficulty feeding the patients. 'We don't know what will happen. Maybe the government will help us, but we won't be able to feed the patients soon. There just simply isn't the money or the food.'

Joth and I left the film crew to the authorities and sneaked into a room where three old women were in bed. Yekaterina was sixty-seven but looked older. She had worked in the same factory for forty-one years. Recovering from a heart attack, she sat perky and upright and, through chuckles that revealed a row of gold teeth, explained that she was leaving the hospital in three days. She talked of her lovely son, who came to visit her every day. 'He brings me food so I don't have to eat what they prepare in those disgusting kitchens at the end of the corridor.'

Next to her was Ana, who was sixty-eight and had heart murmurs. Lying in bed, covered in blankets, she took her hat off and fluffed up her hair to talk to us. 'It's all the hard work I've done lifting boxes in the factory that has made me ill,' she said. She had been in hospital for three days and every morning her husband came to change her sheets and bring her food. That morning he had brought a small pile of sausage which lay, wrapped in tissue, on the table next to her bed.

Back on the streets of Moscow, it was slightly warmer and a thin layer of snow had melted. The shops were packed with people, who had come to stare at the new prices and see what was on offer. More traders were selling at the flower market when we walked to the metro and one man even shouted at me to come and buy his tulips. It was the first spark of sales initiative I had witnessed.

DAY 6

The central market, in the heart of Moscow, is run by Azerbaijanis, who impose stiff charges on anyone else who wants to sell there. We walked in to find the stalls laden, but there were no customers. Fruit from all over the old Soviet Union had found its way there and row upon row of stalls were overflowing with grapes, pomegranates and oranges. But no one could afford 65 roubles for a bag of mandarins.

In the covered meat market, we were overwhelmed by the smell of sweet flesh. Small, fat piglets lay outstretched on wooden blocks, their coats covered in muslin. One large, jolly man laughed at my surprise and explained how to cook them. 'Gut them, fill them with apples and shove them in the oven,' he chuckled. But, at 3,000 roubles each, there were few takers. Two days before, I could have picked up the same for 500 roubles. Calves' heads, their ears already cut off and sold, looked at me; large, maroon slabs of liver, priced at 20 roubles a kilo, expanded on the wood. The stall holders stood around smoking, ash falling at random, their meat cleavers embedded in large, round tree trunks. Trotters, whole geese, lambs' heads and a range of internal organs all lay gently sweating, waiting to be sold. One woman tried to interest me in a skinned calf's head. Stuffing her finger into its loose mouth, she laughed when I balked.

A tiny woman, her head bound up in a scarf and carrying a walking stick, poked me in the ribs and cackled, 'My life is terrible. I'm on a pension, I have five children at home to feed and now everything is so expensive I've no idea what I'm going to do. I tried to buy some apples today, but couldn't – they were 5 roubles each. 5 roubles each! Can you believe that?'

Returning to the flat on Moscow's immaculate metro, with its chandeliers, its mosaic-covered hallways and trains that run every thirty seconds, we came to a group of men selling pornographic magazines at 17 roubles for two. Every photograph was amateur and out of focus. Beside them was a young man in round glasses selling Pamyat (meaning 'Memory'), a magazine distributed by a nationalist, anti-Semitic group of the same name. Surrounded by posters written in Old Church Slavonic, he was selling year-old copies of the magazine for 3 roubles. The most recent issue was six months old but, since he had no more than a handful of copies, he would only sell them to committed members of the group.

That evening Kolya and Anka came round to see Milana, along with Ygor and Vladimir. We sat drinking vodka and talking. Like Milana, Kolya worked for WTN. He had long, blond hair and bright blue eyes, spoke immaculate English and had spent time in London. Anka, his girlfriend, had thick, black hair and creamy skin. She was shy, and sat with legs scrunched up on the sofa. Ygor was wickedly funny and had a mania for learning obscure English words from the dictionary. Vladimir was gentle and quiet, with a twitch and a stutter. He played classical guitar and was currently studying in Germany. They all took great pleasure in watching us force down shot after shot of vodka, laughing as our eyes watered and our bodies shook with each slug.

DAY 7

It was 2 p.m. and Natasha had just woken up. She was dressed all in black, wore no make-up and had long, thick, blonde hair that fell in curls around her face.

Fiddling with a Marlboro packet, she refused to catch my eye while she spoke.

We had met through Ygor – Natasha and he had grown up together on the outskirts of Moscow, but had since gone their separate ways. Ygor had some sort of business he would never talk about, Natasha became a prostitute. She works in Red Square and the Intourist and Metropol hotels in the centre of Moscow, sleeping with foreign businessmen for hard currency. Her black Levis and warm, woollen jumper reflect her wealth; her boots could never have been bought for roubles.

Natasha's voice was gentle and she had a fragility about her that made me want to squeeze her hand. She had spent a year in Byrtirka, a juvenile prison in Moscow, before being moved to a hard-labour camp for a further twelve months. With a girlfriend, she had stolen and then sold another friend's clothes because the friend had stolen from her the week before. The whole thing had just been a prank, but Natasha and her girlfriend had been caught selling the stolen clothes.

'I was put into a cell with three other girls,' said Natasha as she lit her fourth cigarette in about as many minutes. 'Of course, I went through the "initiation ceremony".' One of the girls in the cell went for her and when Natasha pushed her away, 'She fell and split her head open on the sink. There was blood everywhere. I immediately covered my face because I thought, if she's going to attack me, I want to save my face. Instead, the girl came over and said, "You'll do all right here."'

Few of the girls in the prison were criminals by nature. 'There were so many really tragic cases,' said Natasha. She shared a cell with a girl who, at fourteen, had been thrown out of the house by a new stepfather. 'She lived on the streets for a bit. Then, one evening, she returned home to steal some food because she was hungry. She took two cans of fish and got two years for breaking and entering.'

The other girl in her cell had been raped by her stepfather. One night he returned home and tried to rape her again. She tied him to a chair in the kitchen, tortured him and eventually cut his throat. 'She went to the police, but they didn't believe her. They told her to stop wasting their time with childish inventions,' explained Natasha. 'It wasn't until her mother came home that she was finally caught. She's doing ten years for first-degree murder.'

Natasha spent her time singing in her cell and once a day, for an hour, she would walk around the enclosed quad at the top of the prison. 'I didn't go outside for a year. The worst thing was the boredom.' It was impossible to knock messages through the cell walls, so to talk to the other girls, Natasha would shout through the hole in the cell door that the wardens used for delivering food. But, 'I had no one I could really talk to. My girlfriend and I were kept apart and the only way we could meet was if we could get into the hospital.'

There were various tried and tested methods. 'One was to swallow a piece of fat on a string wrapped round a back tooth. The fat sticks in your throat and your whole face swells and goes yellow. They think you're seriously ill and take you to the hospital. If you pull the fat out, the swelling goes down.' Natasha gave a cunning giggle and reached for another cigarette.

'But,' she went on, 'there were those who didn't get it right. There was one in the next-door cell to me. She swallowed ground glass.'

'Ground glass?' I asked, my toes curling.

'You cough up blood and they think you have TB. The only problem was she swallowed too much and died of internal bleeding.' Natasha flicked her ash determinedly, as if to dispel another thought.

Teenagers in the prison were treated slightly differently from the adults. 'Our food was better,' said Natasha, dismissively. 'We had five sugar cubes a day, one piece of bread and a small cube of butter.' Once a month, parents were allowed to send a food parcel weighing not more than five kilos. 'But my parcel was nearly always taken from me as punishment.'

As further punishment, Natasha also spent time in solitary confinement. 'My main crimes were arguing with the wardens and singing after lock-up.' Gazing into the middle distance and curling her hair round her fingers, her voice was expressionless as she spoke. She described a small, bare room in which it was impossible either to stand up or lie down. The ceiling was low and domed, there was no heating and water overflowed from the open drain in the corner and lapped around her ankles. Since she could not sit on the floor, she would spend the day squatting against the rough cell wall. A small bench, which was kept folded away between 6 a.m. and 10 p.m., served as her bed. She had nothing to wear apart from a short, cotton dress and her boots. For food, she was given a small hunk of black bread and some weak soup. Dividing the bread in two, she would chew one lump to make it sticky and then use it to stop the wind blowing through the broken window. The second lump she gave to the rats so that they would leave her alone.

'That was where I used to hang out for ten to fifteen days at a time,' she said, turning and staring into my eyes. Her face was pale: her skin a toneless yellow, her eyebrows and lashes transparent, her eyes a watery grey.

Suddenly she changed position. Jerking back into the kitchen chair and taking a long drag on her cigarette, she exhaled and stared at the ceiling. 'The worst time was when one of the wardens dragged me out of the cell and raped me because I was singing "Happy Birthday" at eleven at night. Lock-up is at ten, so I was an hour too late, you see.' She spoke in such a matter-of-fact way that I thought perhaps I had misunderstood her. I had not.

The warden had come to tell Natasha and her cell mates to be quiet. When he came into the cell, they all pretended to be asleep, but he dragged Natasha out of bed by her hair and, tearing out clumps as he went, pulled her along the corridor and kicked her down stairs. In spite of her age he handcuffed her (Soviet law forbids juveniles to be handcuffed), clubbed her with a rubber truncheon, caught her by the throat and then raped her.

'I screamed for a doctor. I wanted them to see my injuries so that he would get into trouble.' But when the doctor saw her, he said that her dramatic hair loss was due to a nervous disorder and gave her a rabies injection. She was taken to a small boxroom a metre square. 'I could hardly breathe. I spent the night curled up, crying and was eventually let out at six in the morning.'

Natasha was only supposed to spend three months in the prison in Moscow, but ended up staying twelve. 'I became the big boss – the girls would stick up for me,' she said with a grin.

On her eighteenth birthday, they came to take her mattress away (juveniles are supplied with mattresses, but adult prisoners are not). She pretended that she was only seventeen. 'I said that I was born in 1973 and told them to look at the records, which I knew they would be too lazy to do. The warden said: "If you're lying I'll stick you back in solitary." My cell mates backed me up,' she said, adding triumphantly: 'I never lost my mattress.'

After twelve months, she was sent to a camp in the Mordovian Republic, eight hours from Moscow by train. The journey took two days. She was given a loaf of bread, a salted fish and some sugar for the transfer. When she arrived, she was placed in a temporary prison and sat on wooden planks for five days.

She still has many friends from the hard-labour camp. Working nine hours a day at a conveyor belt, they sewed prison uniforms and made special army hats. 'At first I couldn't sew, nor did I want to try. I just sat and cried. But eventually I got so good that I would finish my quota in the first four hours of the day.'

If her work was not good enough, she was fined. 'I ended up sponsoring the Red Army,' she laughed. 'I was fined so much that, when I left, I was paid 18 roubles and 63 kopecks for a year's work.

'The camp wasn't as bad as all that. We looked after each other. It was us against them, which made it more bearable.' Natasha left the camp in June 1991.

'What do you do now?' I asked, already knowing the answer.

'I type in the evenings,' she replied.

Ygor, who had been listening to the whole of our conversation, started to laugh. 'She knows what you do Natasha, so why don't you just talk about it?'

Natasha, relieved that she did not have to pretend any more, began to describe what men from various nations were like to sleep with. 'Businessmen from Germany and Italy are the best because they pay immediately and leave soon afterwards. Englishmen are rare but quite sweet; Americans are greedy. The French are very highbrow and start talking philosophy. They think you're privileged to be sleeping with them, and then they haggle over the price.'

'You must know lots of different languages,' I suggested naïvely. Natasha looked stunned. 'What on earth do I have to say to them? All I know is how to count!'

Natasha charges between $100–150 each time. She pays $10 to the doorman to let her into the hotel, which is exclusively for foreigners, and another $50 to the police so that her passport, without which she cannot move, is not confiscated. 'The rest is profit,' she said.

The reasons why girls take to prostitution is the same in Moscow as it is all over the former Union: no other profession is so lucrative. In a recent survey in *Moscow News*, sixty per cent of girls considered it the best career option.

'There are girls from all over the old Soviet Union who all want money, the nice clothes that you can only buy for hard currency, and an easy life. No one else can pay them what they can earn in one night,' said Natasha, adding, 'But you've got to be intelligent and know how to live off your connections in this town to survive.'

'I became a prostitute when I left prison because I never wanted to be poor again in my life. I never wanted to be ordered around again; I wanted to be free.

I wanted to compensate for the time I'd lost inside. I don't want to work any more – I've done enough of that already. And I don't ever want to have to depend on anyone. I've learnt that life's too short to be scrabbling around for roubles in the dust like my mother and her mother, who'd married, had children and were old before they'd opened their eyes. I lie there, close my eyes and think of something else – I pretend that it's not happening to me. It's all over quite quickly. I get the money and then I can go and live,' Natasha blurted, as if this was all some kind of catharsis. She leant back in her chair and looked at me, waiting for me to judge her.

'And all you did was steal some clothes?' I asked finally.

'And I sold them.'

'Was that all?'

'What more do you want?'

DAY 8: Christmas Eve

'So many people get killed on this road that most sane drivers won't use it at night,' said Ygor as we drove down the Moscow ring road. We approached the traffic police checkpoint that blocked the road. Every car in front dutifully slowed down, waiting to be hauled over on some count or other. The police are allowed to fine drivers on the spot – a right that they exercise at every possible opportunity. 'You just bribe them, no matter what you've done,' said Ygor. 'If they catch you drunk, you just pay them off. In fact, you can pay them off for anything, they're so corrupt. Or, if they insist on fining you, all you have to do is say that you haven't got the money. They can't do anything about it because they don't have the computers to trace you.' He chuckled.

It was snowing heavily when we arrived at Zagorsk, or Sergievsky Posad, as it has been renamed. Although it was early afternoon, the light was already beginning to fade as we walked through the archway into the ancient monastery.

Founded in 1340, the monastery grew rich on the wealthy gifts of czars, nobles and merchants all seeking divine support, and it boasts some of the finest icons by the mediaeval painter Andrei Rublyov. A place of both religious and nationalist pilgrimage, it is also a working monastery, with about 100 monks, and houses one of only two seminaries in the whole of Russia. Wandering beneath the spectacular gold and dark blue domes, now covered in a fine layer of snow, we were surrounded by pilgrims who had all made the journey to spend the night praying and breathing incense, celebrating the Russian Orthodox Christmas.

I walked into a candlelit antechamber in the shadow of the golden domes. The small stone room was full of old women gathered around a slowly trickling fountain of holy water. They queued in turn to drink, crossing themselves and muttering rosaries as they either wet their lips or filled small glass bottles. In one corner a hunched, grey-haired woman shoved bread into her mouth with the speed of someone afraid of being robbed. Emptying the contents of her string bag, she turned to me. 'What are you staring at?' she demanded. 'Nothing,' I replied. 'Are you a girl?' she asked. I looked puzzled. 'You'll never get married if you wear trousers,' she said, checking me up and down. I asked her where she was from, to which she replied, 'God knows', and crossed herself. 'Will you spend the whole night here?' I asked. 'God knows', she muttered again, and walked off.

Another woman, buying a candle, had come from Tatarstan and had already spent one night in the church. We began to talk. She had nine children and three cleaning jobs and had left her husband because of his drinking. 'What's everyone complaining about? I've worked all my life and I'm still here to tell the tale. The young are afraid of hard work – all they want is an easy life. They sit and complain. A bit of hard work wouldn't kill them, but they become prostitutes. They sell themselves for hard currency or they become black marketeers. There'll be an apocalypse. God is warning us – He is already making the days shorter as a warning. Look, it's 3 p.m. and it's already dark.' I tried to explain that the darkness was due to Moscow putting the clocks back to have summer and winter time, but she would have none of it. She stood, holding her bag of bread, and shouted, 'Newspapers keep trying to predict the future and they know nothing. God knows. The people must stop trying to predict the future. That's God's work. We must follow what God has said.'

One of the churches opened at five and the crowds poured in. In the semi-darkness the supplicants crawled towards the icon screen. Dragging themselves along the ground, they methodically crossed themselves, waiting for the blessing from the priests. Dressed in long black robes and with long beards, the priests offered the ornate cross for the worshipper to kiss and then made a sign of the cross over them. All the while, a small group of dedicated old women stood in a group in the corner of the church, leading the chanting. Most of them had prayer books, but they rarely looked at them. Along the front of the icon screen a young priest tended the rows of candles that bathed the golden-walled room in a soft, warm light. The candles would have to last until morning. As he walked along, his long robes rustling with each stride, he threw the chalice of incense high into the air. With a rattle of its chain, it swung full circle, releasing the incense in dark, sweet-smelling clouds.

The church next door opened slightly later, but a queue had already gathered outside. Clutching string bags full of bread and bottles of holy water, they were prepared for the long wait. Suddenly, the doors opened and the crowd surged forward, crushing the beggars on low wooden trolleys – wheelchairs are in short supply. We queued again to buy candles and to write names on small pieces of paper for the priest to bless during the service. Old women rushed inside the church, lit by guttering candles, to reserve a place. Spreading out their clothes on the corner seats, they then relaxed, watching while the rest of the church filled up with latecomers, who put down small camping stools. Everyone was prepared for the night.

We returned to Moscow for a concert. Meeting up with Volodya, the classical guitarist, we went into the small auditorium. In the middle of the stage stood a lone guitar player with lank brown hair, wearing ill-fitting, brown, flared trousers and a tight brown jumper. The lights were not dimmed as he began and there was no display of showmanship. He played for an hour and a half, pausing only at the end of each piece to wait for the compere, in a frilly blue shirt and a bow tie, to announce the next item, when he would blow on his finger tips, wipe the sweat on his trousers or handkerchief, and start again. He captivated the audience. A woman with a bad hip lurched out of her seat during the applause, made her way to the front and hugged his knees while he was taking a bow. As I sat on my hard, wooden seat, I wondered if he would have been able to hold the attention of a Western audience, with our short attention spans and our cravings for stimulation.

After the concert we went back to Volodya's flat in Moscow's outer suburbs. It was full of musical instruments: guitars lay everywhere, there were balalaikas on the wall and in one corner stood a piano, with tin trays placed on its strings for a more amusing musical effect. We sat round a table in the sitting room.

There is a Russian saying that the shops are always empty, but the table is full, and in this case it was true. Bottles of home-made wine and vodka lay among the sausage, potatoes and pickled peppers. At one end of the table sat the mother and her two sons, all of whom were classical guitarists; squashed at the other end were Dima, editor of a science journal for the Academy of Sciences, Demitrov, a guitarist from the Ukraine, and Asia and her husband. Asia had recorded an album four years ago with the state-run record company, Melodya, but she was still waiting for it to be released. They had all studied music together at the Moscow Conservatory.

As we ate and drank, guitar after guitar was brought to the table and, amid much laughter and clapping, everyone sang gypsy songs. With exaggerated seriousness, Volodya and Demitrov played duets, contorting their faces and closing their eyes in ecstasy. Then Asia sang, her dark, melancholy eyes fixed on the table.

I talked to Demitrov. He had dark hair and dark skin and joked, saying that he doubted his parentage. 'No Ukrainian can be this dark,' he laughed. He came from Kharkov in the Ukraine, and complained that he had woken up one morning recently to find that all the street names had been changed to Ukrainian. 'I don't even speak the language. It's all a bit much, this independence thing. Soon that's all they'll speak on the streets and I won't be able to understand a word.

'Parents in the West don't help their children, do they?' he suddenly asked. 'Here they'll sweat blood for their children. My family all live in the same block of flats. I have keys to my mother's flat and, when I was a teenager, I'd just walk in, eat all her food and then leave again.'

The party broke up and people drifted into different rooms. In the sitting room, surrounded by the debris from the meal, Volodya's mother played guitar quietly on her own. She had not played during supper but had sat back and listened to her son. Both she and her husband had been classical guitarists. He had been famous when he was alive, but she had given it up once she became pregnant. Now she sat playing a few tunes, but forgot them half-way through. She said that she had made the right decision to give up her career, adding wistfully, 'I'm sad my husband is dead, of course, but I'm so proud of my son.'

DAY 9: Christmas Day

Kolya and Anka had bought their flat from a couple who were emigrating to Israel. It was in a depressed area to the south of Moscow, but, while ugly on the outside, it was crammed full of beautiful furniture, which Kolya had picked up when he was a road sweeper. 'People are so stupid here. They're obsessed with what's new and throw out everything that looks old. My house is full of antiques.'

Kolya and Anka became our closest friends during the next three months: we were in constant contact with them, and they proved to be a lifeline. Kolya was extremely bright, obsessed with film and art, and knew just how to prevent us from taking ourselves too seriously; Anka was soft and gentle, but had a wicked sense of humour. Their way of life was drastically different from that of the average Muscovite, for they both earned hard currency. They could buy nappies and bananas for Koka, their son, and there was always coffee and whisky in the house; they had good quality clothes and found it easier to travel abroad. We spent hours around the kitchen table drinking whisky discussing life and sex. And it was Kolya and his friend, Peter, who told us where we should travel and what we should try to see.

It was rumoured that there was going to be a big surprise in Red Square on Christmas Day. For the first time since the Revolution, the Patriarch had led the Christmas service in one of the Kremlin churches and thousands of people, who had spent the night in the church, were still milling around Red Square. Anka and I went to see what was going on. Behind the ice-cream-like domes of Saint Basil's at one end of Red Square, a large stage had been set up with actors performing the Nativity. This was interspersed with folk dancing and singing in national costume. Although it was entertaining, a weary, depressing aimlessness pervaded the square. Slightly bored and very hungry, Anka and I went to one of the few places where you could be guaranteed food – a hotel for foreigners – and paid hard currency for some orange juice.

While we drank, Anka told me about her first marriage, to a man who was sent to fight in Afghanistan when he was eighteen. 'He suffered a nervous breakdown when he returned,' she said, lighting a cigarette. 'The stupid ones amongst those who went, returned thinking that they were strong and powerful. For the first time in their lives they had power. But those who were intelligent couldn't ever think about it again.

'My husband became obsessive. All he wanted to do was marry me. I couldn't stop him, so I married him, but the breakdowns, the crying, continued. It was impossible, so I left him.' She looked sad and sighed: 'He would never see his friends from the army; they would never talk to each other. He blocked the whole thing out of his mind and never spoke about it.'

DAY 10

Three hours out of Moscow and already the people looked different. Sitting on the train's grey, plastic benches, their clothes were dirty and their faces weather-beaten. After much consultation, with more and more passengers joining the argument, we worked out which was our stop. (We had asked a friend in Moscow to recommend a small settlement for us to visit and, scanning the map, he had found Korovino.)

As the light faded, we arrived at a small station with a platform that did not reach our carriage. We leapt the six feet or so into the snow, rolling down the steep bank into a drift. There was complete silence as night fell. Finding the road, we followed it through the forest to a small town. Knocking on the first house with lights on, we asked the way to Korovino. It was three kilometres in the other direction. Using the light of the moon to guide us, we trudged through the snow towards a cluster of lights on the horizon. Occasionally, trucks rattled by along the track, but they did not stop.

We arrived at the small kolhoz, or communal farm. Silhouettes passed us in the dark but ignored us. Finally we managed to speak to an old woman, who told us that no one would be at home as the night shift in the cow sheds had just begun. Knocking on the door of a wooden house with carving around the window, we were asked into the kitchen. An old man in felt boots said that if we wanted to spend the night there, we would have to ask the chief.

Back out in the snow again, we heard the sound of sleigh bells. Flagging down the driver of the horse-drawn sleigh, we were directed to the chief's house. Vladimir answered the door. Initially unimpressed with our arrival, his welcome became expansive when we told him we were English. He called out his wife and grand-daughter to meet us, but they just stood and stared – they had never seen foreigners before.

Both Vladimir and his wife had spent the whole of their lives on the kolhoz; his daughter also lived there, married to one of the workers. Vladimir had been chief for the last fifteen years, lording it over 120 workers and as many pensioners. He had spent most of his time building his home, which he proudly showed us round. The two-bedroomed house was complete, but the sauna in the yard and the guesthouse, which he was building for his son who lives in Moscow, were not.

We sat down to a huge supper of pickled mushrooms, pickled cabbage and pickled garlic. Vladimir opened a bottle of cognac, saying, 'We live well in the country because there's a lot of food. It's in the town that they suffer.' We drank toasts to friendship and the New Year, which he forced us to knock back in one. Then out came the photo album, full of faded, black-and-white, formal photographs of communal holidays to the Black Sea and the Caucasus. All of them had a date at the bottom; all of them showed the large group from the farm sitting in rows on the steps of a monstrous hotel. Joth and I paid many a complimentary remark about how healthy and fit Vladimir looked. He held in his stomach and patted it. 'I still don't look that bad,' he said, ordering his wife to bring more food and drink to the table.

At 10 p.m. he booted us out, saying that he had to go to town the next day and have his teeth pulled. He said that if we were lucky, we would be able to catch the last train to the next town and find a hotel. We stole back the bottle of vodka that we had so ostentatiously given him. (Kolya had slipped it in our bags as we left, saying that it was the hard currency of the villages and we would get nowhere without it.)

We set off in the snow, barely able to put one foot in front of the other. It was bitterly cold and we resolved to make the three-kilometre walk back to the station and drink the vodka in the waiting room. On the way, we met Sasha. In the dark, we explained that we were from England and that we desperately needed somewhere to sleep. He invited us in.

His small house smelt of cows. In the kitchen, his wife and grandmother lay slumped on the table, their foreheads resting on their hands. The grandmother hacked away, her body wrenching every time she coughed. Their clothes were dirty and their hair stuck to their heads. Sasha led us into a tiny room with a Christmas tree in the corner. He opened the vodka and, sitting on the broken sofa, knocked it back in silence.

He was young, with a red face and stiff, blond hair, and wore large trousers tied at the waist with string. He had married his wife two years ago, 'and we still don't have children', he said, smiling at her. Laya had a soft face with pale eyes. She was shy and, darting in and out of the room, said nothing and refused the vodka. After a while, she came and sat and stared.

Sasha put on some music on an old spool tape recorder. He smiled as he urged us to enjoy the loud music while he sang along. We were introduced to a small puppy, who peed on the floor with excitement. Next came a kitten and then rabbit after rabbit was brought out for our amusement. After that, I was taken outside to a hutch crammed with rabbits. 'They're for food and fur hats,' explained Sasha with a gentle smile, adding, 'Look, we have chickens and a goose.' He pointed into the pitch darkness.

He insisted that we sleep in his bed. We refused, saying that the floor would be fine. The battle lasted around ten minutes. Eventually Sasha appeared at the door, dragging his mattress and sheets with him. He placed them under the Christmas tree. 'If you so want to sleep on the floor, then you can,' he said, laying out his bedding. It smelt of cows, the worn sheets itched with dirt and a small kitten came and slept on my head. Where Sasha and Laya slept, I do not know, for there was no other bed in the house.

At 4.30 a.m. Sasha woke us. It was still dark, but it was time to milk the cows. In silence, we walked through the snow to the cow sheds. Inside, the smell was overpowering and my eyes began to water. Around 3,000 cows were all chained to the stalls chewing hay from a trough, a row of sluices running between them. An old man with a wooden rake walked between the rows, mucking out the animals, while Sasha prepared the pipes for milking. Suddenly, an old woman, rattling her keys to prove her authority, came rushing towards us. 'Where are you from? Why are you here? Who sent you here? Who knows that you're here?' she shouted. I replied, 'No one, no one.' She pushed us out of the sheds. As we left, I turned to say goodbye to Sasha. He smiled and shrugged his shoulders.

The woman in the woolly hat behind the screen at the station told us that we had missed the 6 a.m. train and would have to wait for the 8.20. We sat on the floor of the station hut, clinging to each other for warmth.

Finally, the train arrived, but as we walked to the platform, a truck drew up and a man with gold teeth leapt out. 'Are you the foreigners?' he shouted. 'Can I shake your hands? The whole village is talking about you. Are you writing about us? Can I be in your book?' He slapped us on the back and wished us to go with God.

We got onto an empty train and immediately fell asleep. When we awoke, we were surrounded by people, all staring. 'They're awake,' whispered someone. The crowd stood back as we stretched. 'They're American spies,' said someone else.

DAY 12

In a small house next to the church of St Nicholas in the centre of Moscow, we met Vladimir, a Russian Orthodox priest. In a dark, airless room, where the priests rest between services, we sat beneath a huge, gold-framed photograph of the Patriarch. An old woman came to serve us tea, piling the table high with stale iced cakes and sugar.

Vladimir was dressed in long, black robes and had a long, pale brown beard that touched his collar. He was softly spoken and paused for thought each time I asked him a question. He could not remember his age when I first asked, but eventually worked out that he was twenty-seven. He used to be a hippy and had played guitar, but gave it all up when he met a monk in Vilnius in Lithuania five years ago and converted to Christianity. He spent two years at a special seminary and one year as a novice, qualifying as a priest in September 1991. He has had to renounce most worldly things, although the Russian Orthodox Church does allow its priests to marry, and he has a wife. 'The world is beautiful and at the same time sinful,' he said, looking down and playing with the fringe of the table cloth. 'We try and live apart from the evil in the world and I've had to give up things that are associated with that evil – all art, theatre, cinema, poetry, music – in order to lead a spiritual life.' He then added, 'Music is the least of the evils, theatre the most terrible.'

Vladimir spends most of his day in the church, administering at baptisms and funerals and listening to anyone who wants to come and talk to him. 'They range from the KGB to old women,' he said, smiling. He is paid 1,500 roubles a month, given to him from donations. 'I don't think about the future,' he said. 'We're praying for the people at the moment. The greater the unhappiness, the greater the dissatisfaction, the more people turn to God. Congregations are getting younger and younger, and many new churches are opening up.'

He explained the differences between the three Russian Christian Churches. The first, the Underground Church, was set up after the Revolution. Its members believe that they are the only Christians untainted by the state but, said Vladimir, 'There's something sinister about them now. I can't understand what's happening. They seem determined to carry on their struggle, regardless.' The second is the Russian Orthodox Church Abroad, who were given legal recognition in 1920 when the Patriarch signed a declaration to the effect that the Orthodox Church would cease its struggle with the state. The third group, and the one to which Vladimir belongs, has remained as part of the state constitution.

With the break-up of the Union has come religious struggle. 'In Lithuania, during the Catholic Christmas, there were disturbances in an Orthodox monastery. Demonstrators attacked the priests, protesting against the Orthodox faith. There have been protests, too, in the Ukraine, with the opening of three new churches there, and there may be worse to come. There's supposed to be an agreement between the Catholic and Orthodox Churches: the political games are supposed to be over. The Orthodox Church has always been tolerant of other religions, even though we don't have formal relations with them. Many are beginning to open schools in Moscow – there are now Muslim and Jewish schools here, for instance.'

As we left the house, the bishop came to bless us. We walked out into the street and Vladimir pulled up his robes and hid them under his coat. 'People still spit at priests,' he said. 'It's only recently that we've been able to grow our beards. We're slightly less of an underground society, but we must still be careful.'

That evening Joth and I took a train to St Petersburg. There were no tickets, so Kolya bribed the woman who controls one of the carriages, paying her 400 roubles to let us on board. We slept in her bed, in a compartment full of perfume, lip sticks and a variety of military hats. Since she would often sleep with passengers to earn more money, she soon found somewhere else to sleep.

DAY 13

We had been given Gabriel's number by a friend of Joth's called Katya. Half English and half Russian, she had moved from London to St Petersburg and had invited us to the city for a rave.

It was 9.30 in the morning when we found Gabriel's flat. He answered the door, a joint in his hand. He had just returned home after months away, working with the crew on an American, low-budget movie and was exhausted, but ready to party.

The flat was a shrine to the West. An expensive-looking tape recorder blasted out the latest tunes; the walls were covered with posters and flyers from different parties that he had helped organize, and a large pot of peanut butter stood, half-finished, on a table in the middle of the room. Two Americans, who had been in the film that Gabriel had been working on, had just arrived for the weekend.

Gabriel held court, telling the gathering about the film and finding out the news from the others who had come round to see him. His girlfriend, Yana, a pretty, slim model with long legs, made coffee while her grandmother cooked up blinis in the kitchen.

Gabriel was an actor. He showed us a portfolio of photographs of him in the title role of Tom Stoppard's fifteen-minute version of *Hamlet*. There were shots of him with Vanessa Redgrave, who directed the play and whom he had coached in Russian; there were also stills from various films that he had starred in. When there was no acting work, or when he was too lazy to act, he earned hard currency as an assistant director on American films.

Along with three others, Gabriel was the focal point of St Petersburg's youth culture. They had brought Acid House to St Petersburg almost three years ago. 'It all happened when we went abroad for a summer. We all came back with tapes,' he explained as he rolled another joint. 'Alexei had a big apartment on the Fontanka and we broke down the walls and made it into a club. We then went round cafés, asking people to play the music and spread the word, and it got out of control. We began charging on the door of the club, equipment came from everywhere – the turntables are from Finland. Then came the magic mushroom season and we realized we needed lights and everything. Katya also has her own radio show, which means that the latest tracks are played there as well.' As he spoke, he fidgeted in his chair, his bright blue eyes sparkled and he exuded a contagious enthusiasm.

Bouncing around the room in time to the music, he then showed me the flyer from a party that he had helped organize ten days before in Moscow, in the Cosmos Pavilion USSR Exhibition of Economic Achievement. Around 15,000 people danced in fifteen acres of dance floor, with lasers and lights bouncing off the cosmonaut models that hung from the ceiling. I was sorry we had missed it.

Katya came to collect us and we went to the market to buy food for the party that evening. The food was expensive and the market empty. As we left, burdened with more alcohol than food, Katya suddenly stopped and knelt down near a man who was selling three light bulbs. 'You can never get these,' she said, as she inspected them closely, rattling them to see if the filament was intact. 'Rule number one in this country: if there's a crowd, check it out; and rule number two: if you see something, buy it, because you'll probably not see it again for a long while.'

Katya had been lent a flat in a beautiful building in the heart of the old city by an artist who was working in London. As soon as we arrived she set about cooking supper of lentils, sausage and salad – an enormous spread. She then laid it out in a long room that smelt of new wood.

The guests arrived in droves. They were all going on to the main party later and an atmosphere of excited anticipation filled the room. The two Americans sat at one end of the table. One, an actor from California, was somewhat bemused by the whole affair; the other, a technician, looked more at home. Beautiful girls, in expensive clothes, willowed their way round the table, while Gabriel forced Katya and I to down tequila slammers. As more and more people arrived, there was soon not enough room to sit down.

After supper we began to dress up. Katya painted her nails green and put on an electric-green nylon wig to match. I borrowed some of her clothes, as I had brought nothing suitable with me. We went in convoy to the party, arriving at midnight. The planetarium was packed. Hundreds of people had paid their 50 roubles to get in. The music and lights were exactly as you might expect in a London club, yet the atmosphere was different. Everyone was there to enjoy themselves; there was no pretension or rivalry. This was a rare event and everyone was making the most of it.

Just off the dance floor was a small room for people to relax in. It was thick with cigarette smoke and people deep in intimate conversation. After about four hours' dancing, I vaguely remember finding a corner in the room and curling up asleep. Katya eventually found me, dead to the world, still wearing a pair of small, round, dark glasses that Gabriel had lent me for the evening.

DAY 14

We woke late, regretting our debauchery, and I spent what was left of the day talking to Katya about her decision to move to Russia. Deep down, she felt that she belonged here and had organized her life so that she could spend as much time as possible in St Petersburg. She sculpted during the day, fulfilling commissions from London, which she then delivered, returning to St Petersburg on the proceeds. Apart from her radio show, she was also involved in organizing cultural events, such as concerts and plays.

We wandered through the city, its baroque, rococo and classical architecture and numerous canals covered in snow and ice. There is a seductive quality about St Petersburg and I could understand why Katya had made it her home. We ate in a small café under the arches, drinking cognac and listening to funky music. On the way home, we dropped in on some artists who had a studio next to the Winter Palace. It was crammed with vast paintings and intricate sculptures. We were introduced to Vladick 'Monroe', a drag queen who, with cropped hair and a wide smile, was rather beautiful, and watched a video, shot and edited by Yuris, of Vladick and Sergei Kuryokhin, a composer, with a group called the Popular Mechanics. We also watched a video about a gay cruise to Paris, produced by a pirate television station that specializes in making films which combine clips from official Russian television with home video. The first programme it made for Petersburg television was a landmark in Soviet TV: a satirical examination of the Communist Party, which stated, among other things, that Lenin's fixation with the colour red stemmed from his being a vampire.

That evening we took the train back to Moscow. We had managed to buy some tickets and fell asleep in our bunks almost as soon as the train had left the station.

We spent the next two days organizing our journey from Moscow to Kiev. Despite the many hearty jokes about our leaving, and the fact that I knew people in Kiev, I was still rather frightened by the time Kolya took us to catch the train. We shared a carriage with two genetic engineers who were returning to Kiev from Vietnam. Just before they fell asleep, exhausted, they offered to take us round the hospital for babies of the victims of Chernobyl.

Ukraine

. . . .

DAY 17

Arriving in Kiev station was, in a way, like coming home. I had studied Russian here three years previously, spending three wild months among a group of artists whom I had often thought about, but had never dared hope to see again.

Iliya had been waiting for us for hours and now ran down the platform towards us. He had shaved his hair off and was thinner than I remembered, but he still had the voluptuous lips that women in the West spend hundreds of pounds emulating and his huge, brown eyes still sparkled. He threw bald scalp back and laughed as he hugged me. I noticed that he was missing four teeth.

'What happened to your teeth?' I asked, shocked that a twenty-four-year-old should have the smile of an old man.

'Oh, I know. Isn't it horrible? They pulled them all out about a year ago,' he said with a shrug and ushered me along the platform, crushing my shoulders with his arms. We negotiated with the army of taxis outside the station, all asking prices that three years ago would have taken a party of ten out to dinner.

It had been summer when I was here last, and Iliya had been rich. Once, we had taken a hole punch to his stockpile of roubles to make confetti and, letting the small circles run through our fingers, we had thrown a month's average salary into the air. We had been obscenely drunk and danced on the grassy hills in the centre of Kiev; we had burnt our noses sitting in the sun in Gidro Park.

This time, Kiev looked altogether different. Covered in snow, the streets were packed with people trying to buy food. It was cold and the light a flat grey.

Iliya's studio lay in the heart of old Kiev on the first floor of an ochre-and-white baroque building. It had four large rooms, the walls of which were covered with Iliya's vast oil paintings. His wife, Tatyana, a large, earth-mother character fourteen years Iliya's senior, greeted both Joth and I with an expansive hug.

We sat down in the largest room at a table covered with cigarettes, black bread, a block of cheese, a small sculpture by Iliya's younger brother, Kyril, abstract pottery, and vases of dried flowers. It was 9.30 in the morning and Iliya began to serve the alcohol. As bottle after bottle of Georgian wine appeared from behind a screen in the corner of the room, we began to talk of old times and catch up on news of old friends. Iliya had aged since I first knew him. There was something urgent, now, about his drinking and the freedom I had noticed three years before had been curbed by responsibility.

Three bottles of wine and a bottle of vodka later, we began to take photographs, throwing our arms round each other and laughing extra hard when the lens of the decrepit camera pointed our way. Iliya, giggling and knocking over chairs, used up a whole film, which we took into the small darkroom he had built behind the kitchen. Crouching on the dusty wooden floor, in the light of a painted bulb, Iliya tried to determine which solution was which. Developed on small pieces of curling photographic paper, the pictures slowly disappeared as we watched and laughed. The solutions were too old and weak to do their job properly.

The loo was used as seldom and quickly as possible. For want of anything more suitable, I was handed a copy of *Novy Mir*, a crisp-papered literary magazine, and shown to a room with damp walls. The loo was orange with rust and water rushed through the system all day. Next door was the bathroom, the floor of which was covered in moist wooden slats. The basin was coming off the wall and the taps ran constantly, the water temperature controlled by some contraption in the kitchen. The kitchen itself was heated by four gas burners that remained alight because gas was free and matches in short supply. It always appeared to be empty, save for rows of half-finished jars of indistinguishable pickled things.

The telephone line had been stolen from a public box in the street. Iliya and Kyril had extended the cable into the flat and, by holding some wires together, they could make free calls, but could not receive any.

That afternoon, Iliya left to spend some time with his two children, David, aged six, and Sasha, four. His step-parents usually look after them during the week, returning them to Iliya at weekends, which leaves him free to paint.

Bursting through the door, Kyril arrived. Tall, his hair long and dark, he was at ease with his body and communicated through his long, slim hands. Leaning forward in his chair, his hair fell over his face and he gripped my knees while he spoke, intensely excited about the new film director's course that he had just started.

The course demanded that he write short stories and illustrate them with photographs – the school did not have enough money to use real moving images. He was slightly perturbed. Since he already had a degree from art school, and since his family's artistic abilities were well known in Kiev, he had been excluded from the first two years of the course. 'So you see, Image, I don't know how to develop photographs,' he said, laughing at his inadequacy.

Kyril, Tatyana and I went out, chatting as we walked along the main street towards the central market. It was full of mandarins and pomegranates, all over-priced in Ukrainian coupons and occasionally in roubles. Stumbling upon a man selling pink champagne and a weird home brew in old vodka bottles, we queued up for twenty minutes and bought three bottles, as well as pickled shredded carrot in a plastic bag.

At one end of the market a whole range of herbs and spices were being sold as medicines, in keeping with the Soviet hatred of doctors. 'I always come here. I'd rather talk to an old woman on her stall than see a doctor. I've never been to a doctor in my life,' said Kyril with a flourish.

Citizens of Kiev, irrespective of their employment, receive 200 coupons a month. But those like Iliya, who make a living from selling paintings and hand-worked clothes, who are not officially registered, have nothing. Tatyana receives 200 coupons a month because of the two children, but with chicken at fifty coupons per kilo, paint at ninety coupons a tube and sausage 150 coupons a kilo, she has to rely on the exorbitant prices in the central market to spend the thousands of roubles that she is unable to exchange. Kyril, as a student, also receives 200 coupons, which he hands over to his brother to look after the two children.

Dusk was falling by the time we turned for home. The wide pavements were full of queues. The milk shop was inundated with people. Tatyana turned and stared: 'I haven't had milk for three months, or any butter. But a friend of mine, Neli, bought some the other day – she managed to get three litres. I had some and it was delicious.'

Iliya could not believe our good fortune at not only coming across alcohol, but alcohol which we had not had to pay coupons for. He shouted at Tatyana for not buying more. Offended by her public scolding, she went into the kitchen to make cheese on toast and we sat down to drink all over again.

Vakhtang, a translator, and his girlfriend Natasha arrived three hours later. They had been looking for alcohol, but had not found any and instead had bought a bag of hard buns covered in a thin layer of icing sugar. 'There's no booze in this town,' said Vakhtang, in perfect English. 'We've been omnipresent and found nothing. All the old haunts have dried up.'

Vakhtang was a small, gingery man with long moustache and soft voice. He had taught himself English and was inordinately proud of his fluency, using archaic words that one would never use in conversational English to show off his range of vocabulary. As he spoke, he hunched over and protected his throat with his hands. I found out later that he had throat cancer, a common disease in the Ukraine after Chernobyl.

Vakhtang had spent a year building a road in Siberia in the early 1980s. 'The KGB were really turning on the heat,' he explained. 'I thought I'd disappear for a bit to ease the pressure. And what better place to go than the place they would send me any way?'

Some friend of his had signed a KGB confession, stating that he had seen foreign magazines in Vakhtang's flat. The KGB searched the flat and confiscated a pile of copies of Punch magazine. 'They took away all the copies and underlined all the anti-Soviet jokes,' he laughed sarcastically. 'Of course, there were thousands of them. I was branded a subversive and followed wherever I went.'

He argued that he needed the magazines to teach and perfect his English, but his pleas fell on deaf ears, so he fled. 'It all seems rather ridiculous now, but that was before Gorbachev, and things were very different then.'

Natasha, an out-of-work ballet dancer, had a sweet little round face, full lips and a high, girlie voice that she used to good effect. She said little, looked through her eyelashes and sucked on a small bone pipe in a manner that a fifteen-year-old boy would have found highly provocative.

More vodka appeared from Iliya's secret drinks cabinet behind the screen and we drank one bottle while Iliya hid another under the table, winking at me as he did so. The three bottles of champagne were hidden behind a curtain and not mentioned until Natasha and Vakhtang had gone.

DAY 18

Midday, and more cheese on toast, accompanied by a thick syrupy coffee that I had to strain through my teeth to drink. We sat around the table with the curtains still drawn, discussing art and looking over Iliya's paintings.

Three years ago, Iliya had principally made clothes, sewing large ethnic shirts from material hand-painted in flowers, birds and pineapples. He made jeans, dyeing them different colours and patching them in his own fabrics; he also embroidered multicoloured, silk waistcoats. His clothes were beautiful and had made him a lot of money, as he sold them to foreigners for hard currency.

As we sat round, Iliya hauled out huge canvas after huge canvas, laying them on the floor and treading all over them irreverently as he showed them off. They were strongly painted with confident strokes. Joth and I, probably for the first time in our lives, genuinely made all the right noises. Tatyana watched and smiled contentedly. She had taught Iliya to paint.

'Look at this,' said Iliya, tearing a letter off the wall. 'I've been invited to represent the Ukraine in an exhibition in the States. The only thing is,' he added dejectedly, 'I don't know whether I'll be able to go because the flight is so expensive.'

We spent the early afternoon wandering around the art institute, a huge building with floor after floor of studios. Everyone seemed to know Iliya. In one room, two slim, young men gossiped together, smoking cigarettes. Maxim's studio was dedicated to paintings of contorted, naked men. They were mildly disconcerting. We sat down to tea from a rusty brass samovar. Once more, the conversation drifted to coupons and the price and scarcity of paints.

'How are we supposed to work if we can't even get the raw materials?' complained Maxim as he kicked a butt across the floor. 'No one can afford anything and none of my old connections work any more.'

We crossed over to an outbuilding, where a mother and son were working together in a small room that stank of linseed. The boy's girlfriend squatted on the floor, smoking, surrounded by grey constructivist canvases.

Returning home, we stopped off at one of the few hard currency shops. There was a large queue of people, most of whom had simply come to stare at things that they could never afford to buy. There was a group of aggressive-looking young men, in tight woollen hats and heavy boots, loitering outside the shop. Iliya explained that they were either mafia or simply thieves, ear-marking for future reference those rich enough to go in. We bought Iliya a bottle of French brandy and his face lit up with excitement. 'We haven't been able to buy this since the Ukraine declared its independence, along with most of the luxuries that we used to have,' he said, irritatedly.

Back at the flat Kyril was being ingenious with food. He had spent the last of his coupons on some eggs, cheese and pickled tomatoes and served them with great aplomb. Iliya brought out yesterday's pink champagne and Natasha turned up. Small and sweet, she perched on a chair and recounted her day. Kyril was all ears, while Iliya, bored by the account, busied himself inventing cocktails. He took some Uzbek grass out of its *Pravda* parcel and, blowing the tobacco out of a cigarette, rolled a joint.

'The only use for these shitty cigarettes,' he giggled as he gripped the long cardboard tube in his lips, blew out the poorly cured sticks of tobacco into the palm of his hand and refilled the tube with grass. Inhaling the smoke, he blew it out onto a glass of champagne so that it cooled in a thick, noxious layer over the pink liquid. He then inhaled the smoke over the champagne and drank it down in one. 'God, that is so beautiful. It's like a Rembrandt,' he said, laughing. 'Does anyone else want a Rembrandt?'

We all wanted Rembrandts. Iliya went around administering them to each of us in turn and the evening degenerated. Sniggering and extremely jolly, we trampled through the snow to wait for a trolley bus. Once on board we took the whole thing over. We enjoyed our captive audience and danced and sang osten-tatiously, our gestures just that bit bigger than necessary, while the other passengers, in a manner that smacked of the English, ignored us and avoided eye contact at all costs. They stared blankly into the darkness, sneaking glances at the reflections in the bus window.

Finally, after missing a few vital junctions, we arrived at Vakhtang's, a modern flat decorated throughout in red-brick wallpaper, giving it an English country house look. Heavy jazz emanated from a darkened room. He greeted us holding a large jam jar of home-made red wine and did not appreciate our already inebriated state: he had planned an evening of erudite conversation, but we were incapable of it. His grandmother produced stuffed cabbage leaves that she had spent all afternoon preparing, waited on us, and then spent the rest of the evening reading in the kitchen.

Throughout the evening, various people arrived. Valeri, a beekeeper from Siberia, sat next to me. He had a strong, wind-blasted face, a long, straight nose, thick hair and an immense beard. His hands were the texture of a cat's tongue. He used to sculpt wood and had had no state job, which in a country of full employment had been considered unethical before *perestroika*. Classed as an undesirable vagrant, he had gone to Siberia, where he had met Vakhtang. He sat emptying the contents of his address book for our future travel.

'The only problem is, most of my friends are criminals because I've spent the last ten years building roads in Siberia,' he said in a voice that was unaccustomed to idle chatter. 'He's a thief ... and he deals in weapons ... ,' he muttered as he turned the pages. Two more artists arrived with a bottle of *samogon* that was so strong that my eyes streamed after one slug. Natasha began to lose control, persuading any man she could to dance with her. Joth was dragged to the floor. Natasha ground her hips into his thigh and tickled his ear with her tongue, while I had to entertain an increasingly irritated Vakhtang.

DAY 19

Genadiy welcomed us and sat us down in his office. A genetic engineer from the World Laboratories Ukrainian Branch, whom we had met on the train from Moscow to Kiev, he began to lecture us about what we were to see, and why he was showing it to us.

'These children are victims of Chernobyl, the victims of nuclear fallout. All of them were born around here after the explosion. After you've seen them, you must tell the rest of the world. If *perestroika* is ever to work, then we must show our souls, even the darkest corners of our souls, so that the West will understand us and help us.' He genuinely believed that if the West knew about what was happening, then they could not fail to help.

Galina, a gentle, plump woman, came with us to the hospital. She had not been before and was nervous. Driving through miles of dense birch forest and thick snow that lay in plump drifts, we discussed literature before the conversation drifted to nuclear fallout.

'There are many people who have throat problems in Kiev. Their goitre glands are swollen, there are endless cases of throat cancer. People in Kiev are lethargic, they find it hard to concentrate and work. They're prone to illness, especially in the soft tissues like eyes, ears and throats. It's very worrying, but no one seems to care about what happens here any more. Before, when we were a union, the state helped – it sent the children on holiday to places like the Crimea – but now we're on our own and I don't think the Ukraine has the money to look after its sick population.'

We arrived in Vozrel, a sanitarium town about forty minutes from Kiev. It is said to have clean air and its narrow streets were lined with wooden, single-storey hospitals. It began to snow as we reached a small, white hospital surrounded by trees. We were met by Dr Tatyana Savilina, a round, jolly woman with a full set of gold teeth, whose sterile gown looked grey against the new snow. She ushered us into the first ward.

As I entered, my face went red and my eyes stung as I tried to stop myself crying. And I had not yet seen any of the babies. The room was small with windows on all sides. Little white cots ran along the walls and in the centre stood a playpen. This room was full of mongol children, with flat faces and heavily lidded eyes. All were severely deformed or paralysed, their skinny limbs lying useless. In the central playpen, a one-year-old boy was bent back double, his head touching the balls of his feet. Rocking backwards and forwards, he was growling and his arms, rigidly straight, jerked at his sides. I walked over and stroked the top of his head. The growling stopped and his arms jerked a little less.

To the right of him was a girl with encephalitis and next to her, a girl born with a large, bloated stomach. Her malformed intestines did not work properly. 'Short of opening her up and rebuilding the whole digestive system, there's very little we can do,' said the head sister, stroking the baby's tummy. 'She won't last that long now,' she said, her lips twitching to form a slight, apologetic smile

In the next-door room we were introduced to Lena, who was just over a year old. Blind and unable to sit up in bed, she lay on her back, cowering, afraid of all the attention she could not see. Marissa was eight months old. She was born with an unnaturally small head and looked wizened, old and frightened.

All the children are intellectually subnormal. They are nursed by one nurse and have one nanny who plays with them. They have a veranda which runs the length of the building, where they are placed in the sun during the summer.

Vladick was one. He has an in-growing penis that is swollen in a red, raw lump just above his testicles. He had already had two operations, but will never lead a normal life and will never have children himself. He was undressed in front of us and, using a tea towel, his weeping crotch wiped clean of urine. He is one of the lucky ones. All the children have been abandoned by their parents to the state, yet his grandmother comes to visit him. The others will remain in the state system, their parents either unwilling, or unable, to look after them.

Vladick was Tatyana's favourite. She spoke to him as one would to a baby. The others, although she loved them, she treated more like interesting test cases.

'This child is, of course, very interesting,' she said, pointing to a baby wrapped tightly in a blanket. It was sound asleep with a dummy in its mouth, unaware of its audience. 'She's called Vitia and she doesn't have a roof to her mouth. Shall I open her mouth and show you?' She moved towards the child but I told her to stop. Vitia appeared happy and it seemed pointless to wake her and remind her of her discomfort.

Another baby was picked out of its cot to be changed on the same surface that Valdick had been wiped down on earlier. She was changed on the same formica table, using the same tea towel. There are no nappies in the hospital, just as there are none in the whole of the Commonwealth. All the babies wear yellow cotton dungarees that stay wet, giving them chapped bottoms.

We moved on through the hospital. Sasha was eighteen months old, but has the facial expressions of an old man. His head is shrunken and the thumb on his left hand is divided in two. Lybia and another Sasha do not have roofs to their mouths. Lybia had three teeth on one side of her mouth; the other side does not exist. She and Sasha lay together in their yellow dungarees. Their brains have not been affected. Tatyana, the head nurse, took Sasha out of the cot and forced a wooden spatula down his throat. He screamed. 'Look,' she said in a matter-of-fact way. 'He has no roof to his mouth – the cavity stretches up to the membrane that protects the brain. We're trying to operate to create a roof to their mouths.' Feeling that I had somehow added to the baby's humiliation and discomfort, I made her put him down immediately.

As we left, Tatyana said that in the twenty-five years that she has been working at the hospital, she has never seen so many deformities and so many extreme cases. 'We have more than 300 children here. I can't say for certain that we have so many problems because of the radiation, but I can say I've never seen so many ill children before. Mongol children are usually born to older women but at the moment, women of twenty-four and twenty-five are giving birth to mongol babies. The mothers all come from Kiev, which is supposed not to have been affected by Chernobyl. They didn't want their babies, so the state looks after them. Ninety per cent of these children will never recover. There's a shortage of medicine and clothes, and while food is available at the moment, I really fear for the future.'

We drove back to Kiev in silence. No one could think of anything to say.

We had been invited to a private view and Iliya was dressing up. He spent an hour getting ready, choosing from an extensive wardrobe, most of which he had either made or had picked up in antique markets and mended. He had rows of suits and jackets, all beautifully looked after. He looked immaculate when he finished, in a dark green suit and a turquoise shirt. He even turned his hand to me, complaining that the clothes that I had brought with me were not smart enough.

At the private view we were introduced to various artists, some of whom we had met the day before. Many of them stood smoking in the ante-hall, sectioned off from the paintings and the cold by glass doors. No one was very communicative. We were by far the most beautifully dressed.

In a sideroom next to the main exhibition, the artist's girlfriend sat making sandwiches of caviar and chopped onion. We had arrived late and most of the wine had already gone. Iliya spotted someone with a glass and ran after them, but having found something to drink, we soon left. We waded through the falling snow, glasses that we had stolen clinking in our pockets. There is a great shortage of glasses in Kiev and, on Iliya's instructions, we had pilfered the ones we had been given, and more.

Iliya, Kyril and Vakhtang went on ahead and by the time we reached the flat, they were engrossed in a game of poker. They had opened the bottle of French cognac and were dressed in the most bizarre of clothes from Iliya's wardrobe. Kyril, clad head to foot in a thick, green, rubber fishing suit with tight balaclava hat to match, looked like a Russian condom. He laughed as we walked in, pinging the rubber on his cheeks. Iliya, in a 1920s KGB uniform and dark glasses, was smoking a home-made cigar. He looked over his glasses and invited us to join them.

A mountain of roubles lay sarcastically in the middle of the table. Three years ago they could have bought a house; now they were worthless. Iliya used 5-rouble notes to light his cigar, which kept going out. He would squeal with delight as the paper went up in flames. 'This is capitalism,' he laughed as he leant forward, rummaging through the pile to find more money to burn. Large amounts of money were lost and won. Vakhtang cleaned us out, but left the money behind as he went.

DAY 20

Walking through the centre of Kiev, Iliya and I came across a small demonstration. Around 250 people had gathered in the main square, huddling together for warmth in the blizzard, their bright pink hands gripping pale blue and yellow Ukrainian flags. Grouped around the naked pillar were Lenin had once stood, they stomped their feet on the packed snow and listened to a poor orator talk about the importance of the Black Sea fleet to national security. He spoke in Russian, while most of the crowd muttered words of approval in Ukrainian. He called them to arms and reminded them to take part in the large demonstration the next day.

I stood listening, fascinated. Iliya was bored. 'Look at these people,' he said, pushing his jaw out and jerking his head back. 'They're like bloody sheep.' He made a few bleating noises. 'They have no idea what they want; they listen to anyone who takes the platform and applaud any phrase that praises the Ukraine. "Long live the Ukraine! Hurrah, Hurrah, Hurrah!"' he said, leaping around. 'It's pathetic. Can we go?'

I left Iliya to do some shopping and returned to the flat, where I talked to

Tatyana. She was in a pensive mood and her wide, heart-shaped face portrayed the blankness of introspection. She began to talk about Iliya.

'Both his parents are alcoholics. His father is capable of living in the real world but his mother isn't. She's in hospital. Iliya has lived by himself since he was fourteen and has always worked for a living. Kyril lives with the grandparents, because he was too young to live with Iliya when it all happened. But the boys are very close. Kyril relies almost completely on Iliya for stability and for affection. He treats us more or less like his parents. We are his family.

'When I first met Iliya, I realized he was remarkably talented, so I started to teach him to paint. I remember the first time we went to bed together: it was after a friend's party and I was so embarrassed at the thought of lying in bed with this small boy that I would not let him take his trousers off all night.' She giggled and then searched for a cigarette on the table, embarrassed at her openness.

'Iliya's father was furious. He kept on asking me, "What's wrong with me, that you want my son?" His mother was too drunk to care.'

As if to bring testimony to Tatyana's words, Iliya and Joth fell through the front door, drunk. They had been at Iliya's father's, mending Joth's camera. The father had welded the broken flash together while polishing off a couple of bottles of vodka. 'He made us.' said Iliya as he met Tatyana's disapproving look.

We had been invited to Natasha's for supper, but Tatyana refused to come. We trooped off to a tiny flat at the top of a modern block and sat squashed round a table in a studio surrounded by mirrors.

Natasha is Greek Orthodox and produced a speciality dish of fried curd dumplings. She tried the same routine of persuading men to dance with her and grinding her hips into their groins, much to Vakhtang's irritation. Iliya decided that it would be a good thing to leave early, before it all went horribly wrong.

Tatyana was in a better mood when we got back. Triokh, a photographer, had turned up. He was a tall, bald, shy man with an endearing giggle that punctuated nearly every sentence. He was intensely talented, but could not afford a camera. He had entered a competition to find the best photographer in Kiev, because the first prize was a camera. But due to the price rises, the prize was changed to a telephone. Triokh won, but the telephone was useless to him because he could not afford to install it.

He had never made any money from his photographs. He once had some printed in a magazine, but was never paid. He is a cult figure in Kiev, with a fan club of women who hang on his every word. Martina, his model for the past two years, was sitting next to him. In her mid-thirties, she had a strong face with entrancing eyes and badly dyed red hair, and had clearly been beautiful at one time. She made jewellery and was covered in it. Next to her was Luci, with blonde, frizzy hair and bright pink lipstick. I had met her three years previously, when she greeted me in a pair of white briefs after she had invited us round to supper. This time she was wearing clothes, but she still had the same high, affected voice that had irritated me before.

They had all been drinking heavily. Empty bottles littered the table and Luci lolled on her elbows and insisted on speaking French. Martina was morose and Tatyana flirted with Triokh, who chuckled gauchely. They were all disappointed that we had not managed to bring more alcohol back with us.

DAY 21

Tatyana was cleaning the wooden floors of the studio. Wrapping a grey tea towel around a piece of wood, she patiently mopped up the slush brought in by hordes of pairs of snow-covered feet.

There was a demonstration in Saint Sophia's Square, a mass rally calling all the retired soldiers to join the Ukrainian army. The square was packed. The day before, it had been teeming with Ladas and trolley buses; today it was sealed off and filled with between 2,000 and 3,000 people. In one corner, in the shadow of the gold and turquoise domes of the cathedral, was a small platform.

The crowd stood in the falling snow, waiting for Vyacheslav Chornovil, a nationalist who had been narrowly beaten by Kravchuk in the Ukraine's presidential election. Ukrainian flags made of patchworked pieces of material were agitated wildly as soon as Chornovil took the stand, and the crowd advanced towards the platform to hear what he had to say. As the snow speckled their thick fur hats and coats, they listened, shouting, 'Long live the Ukraine' at appropriate moments and punching the air with clenched fists.

The demonstration lasted well into the mid-afternoon, with the crowd thinning and expanding as passers-by joined in and those less dedicated to the cause, or unable to stand in the cold any longer, drifted away. At the end, there was a Christian procession down the street past the studio. Tatyana and I watched from the balcony. The group was headed by a row of portly women with power- ful voices who sang hearty songs. Holding banners and wearing traditionally em- broidered shirts and skirts, they walked slowly towards the main square. There, in sub-zero temperatures, they stood singing Ukrainian Orthodox songs for a while, until they, too, dispersed.

'They're always processing down this street,' explained Tatyana, rather bored by the whole scene. 'Today is a holiday according to the Ukrainian Orthodox calendar, which is why they managed to get so many people out onto the streets. Once, there was a demonstration on Iliya's birthday,' she laughed. 'We stood out on the balcony and serenaded them with balalaikas as they marched past. They were not amused.'

Iliya, Kyril and I set off on a vodka hunt, fully equipped with empty Martini bottle, and a plastic bag to hide the spoils from envious gazes on the way home. Arriving at the small café at the bottom of the cable car run, just off the main square, we saw that a queue had already formed. The café was not yet open, but word had got round that there would be vodka on sale. About fifty men in heavy winter coats stood smoking cigarettes in the cold, stamping their feet to keep warm. It was beginning to get dark.

Eventually we were allowed inside. The café sold newspaper cones filled with peanuts toasted in their skins, hunks of bread with pieces of meat covered in large white lumps of congealed fat, as well as small plastic mugs of jam and water. No one was interested – they had come for vodka and nothing would distract them. Most could only afford half a milk bottle or a glassful. Iliya filled up his Martini bottle almost to the brim for 90 roubles and quickly hid it in the bag. As we left, most of the customers were already tucking in, draining their milk bottles and rummaging through their pockets to find more money, before rejoining the queue.

We walked up to the stadium, where some children were playing in the snow. Skirting two extremely drunk men who were using each other as a precarious support, we went and sat in the stand. 'Shall we sample our purchase?' asked Iliya, with a wicked smile. Both Kyril and I agreed that it would be embarrassing to return home without first checking to see if the vodka was passable.

Tatyana was pleased with the vodka, but not as excited as Platon, who had arrived while we were out. Platon stains glass, but is also involved in numerous dodgy scams, for which he has a wide network of contacts. He has wild blond hair, wild blue eyes, a large mouth and is missing a front tooth, which makes him whistle slightly as he talks. The last time I had seen him, three years before, he was crawling, naked, through a flower-bed. He used to call me *sistrioshka*, 'little sister', and all he could do now was stare and giggle in disbelief that I was sitting opposite him.

He had just come back from Poland, where he had gone to sell his saxophone; but he had got drunk on the train and had it stolen even before he arrived. He screamed with laughter at his own stupidity and toasted his return in vodka. He, too, had fallen on hard times. 'It's these coupons. How can a man do business when the only currency around are these stupid coupons?' he exclaimed. 'My caviar days are over.'

We sat mulling over old times. Platon shouted at me for not smoking my cigarette right down to the butt. 'You can tell you haven't been here very long yet,' he laughed. 'You won't be wasting tobacco like that when you get to the Southern States.'

Platon had to leave because he was expecting guests at home. We went to a neighbouring studio, a group of huge, connecting rooms with parquet floors and high ceilings, lit by naked bulbs. My footsteps echoed loudly as I walked. There was one chair to sit on.

A youth with a skin problem dragged me to his studio, where he showed me his canvases – aggressive, depressing paintings, in blue, maroon and red, of death screams and suicides. 'These are not commercial paintings,' he said as he unscrolled yet another. 'They mark the height of my self-analytical, self-expression stage. We live in depressing times and I think this ought to be expressed. The only thing is, I find them hard to sell.' Pleading extreme tiredness, I escaped to join Tatyana and Iliya, who were sitting on the floor, drinking red wine. It was in short supply and there were no glasses, so they were using egg cups.

DAY 22

It was fifteen degrees below freezing but the open-air swimming pool was doing a brisk trade. Rubber-capped heads bobbed up and down in the water, disappearing under great clouds of steam that the wind whipped across the pool. The swimmers changed below ground and then went through a series of passages that led directly into the pool, thereby avoiding exposure of flesh to the elements.

The clientele was not that different from any seen in public baths in the West – old women in flowery rubber hats doing their lengths, middle-aged men worried about their midriffs, keen lads letting off steam – except each and every one of them was bright pink. Any part of their skin that was not fully submerged – faces, backs, shoulder blades and even, for the adventurous doing backstroke, stomachs – was crimson.

Next door, in the smaller pool, were the water polo players. They had just finished training when I arrived. The presence of a girl immediately made them show off: they bounded around, leaped in and out of the water, dived from the side, rubbed themselves in snow and beat their breasts. I had never before seen firm, purple bodies in small, tight trunks throw themselves into water and then cover themselves in snow. Such masochism was fascinating. Their trainer came back and angrily ushered them through the watery tunnel to change. Disappointed, I moved on.

Kyril and Joth went off to buy bread, using Kyril's coupons, for our twenty-two-hour train journey to Rostov on Don. They arrived home four hours later with only one loaf. They had queued for an hour in one line, only to watch the last loaf go to the man two people in front of them. They had to find another shop and start all over again.

Iliya sat at the table, beaming. 'Look what I've found,' he announced proudly. He had been back to the central market and bought three more bottles of the pink champagne that Tatyana and I had found a few days before.

We all gathered round, ready for the ceremonial bang as the cork shot out. Iliya took up position, everyone stared, and the cork plopped as if from a flaccid lemonade bottle. Iliya, disgusted, opened another. No bang. They were all the same. 'Oh well,' said Kyril, optimistically. 'I'm sure if we pretend that it's wine, then it'll taste all right.'

'Do you want a glass of wine?' asked Iliya, picking up one of the glasses we had stolen from the private view. 'Don't mind if I do,' I replied with a nod.

As the evening wore on, all the people whom we had met over the last couple of days arrived to say goodbye. Iliya frantically went around filling everyone's glass and there was the ritual exchanging of presents. Martina, Triokh's model, made me sit down and translate the traditional list of Russian obscenities into English, for future reference. I had to explain when and where such phrases could or should be used, which caused much confusion and hilarity.

Triokh arrived, complete with blindfold and a camera that he had borrowed from a friend. Within ten minutes, he had Kyril, Iliya and me all topless, contorting ourselves into different positions. He then bent over the camera while I stood blindfolded, being caressed by the two boys. At this moment of 'drunken creativity,' Vakhtang walked in, totally sober. I was glad I could not see him, but I heard him express shock and then fall silent. We all carried on, unaware that what we were doing was anything out of the ordinary.

I hardly remember packing, or even getting to the train. As I said goodbye to Iliya, he whispered: 'It's much better to do horrible things like leaving when you're drunk, because then you don't get unhappy.' Iliya did not understand that alcohol also makes you over-emotional. I remember crying and Iliya laughing. 'You'll come back. I know you will,' he said. 'This country has your soul. It takes it away without you realizing and then you have to come back.'

Russia

· · · · · · · · · · ·

DAY 23

There was a shortage of tea and for twenty-two hours we drank nothing but hot water from the coal-burning samovar at the end of the train corridor. Over a cigarette, we met a Georgian couple who were on their way back to Tbilisi. They seemed unaware of the civil war that was tearing the capital apart and the rise of Gamsekhurdia's support. However, they were finding it difficult to return. All train links had been severed; the airport runway had been mined and the roads were impassable. The only way they were going to get home was by taking a boat from the Crimea across the Black Sea to a small port, from where they hoped to find a local train to take them to the outskirts of Tbilisi.

They were both so excited to meet foreigners for the first time in their lives that they insisted we come to Tbilisi. 'The Georgians are the most hospitable people in the world. They won't harm you once they know you're English. There may be a bit of fighting at the moment, but it's nothing we can't handle,' the husband laughed.

He was sixty years old, with dark hair, almost-black eyes and a long, hooked nose. He had been a builder all his life. 'All I need to do is tell my boss that I have English people at home and I'll be allowed a holiday,' he said, fidgeting with excitement.

His wife was small and dark, with the round figure of a woman who has had many children. She had borne nine. Dressed in a grey-blue dress, with a thick, black scarf wrapped around her shoulders, she was convinced that Joth and I were brother and sister because of our freckles. 'You will be our English daughter and son and we will look after you,' she said, exuding delicious maternal warmth.

Joth had a sore throat and she offered to cure it. 'They call me a white witch. I have healing hands,' she said. Stretching out her pink, gently wrinkled hands, she placed them around his throat and began to rub. She tapped his shoulders to release the 'bad energy' and brushed it away down his arms, drawing it off his fingertips. Then she moved her hands in circular motion just over his neck, feeding in 'good energy'. Taking each fingertip, she bent it backwards and, pressing his wrists together, bent them backwards and forwards too. Then she clapped her hands together. Joth did, indeed, feel better.

After that they would not leave us alone. They fetched a jug of hot water and home-made strawberry jam. Mixing the two together, they then made us drink glass after glass of the hot, sticky, sweet drink, promising that it would be good for us. While we drank they sat and talked about their nine children. The six sons worked for the same building company as their father; the daughters were all married and lived in Tbilisi. They had six grandchildren. Then came the toasts in Georgian wine from an old apple-juice bottle. We raised a blue plastic mug to 'our meeting' and 'friendship'.

Natasha and Kolya had been waiting for us at the station for two hours – the Ukrainians had refused to change their clocks along with the Russians and had kept the train waiting on the border until it was the 'correct' time to leave. The couple had borrowed a car from a friend and drove us to Natasha's parents' home in the centre of old Rostov. It was a small, second-floor flat, the only access to which was a steep, metal staircase all covered in snow. It was lethal and I clung to the shaky banister. Inside, the sitting room was full of the complete works of Lenin in a glass bookcase. They were covered in dust.

Natasha had a flat face, thin, dark hair and blue eyes. She rarely laughed, let alone smiled. Kolya was of Cossack descent and tall, large and strong. He was docile and hardly spoke. Both were majors in the police force: Natasha worked for the intelligence police, Kolya for the traffic police. Both had been married and divorced.

Natasha's parents were like shadows, rarely leaving their small room, which was just off the kitchen. The mother, who was eighty, with thin, balding hair, tied in a loose bun at the back of her neck, prepared all the food, but never spoke. The father, in his mid-eighties, was a good-looking old man with skin that was cracked and creased. Hunched over, he wandered backwards and forwards silently from the small room to the veranda to smoke his cigarettes.

They were nervous about us being in their flat and avoided eye contact at all times. They disapproved of Natasha inviting us to stay, perceiving our presence as something dangerous. Their logic was: the less contact they had with us, the fewer the repercussions. Natasha and Kolya were more welcoming, but they, too, were frightened. They had asked their superiors if we could stay and had taken a week's holiday in our honour, but they were still afraid. Natasha would not tell me her surname.

She was from an old aristocratic family. During the Revolution, most of her family had fled to France and Canada; only her grandfather, who had just returned from England, remained behind. 'I think he regretted the decision for the rest of his life,' said Natasha with a brittle laugh.

When Natasha was young, she kept in touch with her relatives in France, writing letters that were attached to the end of her grandmother's. 'She was too old to care or be frightened by the regime, and I was too young to know better. My father never once put pen to paper. He wasn't frightened for himself, but for the rest of us. He wasn't prepared to take any risks, so he kept quiet.' Her voice sounded desperate, as if seeking some sort of justification.

When Natasha's grandmother died, however, Natasha lost contact with her relations. It became too dangerous to write and receive letters from abroad. She wrote one final letter about twenty years ago, telling her relatives not to write any more and that she would no longer be communicating with them. 'And that was that. I've never heard from them again.'

Natasha went to school in Rostov and passed with the second-highest marks in the year. She wanted to go on to the town's Institute of International Affairs, but her background was not ideologically sound enough. 'They told me that, because of my ancestry and the fact that I had relatives abroad, I'd have to spend two years in a canning factory, so that I could then genuinely call myself a worker. I would have all that bourgeois affectation beaten out of me.' Her voice was flat. 'I wasn't the sort of person they wanted at the institute,' she added.

She refused to go to the canning factory. 'I would have had no brain left if I'd gone. But then, I suppose that was the general idea.' Instead, she went to the Institute of History. She finished in the first five in her class, which entitled her to stay in Rostov to teach rather than being sent to a provincial backwater. 'If you go to the Institute of History, you automatically become qualified to teach, but whether you stay in Rostov, or go to another town depends on your grades.'

However, there were too many history teachers in Rostov, or that is what Natasha was told, and she was offered a job in the police force. 'You don't refuse jobs that are given to you, otherwise you'll never work again.'

Natasha toed the line. Having witnessed the failure of her parents – Natasha's father has never worked and they have lived in abject poverty all their lives – she decided to reject her upbringing. 'I became the first member of my family to join the Communist Party,' she said, half closing her eyes and looking at the floor. 'It was the only way to get promoted and have a successful career. I learnt the propaganda and said it in the right place at the right time. I also work hard and I'm good at my job,' she blurted.

In May 1991, however, at the height of *glasnost*, Natasha, Kolya and three other policemen took the decision to leave the party, much to the consternation of many of those with whom they worked, who told them that they were fools and would regret their decision. 'They told us to stay in the Party until it was safe to leave, but I couldn't live the lie any longer.'

During the annual August police holiday to the Black Sea, they heard about the hardline putsch. 'We were terrified. We sat huddled around the radio, tuned into the BBC World Service, trying to understand what was happening. We agonized over our decision to leave the Party so soon, and all our workmates were triumphant. We could get no other information: they only showed *Swan Lake* on television and no one would tell us anything. Those were horrific days.'

But when the putsch failed and Natasha and Kolya returned to work, it was a different story. 'We walked around smugly, saying we'd been right all along and we were in a much better position than most people,' she said with a laugh.

'It's the KGB that's the problem at the moment. They had so much power and now no one knows quite what to do with them. They themselves have no idea what they're supposed to be doing. They work next door to me, as good as in the same building, and I think there'll be a merger – crime intelligence and them. They don't want that, of course, because they'll lose their power, and we don't like them. Half of them will probably end up working for the mafia.'

Rostov on Don is known as the 'father of the mafia', with Odessa, in the Ukraine, its 'mother'. Rostov is the gateway to the Caucasus, traditionally one of the richest trade routes. Here, where Asia meets Europe, there is a swift trade in luxury goods such as champagne and wine. With the political instability of the regions to the south, it is the mafia who can guarantee orders, organize shipments and will exchange weapons for champagne. Intensely powerful, they are a law unto themselves.

Life as a policeman has its perks. Natasha and Kolya get whatever they want through connections, as was demonstrated on our first evening, when we sat down to a champagne tasting. The first was a fruity, white champagne, which had in the past been reserved for those high up in the Party; the second was a delicious, dark red champagne, also not on general release. The Rostov police, apart from having their own holiday camp on the Black Sea, also have their own hospital and clinic, which guarantees them drugs and attention and prevents the need for bribes and queuing. 'The Party looks after its own,' said Natasha.

DAY 24

Early in the morning, we were taken to market. It was full of Koreans selling pickled, shredded vegetables, Cossacks from Sevastopol selling potatoes out of the back of large vans, and people milling around, looking. Few could afford to buy anything. Next door to the market was a church. Three old women were sitting in a row on a bench, begging. Their faces turned to the ground, they held out their hands, maniacally crossed themselves and muttered rosaries under their breath.

Neither Natasha nor Kolya had ever been inside a church. 'You see, it was always forbidden, and as a good Communist, I followed the rules,' said Kolya. The church was crowded with old women in long, thick coats and flowered headscarves. Some were kneeling in front of the golden icon screen, others in front of the huge paintings of saints, their heads bowed as they lit candles and prayed.

Kolya was moved by the whole experience and went looking for the painting of Saint Nicholas, his namesake. Asking the first old woman he came to, he bought a candle, followed her directions to the painting and, bowing in front it, began to pray. Natasha was less moved and found Kolya's enthusiasm slightly embarrassing. She wandered around, commenting upon the architecture and the amount of gold used in the icons, but ignored the building's religious significance.

We left the church and drove to Asia. Crossing the River Don, the official border, we made our way across the steppes which, flat, treeless and wild, stretch as far as the eye can see. Arriving in Vartaisk, a small town about twenty kilometres from Rostov, we wandered through the narrow, snow-congested streets, lined either side with fat dachas that exuded a warm, territorial homeliness. We stopped off at the police station to meet a friend of Kolya's and were introduced to the head of the station, who sat below a faded chocolate-box-style painting of Lenin leaning forward with clenched fist.

'There was another Cossack attack on the Georgians and the Caucasians this morning,' said the chief, an enormous man with a huge moustache. 'They went into the market with whips and attacked the store holders, tearing down the stalls, threatening and whipping the people,' he continued, nonchalantly. He explained that, since the new land reforms, which entitle people to own land, racial tension in the area has grown. The Georgians and the Caucasians are buying more and more land in the extremely fertile steppes, bringing in fruit and wine, which cannot be grown in the area, from their orchards further south, and buying up land with the profit. 'I think it's much more to do with jealousy than pure racism. The Cossacks are nothing without their land, and they can't stand it when people take it away from them,' he concluded.

As we sat in his office he brought out a bottle of vodka from underneath his desk, ordered an underling to get some shots glasses and began to cut up a lemon with a penknife, using a couple of files to lean on. 'D'you have lemons in England?' he asked, as he chopped away. 'You do? Oh. I bet they're not as nice as these – these are from Georgia,' he said, handing me one to taste. 'D'you have vodka?' I replied we did. 'Ah, but not real Russian vodka!' he replied, knocking it back, his eyes watering, his face grimacing. 'Not as good as this – it's forty per cent proof.'

He then handed round some chocolate, cut up into small cubes, and we sat and savoured the taste. I melted mine on my tongue and felt it trickle down the back of my throat. Michael, Kolya's friend who had lent him the car, arrived. Embarrassed to find us all drinking with his chief, he sat in silence as the large man continued to explain the virtues of Russian vodka.

Michael invited us home. The light was already fading as we walked through the snow to a small house in one of the narrow roads in the village. The house had a sitting room, where the parents slept, a kitchen and one bedroom. Two small boys, overcome by the arrival of guests, began to show off on the ropes in the bedroom. 'I built them that gym,' said Michael proudly, as he showed us how the two ropes were attached to the ceiling.

His young wife was not expecting visitors. She sprang into action, laying the table, polishing vodka glasses and cutting up the tongue. We toasted 'meeting', 'friendship' and 'international relations' and left early, having eaten platefuls of pickled peppers and tomatoes.

On the way back to Rostov, we passed a school where Natasha's brother used to teach. 'He had to give it up – he had a heart attack because of the stress.' She explained that teachers are under pressure because their promotion depends on the grades of their pupils. If the pupils do badly, then it is the teachers who are punished. So they have one of two options: either they rig the marks so all the pupils are seen to be doing well, or they stay behind after school and give extra tuition.

'But if students don't want to work then there's nothing the teachers can do about it. The pupils know it's the teachers who'll get blamed if they do badly, so what do they care? Or they know the teachers cheat – so what do they care again?' said Natasha. Her brother is now a driving instructor.

'School,' snorted Natasha. 'What did they teach me? History, now that's a joke! I've no idea any more if what I learnt was true or just propaganda. My brain is so confused. Who knows whether I spent all that time learning rubbish? I'll never know. What can you believe in?' She did not speak again, but instead stared out of the window, her sad face deep in thought.

DAY 25

In Novocherkassk, a small, modern town just outside Rostov, we met Katya and Ygor.

Katya was a short, plump woman who never stopped talking. She had a strong face, crudely dyed red hair and fierce lipstick. Her husband, Ygor, was also short, with thick blond hair and thick spectacles that made his eyes seem minute. He

Natasha, prostitute, Moscow

Christmas Eve, Zagorsk

New Year's Eve, Red Square

Iliya, artist, Kiev

Natasha, ballerina, Kiev

Cossack boy

OPPOSITE Zagorsk, Christmas Eve

Old man, Nalchik

Cossack, Rostov-on-Don

Political rally, Kiev

Farmer, Balkar people, Caucasus

Katya and Ygor, Novocherkassk, near Rostov-on-Don

Woman, Caucasus

said nothing unless his wife was out of the room and was made to stand in the corner to smoke his cigarettes, balancing the ash tray on top of the television. 'He's one of those mucky pups that spills ash everywhere, and I just can't clean it up the whole time, can I?' She looked at me for some vote of female solidarity. I looked away.

They had two children. Ira, tall and painfully thin with long, thin, mousy hair and turquoise eye shadow in two crescent moons above her eyes, worked in the post office. She lived with the grandmother because there was not enough room in the family flat. Sergei, the younger, was gentle, blond and intelligent-looking.

We sat in the sitting room of the two-roomed flat, with its photographic panorama of Sweden in spring papered on one wall, and drank coffee. The tin of coffee was ostentatiously opened in front of us. 'This is imported Cuban coffee,' said Katya, showing us all the tin. 'We have lots of friends who live in the major towns and send us presents.' She puffed up her hair. We all drank noisily and appreciatively.

Walking around the town with Katya's arm entwined in mine, we were introduced to everyone she knew. 'These are people from England,' she said dramatically. 'They're foreigners and they're staying in my house.' I would smile and introduce myself.

Finally, after numerous introductions, we arrived at the Soviet, the town hall. There we met the Cossack council: three men in military uniform of blue trousers with red stripes down the leg. Each had a wind-worn face with a long, Roman nose, a long moustache that curled up at the end and a flick of hair that protruded from his lopsided cap. They bowed as I introduced myself. Their office was almost empty, with nothing but a clear desk, a few chairs and an antiquated telephone, which one man was shouting down. Thick, strong cigarette smoke hung in the air. I offered them a Western cigarette, which are usually prized and devoured. They refused. 'Only women smoke those,' said the tallest man with the longest moustache and the longest hair. He took out a filterless stick, which he rolled between his fingers to loosen the tobacco, and placed it under his moustache.

They listened in silence as we explained our business and then telephoned the Ataman in a nearby village. After shouting down the telephone for ten minutes, our meeting for the next day was arranged.

As we left, a short, irritating guide attached himself to me and insisted that he show me round the museum of Cossack culture. It seemed rude to refuse, but afterwards I wished I had. He began his tirade about the ugly and uninteresting town almost as soon as we left the Soviet. I lost count how many times he told me that they planned to take down the statue of Lenin, clutching a rolled-up newspaper, and replace it with one of Ataman Platonov, the famous leader who, during the Napoleonic War, led the Cossack horsemen to Paris, where their horses drank from the water of the Seine.

This boring, humourless guide took it upon himself to monopolize the whole day. It took us twenty minutes to get to the Cossack museum. I was then forced to spend another hour going round, admiring every reproduction photograph and piece of armour. By the time we reached the paintings, we had a whole party following us, not to look at the objects, but to watch my reaction to everything. Every so often, Katya would link arms with me and say, 'Isn't it wonderful, you understand everything! She's English, you know,' she would say, turning to the crowd.

At last we left, only to be dragged through the town to visit the cathedral. It was, it has to be said, genuinely beautiful both inside and out; but once more the guide got hold of me and hauled me across the square. He pointed to a piece of rock on which, he informed me, there had once been a very beautiful statue. I feigned fascination and made to rejoin the group. Undeterred, the guide opened his suitcase. Standing in the gnawing cold, he showed me card after card from a distant Cossack relative in Nottingham, whom he asked me to contact. A few photographs later, I was eventually allowed to leave.

Katya grabbed hold of my arm and began discussing hair dye. It was hard to get hold of and you could never guarantee the colour, she explained. We went on an abortive shopping trip to buy some bread and returned home in a 'communal taxi', or minibus. Katya enjoyed the treat of travelling in such luxury.

After some clattering in the kitchen, Katya produced supper. She explained how to bottle tomatoes to make them last through the winter – a recipe of which she was particularly proud. The tomatoes were grown on their allotment just outside the town. 'With all these price rises, the only way we can afford to live is through our allotment,' said Ygor, much to Katya's shame.

Ygor joyfully brought out some vodka in a green, unmarked bottle. He poured out the toasts and put the lid back on – the first time I had seen a Russian not want to finish a bottle. We toasted 'friendship', knocked back our glasses, and fell silent. Ygor went for a bottle again, but Katya stepped in. 'You know you're only allowed one glass, otherwise you get drunk,' she said. Humiliated, Ygor did not retaliate. Instead, he left the table, collected his ash tray and perched in the corner by the television. 'Don't flick your ash on the floor,' said his wife, her hands clasped under her bosom.

As soon as she left to wash the dishes, Ygor came alive. He works in radioelectronics and his hobby is making radio contact with people around the world. He showed us his collection of cards, sent to him from people whom he had managed to reach. Each short-wave radio fan had a special card printed, indicating the time contact had been made, the frequency, and what the message had been. Ygor had hundreds of cards and we looked through them all. 'It's my little hobby,' he said. 'I sit for hours in my son's room and fiddle with the dial, talking to other countries.' Ygor could not afford to have a special card printed, so he sent fellow fans postcards of Novocherkassk.

Joth and I were packed into the matrimonial bed in the sitting room, partitioned off by a half-drawn curtain. Katya, Ygor and Sergei shared a room that would have been just bearable for one.

DAY 26

Katya whipped the pillow off my head at 7 a.m. 'Oh look! She sleeps with a pillow on her head,' she squawked. 'That's terribly dangerous,' she said to whoever would listen. Then, moving her face rudely close to mine, she repeated: 'That's terribly dangerous, you know.' 'I've done it for the last twenty-four years and I'm still alive, so it can't be that dangerous,' I moaned, snatching the pillow out of her hand and placing it back on my head.

The sausage and bread for breakfast were so unappetizing that we told Katya we would take them for a packed lunch. She wrapped them for us and popped them in our satchels.

We sat for the next two hours in the Soviet, waiting for the car to take us to the village of Aksai. The three Cossacks we had met yesterday questioned me as to why I was not married and did not have children. 'I have three,' said Sasha, a blond Cossack with pale blue eyes nestling below thick eyebrows. 'And I'm also twenty-four. Women should have babies and stay at home, and the men should go to war and look after the land and their horses,' he said defiantly.

When the car arrived, we piled into the back with Sasha and two more Cossacks from the village. After an hour's drive across the snow-covered steppe, we arrived in Aksai, built on the banks of the Don. At the Cossack headquarters we were greeted by the Ataman of the village. A statuesque man with a rough, chapped face and laughing eyes, he wore the obligatory blue trousers complete with red stripe, the long, curling moustache, and the askew hat with the curl of hair. He also had a long, silver sabre at his side.

Next door to the headquarters was a Comsomol museum, dedicated to the achievements of young Communists. The Cossacks were tearing it down to replace it with a museum celebrating Cossack achievement. Rusty old sabres lay on the floor; large pieces of pottery and yellowing photographs were strewn among jaded red flags, icons of Lenin and propaganda photographs of smiling youths at summer camp. The museum curator was enthusiastic. 'The Cossacks are re-establishing themselves. Everyone is looking through their possessions to try to find things for the museum,' he said with a broad smile that barely broke through his moustache. 'Soon, I don't think this building will be big enough to house all the artifacts.'

We moved on in convoy through the village, past lovingly maintained wooden houses, each with a fenced garden containing fruit trees and a well. Small huts at the end of each garden protected holes in the ground, and were supplied with strips of *Pravda* attached to a nail. Speed is of the essence when negotiating these open-air loos in winter, but at least the cold keeps the smells down.

Our group had grown to thirty by the time we arrived at the small excavation of an old Cossack dwelling. The roof of the former house was covered in grass and snow. The Cossacks used to grow grass on their houses as camouflage against enemy attack. We trooped up onto the hill-like roof to see the vast steppe below and the motionless Don, which stretched haphazardly into the distance. Down on the ground, a small group of Cossacks were firing up a huge samovar, filling the central funnel with newspaper and small pieces of kindling wood. Black, acrid smoke spiralled skywards in the flat calm. The sun reflected weakly on the snow. The only noise was the chatter of the men below as they built the fire.

Inside, twenty feet below ground, a long, low table had been laid beneath the domes of peachy rock. Bottle after bottle of home-made vodka lay in a regimental line down the centre of the table. As the only female, I was given place of honour to the right of the Ataman with the laughing eyes. The other thirty or so Cossacks crammed together, sabres clunking as they jostled for space around the table.

To my left sat a dark Cossack with deep brown eyes and thick lashes, who said nothing and knocked back his vodka without flinching. The feast lasted about three hours and, throughout, there was much clinking of glasses, much toasting of gratuitous causes and much beating of chests as the vodka went down. Their initial, frosty reaction to a female drinking partner melted away as I downed my vodka with masculine purpose. I made a speech extolling the greatness of the Cossack nation and glorifying their war-like spirit, and finally clinched their approval by quoting a passage from Sholokhov's *Quiet Flows the Don*.

The feast over, we moved with unsure feet out of the dark cave, our faces florid with alcohol, our eyes red-rheumy and puffy. We slithered down the hill towards the Don, arms linked as much for mutual support as in jolly camaraderie. A group of small children were skating on the river, competing with each other on their makeshift race track.

'Let's hit the ice,' I shouted, completely carried away. The Ataman followed me. The children stopped skating and stared as thirty drunk Cossacks, in full military uniform, careered down the hill and skidded into the middle of the Don. Juvenilia erupted. I pushed the Ataman over, blue bottoms with red stripes hit the ice and tears of laughter ran down the pink cheeks. But it was soon over. The Ataman was the first to grow up and, remembering his position, ordered the men off the ice.

Returning to the headquarters, spirits were still high. Joth and I were both made honorary Cossacks and given passports, which not only entitled us to carry sabres, but also stated that our offspring, too, would be Cossacks. Although written in jest, these passports were valid and it was therefore illegal for us to have them, but the Ataman was completely carried away.

Back at Novocherkassk, more Cossacks arrived from Moscow. Dressed in black fur hats and black fur capes to the floor, pointed at the shoulders, they looked wild and terrifying. Through a moustache that hung like some limp, hairy animal on his top lip, their chief spoke with a deep, gravelly voice. I exchanged cigarettes with him, but he was as unimpressed as the man behind the desk had been, and handed my packet back to me.

Accompanied by Sasha, the blond Cossack who had spent the day with us, I went off to the cultural centre to find some Cossack dancers. Instead, we were confronted by a sewing class. Large women in larger bras sat at desks, learning how to make shirts. The largest of all was being used as a model at the front of the class. They squealed with embarrassment as we walked in, and giggled into their ample bosoms.

Then followed the dress rehearsal for the Cossack folk dancing. The dancers were practising a wedding scene, but were one man short – the best man. Sasha, very much the worse for wear after all the vodka, was roped in to help. A row of portly women in ill-fitting dresses and clutching brightly coloured scarves burst into reedy song. Swaying from side to side, flapping their scarves, they clapped their hands and displayed rows of gold teeth. Sasha trotted uncertainly from one foot to another with little enthusiasm as he escorted a plump girl from one end of the hall to the other. The more I laughed, the redder he became and the more he looked at the floor. As we left the hall, the ensemble followed us into the street, singing. 'It's a Cossack tradition,' explained Sasha through gritted teeth and, turning to me, added, 'I've never embarrassed myself so much in my life and all you could do was laugh.' I laughed some more, and hugged him goodbye.

Joth and I waited at Katya's like two small children desperate to leave school at the end of the day. As soon as Natasha arrived to collect us, we ran with relief to the car, but not before Katya had kissed us goodbye and smoothed down my hair. She meant well.

DAY 27

We made an early start. Natasha and Kolya drove us through the 'striped forest' just outside Rostov. The forest, growing in unnaturally straight bands, had been planted to prevent both soil erosion and the dust bowl that engulfs Rostov during the summer.

'This was the home of the striped-forest murderer,' said Natasha. 'Our department looked for him for almost twelve years before we eventually found him just over a year ago. He murdered over fifty children here, sexually assaulting all of them before cutting them to pieces. He'd take them off the streets in his car and then drive them out here to assault them, kill them and chop off their sex organs. He cut out the girls' wombs and removed the boys' penises. It was horrific. We finally caught him through blood tests. He was a teacher, you know.'

Andrei Chukatilo was put on trial in April 1992 for cannibalism and torturing, murdering and mutilating fifty-five children in the woods outside Rostov. He has confessed to all the crimes and, if judged sane, will be sentenced to death by firing squad.

We left the blood-stained forest and headed out for the steppes. Flat snowscape lay all around as far as the eye could see, interrupted only by the icy black road stretching ahead like a skinny triangle. Large black crows dotted the road, pecking up the grain that was pouring from a truck that we overtook a few miles ahead.

In Kislyakov we were to meet Ataman Nikolai Alexandrovich, who ruled the whole of the Besarabsky region. He kept us waiting in the snow because he wanted to escort us personally over the headquarter's threshold. This is a great honour, rarely bestowed on strangers, but he was a friend of Natasha's brother.

Ataman Nikolai was a huge man with white hair and a long white moustache. He was dressed in the traditional Cossack uniform and his blue shirt, taut around his stomach, was decorated with medals that he had won in Afghanistan. A trained lawyer and former head of the military police in the area, in September 1990 he had been elected ataman of the region by the Inner Circle, a small group of prominent male Cossacks. He will hold the position for four years before handing the job over to someone else. Sitting at his desk, with a large portrait of Ataman Platonov behind him, he summed up his council's aims. 'Our main programme is that of rejuvenation and regeneration of Cossack culture and the patriotic movement. Most of our children have forgotten our traditions. We want to teach them to be true Cossacks again,' he said, leaning back in his chair and twiddling his moustache.

We walked with him through the snow to the new Cossack school, which was run by his brother-in-law. There, for the price of 17 roubles a month, or three loaves of bread, the children learn the old traditions that have been suppressed by a Communist education. We went into a ballet class and about twenty six-year-olds in white fluffy skirts and candy-floss bows in their hair immediately stopped and paid their respects to this huge man. He begged them to continue and, embarrassed, they carried on dancing in their circle, ever aware of his paternal eye.

'We have also started up the old riding festivals, teaching boys to ride from the age of five. After all, what is a Cossack without his horse?' he asked with a wry laugh. 'We don't want independence – we just want to be left alone. The most important thing we're trying to do is to get the 1919 law against the Cossacks repealed. This states that the Cossack people must be wiped out and the land returned to Russia. But everyone knows,' he said, quoting Tolstoy, 'that if the Cossacks leave, then Russia will die.'

Descended from free or runaway serfs who made the wild steppes their own, the Cossacks now inhabit the whole of the southern borders of Russia, from the west to the far east. In exchange for being left alone, they formed the backbone of the czars' armies, remaining loyal after the Revolution and fighting for the White Army during the Civil War. They did not respond well to the strictures of Communism, having lived off the land, fetterless, for centuries, and fought hard against Stalin's collective farms. They paid the price.

'The word Cossack was banned from 1919 until the Second World War, when the Red Army desperately needed us to fight for them again. No Cossack could be a chief of a communal farm – in fact, I'm the first Cossack leader in the area since 1919. To be a Cossack, you must be of pure Cossack blood. The men hunt, wage war, protect the women and their land. The women look after the home.'

We went to a neighbouring village, or *khyta*, called Yolkin. Walking up the steps of a wooden hut and turning the corner, I was met by about thirty old women, dressed in traditional, embroidered clothes, who suddenly burst into song. They sang in honour of our arrival and danced around, shaking their fringed scarves. One of them approached me with a loaf of bread and a small bowl of salt and, as guest of honour, I broke the bread and tasted it, and took a pinch of salt and threw it over my right shoulder. I then sat down at a long table, surrounded by the elders of the village. The small room was packed with old women and a few musicians, who sang for about half an hour, led by a tiny old woman in the corner of the room who knew all the songs, words and gestures. Then, while we drank tea, sweetened with apricot jam, the old woman talked about her life.

Anna Alexandrevna was, at eighty-nine, the oldest member of the village. She had a back rounded through work, a heavily lined face, and wore a cream and pink scarf wrapped so tightly round her head that it squashed her cheeks slightly. She remembered the Revolution and the Civil War and had lived through collectivization, the famine, the German occupation and Stalin's purges.

Her family had been wealthy. 'My father had six horses for war, and four for riding and work; he also had ten cows and some poultry,' she listed, counting off on her bent, red fingers. 'I can read – I spent four years at school – and I've had thirteen children, four of whom are still alive,' she said, puffing herself up slightly.

During the Second World War, when the village was occupied by the Germans, Anna remembers how the women alone held the village together. 'There were no men you see, they were all at the war. But we Cossack women are strong and we're used to hard work. I brought the harvest in last year and I intend to bring it in again this year.' She had tears in her eyes and her comment sent a ripple of applause around the airless room.

An old man, who had crossed himself before drinking his tea, suddenly began to speak. 'We don't have any food shortages at the moment. We Cossacks produce everything we eat, except sugar of course – there's none of that. We've never employed anyone: we look after our own land ourselves, it's the source of our strength. Land, the family and our deep respect for women, the old and children are what keeps us great.

'We are a truly religious people. When religion was banned all over Russia, we still had baptisms and Christian burials. All our icons from the twelfth century, which we've hidden for so long, are now on display.' He pointed to a small golden icon in the corner of the room. He then broke down, tears falling slowly down his face, and stared into his tea.

There was a time when the young used to leave the village for the towns, only to return when they were too old to earn a living. But with the price rises and the poor standard of living in the cities, they now stay on the land. 'It's the only way we can feed our families,' said a young man with a balalaika, leaning against the wall at the back of the room.

The meeting turned confessional. An old man opposite me admitted that he had been a tax collector under Stalin. He wept as he spoke. 'When I came back from the war, I was offered one of two jobs – the first a policeman, the second a tax collector. I became a tax collector, stealing money from my own people for Stalin. The people were starving but they still had to hand over 44 kilos of meat, 380 litres of milk, 300 eggs, a pig skin, wool from every sheep and between 300 and 400 roubles per fruit tree, to the state. And I had to make sure they did it. On the communal farms, the people were paid in kind, so the only way that they could pay the fruit-tree tax was by selling their own food to pay the state. Most of the Cossacks cut down their own trees because they couldn't afford to pay.' The room remained silent as he spoke and he bowed his head and shuffled his feet, uncomfortable at the attention. 'But,' he added, relief in his voice, 'I was dismissed. There were ten families who just couldn't pay, so I wrote to Moscow to excuse them from the taxes. They dismissed me, and made the families pay up.'

We were serenaded out of the building, the thirty women and musicians following us into the snow, swirling in circles and singing. Clapping their hands, they poured blessings upon us. One old woman caught my hand and spun me around with her, goading me to bounce up and down in the snow. The religious man clasped both my hands in his and made the sign of the cross over my forehead: 'I'm not afraid of anything any more,' he said, smiling, his eyes bloodshot with emotion. 'I've nothing left to lose. Everything's possible now. Give the Cossacks back their freedom and their land and they'll feed themselves and half of Russia, as they did before.'

After lunching with the Ataman, where I drank toast after heart-warming toast to peace, international relations and the veterans of the Afghan War, we drove back to Rostov. On the way, Kolya was hauled over by the traffic police, who did not recognize their boss in someone else's car. There was much apologizing and bowing, to Kolya's evident amusement. He mildly castigated them for their impertinence and told them to keep up the good work.

We were to catch the train to Nalchik, but since it had come from Moscow, there were no tickets to be had. We went to the traffic police headquarters, where we sat for an hour or so, watching television in the shadow of Derzinsky's portrait. Then we were taken to the train. Surrounded by police, we were escorted to a first-class compartment. Miraculously, where there had been no tickets, there were now two.

Kabardinsky Balkai

DAY 28

Yura met us at the station with his two small sons, Dima and Dennis. He had a telephone description of us from some friends in Moscow and grabbed my shoulder as Joth and I stood vacantly on the platform. Yura's neighbour, Artur, drove us home, his eight-month-old daughter, Anilana, sitting on his lap. The two families lived on the outskirts of Nalchik in a hideous, pale blue, prefabricated apartment block housing around 2,000 people. There was only one entrance, and one telephone line.

Yura was tall but stooped, with grey, lank hair, brown, crooked teeth and bright blue eyes. His hand gestures were fussy and his manner frenetic. He has two jobs because one does not pay enough to keep his two sons. A geologist, he is a researcher at Nalchik University, a job he loves; the rest of the time he works at a publishing house, which he finds dull. He earns a total of 1,000 roubles, or $10, a month.

When we arrived at the two-bedroomed flat, Yura's wife Olya was in the kitchen, a place she rarely left throughout our stay, making stuffed cabbage rolls. We sat down to breakfast, drinking the last of the coffee, which Olya had been saving so long that it had gone stale in the jar. The couple have no connections and have never seen hard currency; they queue in shops and buy in bulk when they can. They have no car and bicycle to work in the summer.

Olya was slim, with long, curly hair, large blue eyes and thick oval glasses in white frames. Like Yura, she is a geologist. They met at Moscow University, moved to Nalchik when they married and now work together at the University.

Sitting around the kitchen table in silence, Yura stared at our Western cigarettes. I gave him a packet, which he snatched. 'These cost 80 roubles, you know, or sometimes 100. I could never afford to smoke them,' he said as he lit up, half closing his eyes in pleasure.

Nalchik is the capital of the Kabardinsky Balkai Autonomous Republic, in the heart of the Caucasus. Geographically divided into mountains, inhabited principally by the Balkar, and planes, populated by the Kabardinsky, the republic is home to some sixty-seven racial groups who rarely, if ever, mix.

We took the bus to market. Olya, like every Russian, carried her bag with her just in case. The market was full of fruit and pickled vegetables sold by South Koreans and Azerbaijanis. It was all expensive. Olya wandered around, looking at all the produce on sale, walking up to stalls and asking the price, shrugging her shoulders and walking away. Eventually, under much pressure from the children, she bought half a kilo of green mandarins for 38 roubles. The two boys bounced around her like puppies as she handed one out at a time, holding a few back for treats later.

Sitting on some steps waiting for Olya while she talked to a friend, I was shouted at by an old woman: 'Stop sitting there, girl, you're chilling your ovaries, you'll ruin your reproductive organs and you won't be able to have babies for the state.' I stood up immediately so as not to offend her, and sat down again after she had walked by. Next an old man, covered in medals, castigated me for the same reason. 'I did that during the war and it ruined my fertility,' he added. He then removed his false teeth. 'That also happened in the war – I was shot through the mouth.' He laughed at my surprise, displaying his naked mouth. Then, sniggering to himself, he walked off.

'What did they want?' asked Olya. 'I've no idea,' I replied. 'It's your clothes, you see. You look strange and that makes people want to talk to you. We never see foreigners here,' she explained.

Walking on, we came across a courtyard crammed full of makeshift wooden shacks. I wanted to talk to the inhabitants, but Yura was afraid. I went in and eventually he followed.

Sitting in the courtyard was a man playing with his son in the snow. He invited us in. In the first room was a small table with two chairs and a sofa; in the second was a bed. Radiora was a driver and earned 5,000 roubles a month. Tamara, his wife, used to work in a shop. Their two children were scantily clad and grubby; the baby crawled around the floor, putting cigarette butts in her mouth. They had come to Nalchik to look for work and were living in the shack until they received their communal flat, which they would eventually get in six months.

Tamara boiled some water on the wood-burning stove, which also heated the room. She then poured it into glasses, sweetening it with jam. We ate bruised apples from their allotment outside the city. 'Life's appalling here,' said Radiora. 'We have nowhere to live and we can't buy anything in the shops. Life was so much better before — as a driver, I was always in work. Now, there's no petrol and no one can afford drivers. I could earn a lot of money if I tried, but what's the use when there's nothing to buy?'

We ate supper with Olya's parents. Her mother was a Russian literature teacher who gave private lessons for 7 roubles an hour; her father, who had been a radio operator during the Second World War, talked about getting drunk in Finland when it was all over. 'That's the only time I've been abroad, during the last days of the war,' he smiled. 'It was fantastic.'

He had spent the day working on their allotment. 'It's going well,' he announced. 'After all, everything on the table has come from there.' We drank home-made cider and damson wine, with pickled peppers and tomatoes. While we ate, the children played an uninspiring board game that they had invented, using a home-made dice and buttons for counters. 'It's impossible to buy games for children, and if you do find them, they're too expensive,' said Olya as she saw me look over at the two boys.

Running for the trolley bus to take us home, Yura slipped and fell on the ice, breaking the bottle of damson wine that Olya's parents had given them, which soaked the bread in the bag. As soon as we got back to the flat, Olya washed the wine off the bread and put it in the oven to dry. She then filtered the wine of glass and decanted it into another bottle. 'I couldn't throw it away,' she said as she washed out the plastic bag and hung it up to dry. 'You don't know when you'll be able to buy any more.'

Artur, the next-door neighbour, had invited us to stay with his parents, who lived in a village on the plane, and Olya decided that we should make a cake for the trip. Walking out onto her balcony, she brought in a huge slab of butter that she had bought before New Year and the price rises. She had three kilograms of butter and two of margarine. 'I queued for about six hours for all this about seven weeks ago. I keep it on the balcony because it's always freezing there in the winter. In the summer we grow tomatoes there, which I pickle for the winter. Without the balcony, I think we would starve.'

She cut off a small cube of butter and brushed it over the frying pan, but made the cake without butter. She complained about the quality of the flour. 'It was much better last year,' she said as she opened a tin of condensed milk that she had been saving for months. She pulled out a carrier bag of sugar from under the sink and mixed everything together with water. Then she poured the mixture into the frying pan and placed it in the oven. 'I hope that works,' she muttered. 'It usually does.'

Olya's fridge was full of bottled and pickled vegetables. Huge jars contained grey, shredded cabbage that tasted of nothing but vinegar and large tomatoes swam around in the golden liquid. All the food was from her parents' garden or her balcony. 'It's the only way we survive. We can't afford anything in the market — you saw how expensive it all is.'

DAY 29

I spent the morning talking to Olya. We sat drinking tea — we had finished the coffee yesterday and had not managed to find any more. She talked about giving birth. 'Our hospitals are terrible places,' she said, playing with her teaspoon. 'You can only get help if you know or bribe someone. When I had Dima, he cost us three bottles of cognac, a bag of sweets and a packet of coffee. You have to give something to everyone involved — a bottle to the doctor, a bottle to the head sister, presents to all the staff — otherwise no one will look after you.' She leant back in her chair and looked out of the window, taking her glasses off to clean them on her jumper. 'I was sitting in the corridor waiting for a bed and I knew I was just about to give birth. I shouted, but no one listened. I carried on shouting, but no one came.' She screwed up her face as she spoke and shook her head gently from side to side. 'Then eventually a girlfriend who works in the hospital heard and rushed me to bed. I gave birth almost immediately. If it hadn't been for her, I'd have had Dima right there in the corridor.' She looked at me for a reaction. I shook my head.

'The same thing happened when Yura had toothache. He'd been unable to do anything for two days, he was in so much pain. But when we went to the polyclinic there were no doctors available. We were told they were "all booked up until tomorrow". Fifty roubles and a bottle of vodka later, suddenly the doors opened and someone looked at him.' She threw her hands in the air, as if witnessing the 'miracle'. 'It's the same everywhere. You have to know someone, or you pay. That's our national health system — *very* free!'

Olya spent the rest of the morning making a salad for the people we were to stay with. 'It's a tradition, you know. They have nothing and we at least have something. You can't possibly go to stay somewhere without taking presents.'

As dusk was falling, we piled into Artur's car, with Fatima his wife, Anilana and Yura. The car was packed with people and food. The only thing missing was the alcohol. We went in search of vodka. In the outskirts of Nalchik we passed a clandestine market and in the dark I could see a group of people gathered around a man with a plastic carrier bag. 'Look there!' shouted Yura. Artur pulled in. No luck: the man was only selling cigarettes.

We drove on, stopping about an hour later at a small village just off the main road, where Artur knew there to be a black market. It had closed for the night. Further up the road, we called in at some relations of Artur's. An old man appeared at the sound of the car horn. They, too, were out of vodka, but he was sure that next door had some. Three houses later we found a man selling vodka in old Pepsi bottles for 50 roubles a throw. It was expensive, but we could not arrive without any.

Kuba is a small village that belongs to a Kabardinsky collective farm. Arriving at a small house, we were greeted by the grandfather, Tolya, a large man with a florid complexion and a heart problem. By his side stood his diminutive wife, who spoke no Russian, only Kabardinsky. I had learnt a few words that afternoon and said, 'Good evening'. She smiled and bowed.

They had a two-roomed house and a yard, over the other side of which was a guest house that they had not quite completed. In the main house stood an iron bed covered in a patchwork quilt, a table and a coal-burning stove on which warmed a tin of water. In the guest house, a huge stove burnt high and snug. Sitting at the table in one of the two rooms of the guest house, next to a huge bed covered in pink satin and white lace, we were waited on all evening by the grandmother, Nefasset, and Lyba who, as the wife of the youngest son, came lowest in the family hierarchy and was supposed to do all the work.

Lyba was twenty-two years old and had two children, one aged four, the other three. She was from another village further south and had met her husband at seventeen, when he came home with her brother on leave from the army. She was rather beautiful, with long, black hair tied up in a scarf, creamy skin and bright brown eyes, which she lowered every time she approached the table.

We sat eating course after course. The table was crammed with salads, bread and fried batter rings. The men, once they had sat down, never left the table. We finished the vodka and then a bottle of cognac. The grandfather, unable to drink because of his heart, made the toasts.

Life in the village had been hard recently, he told us. The village depended on apples for its livelihood, and last year's crop had been completely destroyed by freak hail that had killed the trees, as well as some of their animals. The state had paid a little compensation, but no one had anything to sell or live on at the moment.

Tolya had been born and spent his whole life on the collective farm: it was the only way of life that he could understand. He began to talk politics. 'Life is terrible at the moment,' he said, handing out his glass for his wife to fill with more tea. 'Bring back Stalin, is what I say. We ate well and life was peaceful then. We had no problems and our rouble meant something. In fact, everything started going wrong with perestroika. I hate Yeltsin and I know that soon there'll be civil war, and it won't be until we all kill each other that there'll be calm in this country of ours.'

Tolya was a forceful man, with dogmatic notions about the position of women. His wife and Lyba did not sit or eat with us until he had gone to bed. Yet he was also my host. I did not argue with him, and dutifully drank my toast to Stalin, clinking my glass with everyone else around the table.

As soon as Tolya had gone to bed, Lyba came alive. She brought out her accordion, took her scarf off her black hair and began to sing. Artur danced in the small room, his body boldly erect as he swirled around, clapping his hands, throwing his head back and staring down his long nose. He gained a proud elegance with each step.

Lyba intrigued me. Behind her quiet subservience lay a bold vivaciousness that lit up her face as she played. I wondered what she would have done with her life, had she not lived here. Then I pulled myself off the fat, judgmental cushion of capitalism and began to clap along with the music.

The children were already asleep, three in a bed next door, as the evening drew to a close. Lyba and Fatima curled up with their babies; Joth and I, as guests, were given the pink and lace bed, while Yura and Artur slept together in the single bed next to the grandparents.

DAY 30

I stood in the snow as Lyba poured tepid water over my hands from a small pewter jug. She handed me a hard bar of soap and an embroidered cloth to dry my hands. Then she once more poured water as I brushed my teeth.

Lyba went backwards and forwards to the well, climbing up and down the metal ladder. All around the well, spilt water had frozen to smooth ice and she skidded slightly as she pulled the heavy metal churns to the surface. Another girl from the village, in a long skirt and shawl, stood at the top of the steps, a yoke across her shoulders. Next to her was a small sledge which she would use to carry the churns home.

Again we were waited on by the grandmother. We sat in a row on the matrimonial bed beside the stove, the table pushed in close. She served last night's leftovers, accompanied by a pickled beetroot salad and large cups of tea. Lyba washed up as we went along, rinsing the plates in the metal bowl that sat warming on the stove. Her hands were already pink with cold.

When we came to leave, the grandmother pushed presents into my hand – a pink, nylon, extra-large nightie, a bar of soap and a bottle of shampoo, which she had obviously been keeping as treats for herself. I thanked her and she clasped both my hands in her own. They were chapped through hard work and trembled slightly. 'Go with God, and come again to stay,' she said, brushing my cheeks with the smooth, thin skin of her lips. I kissed Lyba goodbye and squeezed her shoulders. She blushed and looked down at the snow. The grandfather had already gone to work.

We drove through the village. Someone had slaughtered a cow and a queue of people had lined up alongside a pony and trap, squabbling over huge slabs of fresh meat that glistened red and blue in the snow. We passed the black market that had been closed the previous evening. Now it was full of bottles of vodka decanted into smaller Pepsi bottles. Each stall also had a consignment of packets of Dutch cornflakes, which were covered in humanitarian aid stickers. Artur had no idea what they were. 'Can you eat those?' he asked. 'Well, they must be good because they cost as much as a bottle of vodka.' Yura saw coffee beans and ran to buy some. They were 200 roubles a bag, so he just smelt them, breathing the aroma deep into his lungs before putting them down again. We all bought some beer, but there was so much silt lying in a heavy layer at the bottom of each bottle that it would have to be filtered before it could be drunk.

On the way back into Nalchik we stopped off at a commercial shop selling an odd assortment of clothes, tights and lipsticks. There, gathering dust in a corner, was a pair of Pretty Polly tights with a Tesco price tag – 86p. Perhaps some benevolent woman had given them away as a present, little thinking they would end up, several years later, in a commercial shop.

Fatima's brother had given her some tracksuits to sell. He made frequent trips to Tallin to buy Western clothes, which he then brought back to Nalchik to sell at a profit. But the shop was not buying today. At least, they were, but not at the right price. Someone else had come from Tallin the day before, and had just sold them a bundle of tracksuits. 'I'll have to wait until there's a shortage, then we'll sell them for a good price,' said Fatima, folding up the bright blue and red nylon jackets and putting them back into her bag.

That evening we sat down to pickled cucumbers and cold spaghetti, washed down with vodka and some cognac. Olya became quite giggly and began to talk about her time at Moscow State University. 'I lived off fried potatoes and tea, with my girlfriend, in our student hostel,' she said, laughing.

'D'you remember that place in the woods where we all used to drink, buying illegal vodka from that kiosk on the way?' she said, turning to Yura. There had been nowhere for the students to gather and talk freely, so they would go into the woods near the university and sit around a camp fire. 'There would always be people there, and even in winter we would go with rugs and sit in the snow around the fire, get very drunk and discuss things,' she reminisced.

'D'you remember Marxist-Leninist theory?' she asked Yura. 'We had this great teacher who knew that it was a load of rubbish, but we had to learn it. The Marxist-Leninist theory about geology ... what did *they* know about rocks?' she laughed. 'We all cheated in our exam,' she said. She explained the system of verbal examinations. Standing in front of a panel of examiners, the student had to pick a question number out of a hat. The examiner then read out the question. 'All the question numbers were on pink paper, except for number eight, which was written on green. They could never understand why everyone chose number eight and kept on getting the answer right.'

She went on to recount the story of another friend who had been so drunk when he had gone into his exam that he had passed out on the floor in front of the examiners. 'And they passed him,' she squealed.

I left them listening to old records and talking about their student days.

DAY 31

We spent the first three hours that morning looking for petrol. Almost every station had run out, and those that had any were inundated with rows of cars and people armed with petrol cans. Eventually Ygor, a friend of Yura's and our driver, managed to persuade a friend to part with some of his and we set off to the Balkai region, high in the mountains outside Nalchik.

The Balkar are a strange-looking people, with pale, freckled faces, thick, black hair and pale eyes with hooded lids to protect them from the glare of the sun that constantly shines in the mountains and reflects off the snow. Arriving in Kashkhatad, the region's main town, I bought some salted cheese, which was less expensive than in Nalchik, to eat on our journey.

From Kashkhatad we set off high into the mountains, along snow-covered roads and narrow tracks that cut into the rock, climbing the Chegem Gorge, where frozen waterfalls glistened in the sun as they clung to the pink rock. The gorge plummeted below us on one side of the road and at the bottom, a river flowed irritatedly around its own icebergs. Arriving at the Blue Lake, a deep-turquoise lagoon fed by an underground spring, we threw in some kopecks and watched them glint as they spun down to the bottom.

The villages in the mountains are relatively new. In 1944 the Balkar were rounded up by Stalin and sent at gunpoint in sealed trains to Kazakhstan. Still in their nightclothes, they did not have time to collect their belongings. Thousands died of cold and hunger on the journey, but those that survived returned to their villages in 1957, to find them in ruins. Undeterred, they started again, rebuilding their homes and their lives.

We stopped at a small village high on one of the peaks. Woolly cattle and sheep roamed the streets and fat donkeys stood dozing in the sun. As we drove through, all those who stood gossiping in the road stopped and stared. 'They never get cars up here,' said Yura. 'There's no petrol, no cars and these people never go anywhere – they have all they want here.'

Sasha and his family farmed one hectare of land that had been given to them by the kolhoz. Tradition has it that the youngest son will inherit the land – the older sons either have to apply to the kolhoz for more land or move to another village. 'No one owns the land here, except for the state,' said Sasha, blinking his pale eyes.

Sasha and his wife, both in their sixties, had met on the train to Alma-Ata, the capital of Kazakhstan, on that night in 1944. They had fallen in love and returned in 1957 to rebuild their lives, in a new house, in a new village. 'I originally came from a village higher up the mountains, where I lived in a small house carved out of the rock,' said the mother, pointing out of the window.

We sat on the floor of their large living room, whose walls were covered in dark red carpets. The grandmother, in a rust dress that trailed to the floor, with a skinny grey plait down her back, wandered around muttering to herself and tugging at the black beads that hung round her neck. We then moved to another room, next to the living room, where we were handed large mugs of live curd and crisp apples. The family did not eat with us – it is an insult to guests to eat with them. Instead, we ate alone, waited on by the two old women in the family.

Strolling through the village, which consisted of two rows of houses huddled around the main road, I met Alec. He was sitting in the sun, smoking cigarettes with a group of old men and chatting about the price rises. I told him I was from England. It meant nothing to him. But when he realized that I was not Russian, he immediately ran home and returned with a huge bag of apples. 'You must be hungry if you are travelling,' he said, handing over the brimming bag. 'I grew these myself. The air is clean here and the earth is rich – you will never taste anything so delicious.' He was right.

I sat and talked to him about his animals. 'How do you know whose cow is whose, if they are all wandering around in the street?' I asked.

'We know them by their faces,' he replied. 'See that one with the long eyelashes?' I looked round at the four identical cows munching a mound of hay that lay in the snow. 'Well, she's mine,' he said proudly. I nodded. 'Lovely,' I replied.

He invited me into his house. As we walked through the iron gate, his wife came out to meet us. They lived next door to his parents. I was introduced to his mother – she bowed and so did I. 'This girl is foreign,' he said, throwing his arms in the air dramatically, 'but she can understand us.'

His wife went to the well to collect water for the tea and then began sifting flour. She made a pile of meat dumplings, while Alec and I sat talking. Mixing home-ground flour with water, she made the cases and filled them with meat from one of their cows that they had slaughtered three days before. She cooked on a charcoal-burning stove.

'We live well here. We have everything we need – the only thing we can't grow is sugar and we can sometimes buy that in the one shop in the village. We live in the top five per cent of people in the country. The only people who live better than us are the Communists and the mafia. But then, they're criminals,' said Alec, laughing.

Having eaten meat pasties straight off the stove and slurped our tea, Alec escorted me back to Sasha's house to say goodbye. The whole family came to wave us off, bowing and placing their hands on their hearts as they wished us on our way. Just as we left, Sasha brought out his favourite goat and, smacking it on the head, made it leap into air in our honour. The huge animal jumped on its hind legs and danced in the snow, the late afternoon sun shining through its long curly coat. The family stood back admiringly, and then, clapping and laughing, Sasha made it do it again. To everyone's delight, the goat repeated the trick, leaping into the air, its heavy horns arching to touch its back.

Artur drove us to the station an hour out of Nalchik. We sat in silence in the foggy darkness, alone on the snow-covered road, the light on his petrol gauge flashing red. We pulled in at numerous petrol stations, but all were empty. We stopped and poured the last few drops from the spare can into the empty tank and crawled into one last station. They had petrol and would open in twenty minutes.

We arrived at the train station without any tickets and could not buy any. I went off to seek the help of the police, but when I walked into their office, not one of them took his eyes off the flickering television while I begged for help. After I had finished my spiel about how important we were and how we had to get to Baku immediately, they nodded. I presumed that meant that they would help.

We sat for another two hours in the freezing car, gradually filling it with cigarette smoke. The train's arrival was announced over the tannoy and we returned to the police. They walked us down the platform and opened up the door of a carriage. A screaming woman threw me back off the steps into the snow. The police tried to push me back onto the train. Joth and I stood on the steps of the carriage, laden with luggage, as the woman shouted at the police, refusing to take us on board. The train began to pull out of the station and we both barged past her into the carriage. After much argument and shouting, she eventually moved us from the corridor and let us into her compartment, which was piled high with blankets and sheets. We perched on chairs, leaning on her table, surrounded by luggage.

Despite her vicious exterior, Lydmilla was a kind woman with a nasty job. She made us cups of tea and, running her hands through her cropped red hair, she explained that she had worked the Moscow-Baku train for the last thirty-one years.

'If I look out of the window I know exactly where we are,' she announced proudly. 'I can tell you the next station, and the one after that.' She guarded her carriage like an angry bear would its lair. At each stop she stood defiantly in the doorway, throwing people off the train into the snow. Hurling abuse at them, she would tell them that there was no room. The train stopped about every half-hour and the scene repeated itself every time, as more and more people clamoured to get aboard.

'The train fares are so expensive now, I don't know how anyone can afford to travel,' she said, her voice hoarse through shouting. 'And no one can get tickets at the moment, even if they have the money. I have a famous Azerbaijani film director sitting in the corridor. He has directed fifteen films and he still can't get a bed.'

Lydmilla has a two-day stopover every week in Moscow, where she does her shopping. She showed me some tins of German frankfurters that she had bought to take back to her mother. 'I don't know what they are, but they looked nice on the packet,' she said. I explained how to cook them. 'Moscow is so expensive now,' she said in a tired voice. 'Children's pants are 25 roubles a pair – I earn 500 roubles a month. It's no wonder that children are running around naked. There's something wrong with a government that's cruel to children.'

Lydmilla lives alone in Baku with her mother, a pensioner who receives 450 roubles a month. 'My mother has worked all her life for this country and now that she's old and incapable of working, that's all she gets. Life is awful for her.'

We sat talking, drinking tea and eating bread, waiting for a vacant bed. Nina, a friend of Lydmilla's who ran a compartment further down the train, already had a couple sleeping head to toe in her bed, but said that she would rent it to us when they had left the train.

At 2 a.m. the train stopped and Nina appeared. Grabbing hold of half of my luggage, she stormed down the corridor, shouting that it was better to move while the train was stationary. We barged past row upon row of sleeping bodies piled up in the corridor, Nina occasionally kicking them to move them aside, before forging on.

The bed in Nina's compartment was still warm from the previous occupants. Smoothing down the crumpled sheets, she beckoned us in. She then stood guard outside all night to prevent Azerbaijanis from disturbing us. Joth and I slept head to toe in the tiny, airless room.

During the night, news got out that there were foreigners on the train. We fended off a constant queue of people, as they came and asked for presents. Nina looked exhausted – she had been up for the past two nights, having sold her bed from Moscow to Baku. She sat down and burst into tears and I made her a cup of tea. I think that she had also made some more money by sleeping with a large Azerbaijani the night before, although she would not admit it. But he loitered around, shouting at her, and her right eye was bruised. She stayed in the compartment, hiding, until the train arrived at the station.

We went looking for Lydmilla, to thank her. She offered us another night on the train. 'It doesn't leave for Moscow until the day after tomorrow. Lots of people stay another night – it's like a cheap hotel and you don't need your passport or visa,' she said with a laugh. We said that we might see her later.

Azerbaijan

· · · · · · · · · · · · · · · · ·

DAY 32

The Azerbaijanis are a dark, Arab-looking people, with their own language and a legendary reputation for hard drinking, loud music and wild dancing. Baku, dusty and smelling of spices, exuded the Middle East. Yet it was still distinctly Soviet. Huge, concrete buildings cast shadows over softer sandstone and intricately carved, wooden balconies. There was tension in the streets.

'We are at war,' said the taxi driver, in thick-accented Russian, as he explained why a crowd had gathered outside the main Soviet.

Everyone we met displayed a distinct pride in the battle over Nagorny Karabakh, probably because the territory was far enough away from the capital not to affect them directly. All radios were tuned to the news: it was a war that everyone followed as we would the FA Cup Final – Armenia 32, Azerbaijan, 20.

The central market was packed with fruit and nuts. The Azerbaijanis control the free markets all over Russia: they have a near-monopoly on fresh fruit and a mafia strong enough to ensure a good transport network. Those who are not Azerbaijani must pay for their right to set up a stall in a market. Their own market was probably the best stocked we had seen, yet the cigarette kiosk just outside had more customers. We paid 180 roubles for some mandarins and understood why the market was empty.

That evening we went out to a restaurant. Russians rarely go to restaurants, preferring to entertain at home because, it was once explained to me, they had no idea what was in the restaurant food, you needed connections to get through the door, and it was always unreasonably expensive. 'We can do it better at home,' I was told.

Nevertheless, we went. Sitting on carpets in our own cave, we ate *shashlik*, or kebabs. In one corner of the courtyard, an Azerbaijani band played to the groups of diners in the warren of caves all around. Our waiter was convinced that we were from Poland. 'We don't have foreigners here any more. We used to, but since *perestroika*, our restaurants and hotels are empty.'

We left somewhat the worse for alcohol and flagged down a car to take us back to the hotel. In these hard times, almost every car will stop to drive you anywhere for money. Two Azerbaijanis drew up. They were in a worse state than we were, but the wind was cold and we were extremely tired. As we swerved through the streets, the man in the passenger seat spun round and, breathing cognac fumes over me, asked where we were from. My reply caused great hilarity. 'Margret Tacher!' they screamed with laughter. The driver had to stop the car, he thought this was so funny. 'Where's the Iron Lady now?' he asked, tears rolling down his face. 'In bed with Gorbachev in his dacha in the Crimea,' replied his friend. They paused for more laughter and then drove on, sniggering.

DAY 33

We spent the morning queuing for tickets to take the boat from Baku across the Caspian Sea to Turkmenia. Forcing our way through the crowd that had gathered at the docks, we managed to get to the front. There would be no tickets today, or tomorrow, or any day, for us. 'Foreigners are not allowed to travel on the boat,' said the woman behind the counter. I called the manager, who looked at our visas, said that we could not get onto the boat, and sent us off to the visa office.

The visa office was almost impossible to find. The taxi driver ripped us off and left us in the middle of nowhere; a dozen passers-by all professed to know the way, but sent us in different directions. Eventually we found an ambulance driver, who took us there, nestled in the back amongst the blankets and drips.

The visa office was closed until 4 o'clock that afternoon and yet, at 10.30, a crowd had already gathered. The boat left at three, so some hard talking was needed. The doorman was letting in those who had bribed him, or who were important enough to warrant entry. We barged in behind a man in a smart suit, demanding to see the chief. (In difficult situations, our motto had always been to go for the man at the top.) He was pleasant enough and said that our visas would be organized in a matter of minutes. He rang through, but no one answered the phone. 'They must be on a break,' he said, embarrassed at his lack of clout.

Eventually a man appeared, who then disappeared with our visas. He returned to say that it was impossible; not only did we not have a visa for Azerbaijan, which meant that we were illegal and he would have to inform the KGB, but also Krasnovodsk was a closed town and on no account would we be allowed to go there.

Joth and I had no choice but to return to the docks in the hope that we could persuade the chief of the port authority to let us buy tickets. We had to leave that day: we were illegal and had been found out. Walking into the chief's office, we were all smiles. 'The office is closed and they can't give us a visa until tomorrow,' I lied sweetly. 'Then you can't leave,' he said defiantly, rather enjoying his power. My face throbbed with frustration.

Changing tack, I asked him about business – the first thing I could think of. The conversation drifted slowly but surely to dollars. He offered to change money. Joth and I both realized this was our chance. 'We'll change $20 and give you $30 as a present,' I said, with a delicious smile. He leapt up from his desk, opened the office safe, and handed us a wad of crisp notes. He then sprinted across the courtyard to the ticket office and came back moments later with two smooth tickets to a two-bed cabin. 'The best there is,' he said, laughing. 'If anyone stops you, you've never met me and I'll deny all knowledge of you.' He had done this sort of deal before.

Half an hour later we were sitting at the port, waiting for the bus to take us to the boat. Pale skin and strange clothes meant that, within ten minutes, we were surrounded by a group of about fifty people. They stared in silence. One man, with a blue tracksuit and gold chain, started up the conversation. 'How much for your bag?' he asked, pointing at my rucksack. 'It's not for sale,' I said, trying to avoid his eye. But, with the ice broken, we were bombarded with questions. Where were we from? How much was this? Were we married? Did we have children? Why not? Did we have presents? Why not? I was sitting on the pavement, surrounded by the crowd. Joth told me to stand. 'Look more in control,' he advised. The situation was about to get nasty.

Suddenly, from nowhere, a stocky man and his blonde wife came over. 'Why don't you come and talk to us,' he said, putting a paternal arm round my shoulder and guiding me through the crowd to where a small girl stood dancing up and down in the dust. His name was Syid and he and his girlfriend, Sveta, along with her daughter Alissa, were taking the same boat to Krasnovodsk. They protected us from further interrogation and chatted on the bus.

When we arrived at the boat there was a row of policemen checking passports and visas. Syid saw our nervousness and, taking me to one side, said, 'Just look confident. Barge your way to the front and march past them.'

We did as we were told. Walking up the gangplank, we had only one more official to pass. I felt sick and sweaty. He took hold of our passports. I smiled. 'But you're foreign,' he said, turning to his colleague. 'They're foreign,' he said again. He turned to me. 'You're the first foreigners on this boat. Welcome aboard Great Britain,' he shouted. Everyone laughed, but not quite as loudly as Joth and I.

Our cabin reeked of drains and had a loo that sprayed me in the face with putrid water. Syid and Sveta spent the evening with us. The captain barged in and warned us to keep the door locked. 'People attack, steal from and kill foreigners in this country, you know. A few months ago the Armenians blew one of these ferries out of the water, killing all aboard. I don't want any scenes. Good night.'

There was a constant knocking at our door. 'Hello English, we know you're in there,' said strange voices. I ignored them all and stared out of the window, watching the sun die slowly pink over the Caspian Sea.

Turkmenia

· · · · · · · · · · · · · · · · · ·

DAY 34

The screechings of a woman coming to collect our sheets, which we had rented for the night, woke us up at 3.45 a.m. We had arrived in Krasnovodsk. One of the largest towns in Turkmenia, it hugs the coast of the Caspian Sea, looking westwards towards the Azerbaijani coast. Through the daze of lack of sleep and a headache induced by the reek of urine and detergent that filled the cabin, I was suddenly terrified. We had bribed the authorities in Azerbaijan to let us leave the country. Krasnovodsk was a closed town, they said, predicting that we would be arrested and sent back on the next plane to Moscow. We had no visas and no conception of what we were going to do there, other than that Sveta and Syid had invited us to stay.

I had that gut-churning, clammy-palm, waiting-to-see-the-headmaster feeling as we stood on deck, watching the harbour lights in the chilly dawn. Joth and I had concocted numerous schemes to get past the awaiting officials: the 'I am very important' routine, forging to the front of the queue and acting loudly foreign; the 'head down, foot shuffling and look inconspicuous' trick; and the 'here's $50 and keep quiet' plan. We tagged along behind Sveta, Syid and Alissa, looking obviously foreign with our good-quality boots and well-made rucksacks, rather than the Russian cardboard boxes with string handles. Following the sleepy crowd down the gangplank, we distanced ourselves just enough from Sveta and Syid so that if we were caught, they would not be taken as accomplices.

Turkmenian customs did not exist.

We had wasted hours of planning and a great deal of nervous energy on one half-asleep docker. Syid sighed with relief and took out fifty packets of short, filterless cigarettes, which he had bought the day before in Azerbaijan. He shared them with his Turkmenian friend, a small man with a dark, flat, Asian face, wearing the regulation Russian hat – no matter the nationality or the temperature,

Soviets all wear the same, square, fur hats, which seem tattooed to their heads. The cigarettes were for him to take back to the village. 'They have one shop that hasn't had cigarettes for six months and they live in the desert about fifty kilometres from the nearest town. They're a form of hard currency at the moment,' explained Syid.

We stood in the cold, waiting for the bus to take us to the centre of town. One arrived, but was soon loaded to more than capacity as family after family laden with boxes and children, crammed aboard like sheep. We sat back and hoped we would not have to wait too long for the next one.

When we eventually arrived in the town centre, drawing up to the eternal flame to the unknown victims of war, the driver extorted 3 roubles from each of the passengers. A large-breasted, Arab-looking woman, with two filthy children in tow, began to scream. 'What d'you mean, 3 roubles? This journey should cost half that. I'm not paying,' she yelled, her hands placed aggressively on her hips, as her small children, squeezed into grubby, brown, anorak-material romper suits, mimicked her from the floor of the bus. For a few minutes she continued her tirade, while others sneaked past and off the bus. Then the driver closed the doors and took off, zig-zagging through the town centre with the rest of the passengers screaming, shouting and banging. His protest made, he parked and let everyone off. The fat woman was still screaming, as were her children, who were obviously distressed. Their faces covered with a mixture of snot and dust, they tugged at her stained, calf-length skirt and cheap, high shoes that cut into her heels, and bawled. A large Russian, smelling of stale vodka and pickles, ended the argument. He shoved the woman off the bus and into the dust, called her a whore and muttered through his beard, 'Just fuck off and feed your children.' Humiliated, she walked off.

Shivering with cold, I sat on my bags and watched the sun rise over this dusty port town. It was surrounded by red mountains that slowly became visible as the light grew. Eventually, the teashop in the bus station opened and all the people who had been on the boat crowded in and sat down over small pots of green tea and stale buns dipped in sugar.

The bus for Chiliken arrived and once more a screaming struggle ensued. The crowd made way for a tiny, stooping old woman in traditional Turkmenian dress. Covered in a blanket, with turquoise and silver necklaces and brightly coloured headscarf, patterned socks and slippers, she was pushed up into the bus. Her dark skin was heavily lined, her hands the same texture as the cracked earth that she had tilled all her life. She earned the respect of the crowd, who gave her the best seat on the bus.

The bus was packed with Turkmenian women in coloured headscarves. We sat at the back, next to the fat woman and her two screaming children. As the bus set off into the desert, where wild camels were the only other traffic on the road, the fat woman brought out a large, loose breast and shoved the nipple into the mouth of one of the children. The boy must have been nearly three years old, but with the shortage of food and the lack of any specialized products for babies, the Soviets breastfeed their children far longer than mothers in the West. She soon fell asleep, as did her son, but as the nipple fell from his mouth, what had been a touching scene turned to something strangely grotesque.

For miles there was nothing but flat land and spikey gorse. The sun shone through but gave no heat. We drove through shanty towns of low, concrete buildings that seemed to have been hastily constructed with a complete disregard for the people who would live in them. These shanty towns displayed their intestines – pipes, cables and vents, which are so considerately filed underground in the West, stood twisted and corroded on supports high above the ground. The bus stopped sporadically and I sat and watched as people walked off, carrying their suitcases, into the desert.

After three hours we reached Nebit Dag. It was larger than all the towns we had passed, though its buildings were still made of the same concrete. Its wide streets were almost deserted. The wind whipped up the dust and sent clouds careering down the pavements. We sat once more at the bus station, waiting. I bought some potato pancakes and watched a group of small boys in dark blue school uniforms playing with a metal strip and an inner tube of a bicycle wheel. They ran round in circles tirelessly, seeing who was fastest.

Four hours later, a bus that was even older than the last arrived to take us to Chiliken. It was packed once more with Turkmenian women, loaded down with purchases from the market. There was a shortage of tickets and all those who had bribed the conductor squatted in the aisle as we drove past police checkpoints. As soon as anyone spotted a motorcycle, used by the traffic police, the whole bus shouted in unison, 'Motorcycle, motorcycle', and those in the aisle once more leapt to the floor. We were stopped at one checkpoint and the illegal passengers lay down, their bellies on the floor of the bus, while the policeman wandered around outside. After five minutes' negotiation, he took a bribe from the driver and we continued on our journey. We passed black lakes of oil and water that spilt into the desert from broken oil pipes or crumbling wells, and more wild camels. Turning along the road that ran along the shore of the Caspian, the road began to crumble away. Built on a raised causeway, it is slowly being eaten away by the advancing sea. Quite why the sea is advancing, no one knows; but legend has it that as the Aral Sea retreats, the Caspian advances.

At last we arrived in Chiliken, Sveta's childhood home, where Alissa had been born and where she had met Syid. It was a ghost town: the wind blew paper through the empty streets, no one walked along the wide roads devoid of cars, there was dust everywhere, and a strange silence hung in the air like a heavy cloud. They had been away for a year staying with Sveta's aunt in Zaporozhie, in the Ukraine, searching for work. But they had been unable to find any.

We walked into the two-bedroomed, ground-floor flat where Sveta's parents lived with their younger daughter, her husband and their daughter. The smell of boiled cabbage and pickles hung in the air. The flat was dark: all the windows had been covered in brown paper to keep out the sun and the dust and dark, gaudy carpets hung on the walls. Sveta had grown up here. We were shown to her room. It was covered in faded posters of Russian heavy metal bands I had never heard of. In one corner was a dusty spool tape recorder and in the other, a narrow bed. A curtain blocked off the room from the rest of the flat.

Sveta's mother was a round, good-humoured woman with violent orange hair that peeked out from underneath her scarf. Her father was in his early sixties but looked much older. He could hardly walk and found it hard to speak. He had little or no memory and rattled on to himself in sudden bouts of madness. The family treated him like some irritating eccentric, whom you fed but usually ignored. His life had been destroyed by his work. He had worked for twenty-five years in the chemical factory that supported and, at the same time, suffocated the town. His body ached all over, his insides hurt, his bones were brittle and the doctors had said that it was already too late to help him.

The chemical factory makes chlorine. The workers, most of whom moved to Chiliken because of the factory, do not wear breathing masks. Children born in the town often have weak bones, are small, thin, have breathing problems, or are deformed in some way. Georgi's face was scarred; the skin on his nose had a permanent yellowness; the veins around his eyes stood to attention. He smoked continuously, using a long, plastic holder. It was his only pleasure. But recently there had been no cigarettes in the town or anywhere around. He leapt upon Syid's supply. 'I hate Gorbachev,' he mumbled as he lit up with his shaking, purple-veined hand. 'He's taken away my only joy. First my job kills me and then *he* destroys me. I spit on *perestroika*. I've worked all my life in this godforsaken place. I stayed here after national service to work in this chemical factory, even though I come from the Ukraine. All I have to show for it is a flat that isn't big enough to house my family. Since Gorbachev, there are no cigarettes and no sausage – he has ruined our country.' With this, he burst into tears. 'We are all going to die,' he said, weeping.

'Oh God, why don't you just shut up,' said Sveta as she gathered up her father and parked him in the corner with a packet of cigarettes.

We wanted to wash before supper, but could only rinse our hands briefly in a basin, as the water had not yet been turned on. There is an acute water shortage in Turkmenia – over eighty per cent of the land is desert – and the town has water for only two and a half or three hours in the evening. We sat down to cabbage soup with floating meatballs and dark, heavy bread, followed by slices of thick fat and boiled potatoes. Out came the *samogon*, a lethal form of moonshine that is reputed to send you blind. It was good *samogon*, by Soviet standards – they judge a drink's quality by its strength not its taste. I knocked back a shot, my eyes watered and my whole body shivered in violent protest. One cough and I drank back a glass of tomato and vinegar, the leftovers of the pickled tomatoes we had eaten for supper. I was not sure which was the more wretched.

I was made to explain the social security system in Britain – a tall order at the best of times, but after the *samogon*, almost impossible. None of them, of course, believed a word I said. 'But we're the only country in the world with free health care,' protested Syid. 'Or that's what we've been told. I don't believe anything any more. We've been told so many lies for so long that no one knows what to believe. Our own television will only show what the authorities want us to see and we can only read what they want us to read. We know nothing about your country.'

Gybia, their next-door neighbour, walked in from upstairs. She was Turkmenian, tall, hefty, with long black hair, a flat face and Eastern eyes. She was twenty-four and four months pregnant, and chuckled heartily, clutching her chest. She smoked constantly and drank the moonshine. She was curious about marriage in our country.

'Do you buy brides in England?' she asked. 'The younger and more innocent they are here, the more expensive. If Joth wants a bride, he can get a really perfect one for a few dollars. I can get him one from the village if he wants one.' Joth declined. 'What d'you mean? Everyone should have a bride, especially if you're over twenty.'

The water came on and all hell broke loose. I was ordered into the bath – a large, rusty tub – where I sat as scalding hot water trickled out of a large shower head. Two and a half inches of red water filled the tub. I squatted there, naked, drunk and feeling vulnerable, as a constant stream of people, oblivious to any need for privacy, came to check on towels or soap. After three minutes, with hardly a drop to my armpits, I was hurried out. 'There's a queue. We must clean the whole family and fill up the bath again with water for tomorrow,' said the grandmother as she wrapped me in a towel the size of a facecloth and ushered me through the house to dress.

The series of baptisms continued for the next two hours, as each member of the family dipped themselves into the few inches of hot, red water, dried themselves and returned to the table to carry on drinking. Sveta's sister and her husband, in a royal blue nylon tracksuit, did not join in the fun. They sat in silence, watching the television in the darkened sitting room. They had not moved since we arrived.

DAY 35

We spent the day walking through the town towards the chlorine factory. As we went, Sveta, with her long, bottle-blonde hair and sweetly pretty but tired face, talked about what life had been like in the town. Pointing to a white, columned building with a large, black statue of Lenin and Gorky deep in conversation, at the top of a flight of crumbling steps, she wiggled her hips and said, 'That used to be a discotheque when I was young. We danced and had fun. Now look at it.' The building was covered in sun-bleached posters of jolly Aryans extolling the virtues of toil. Their faces appeared alien in a country whose inhabitants were mostly dark skinned, with flat faces and Asian eyes.

We carried on through the wide, empty streets. Shop number seven had some bread, tea, and a whole counter of matchboxes, but no cigarettes. Sveta walked inside, out of habit, but did not buy anything. A small child crouched over his bicycle, mending the chain in the middle of the road. The only thing disturbing him was the dust and the blowing paper. In the main square stood Lenin, his benevolent, outstretched hand cast over the deserted square. The obscure twangs of Turkmenian music played through loudspeakers on the street corners and echoed off the walls of buildings. The playground was empty except for two Turkmenian children, squealing and spinning on the roundabout, their dark plaits flying.

Sveta directed us to the beach. As we walked along, her grey, plastic, stiletto boots left deep holes in the sand, which was littered with broken bottles, tyres, lumps of rock and lengths of twisted metal. 'There used to be houses along here, but the sea keeps moving closer and closer. The restaurant over there used to be brilliant, but now, as you can see, only its metal foundations remain. The sea took it last summer – I don't know why – the sea used to be far away but now the town is falling into it.'

I saw foundations of houses filled with salt water, rotting wood floating among strips of curling lino. Many of the roads simply disappeared as they neared the sand, covered in the rocks and bricks from decaying houses. 'God has deserted us here,' said Syid. 'What did we do wrong?' He buried some rusty metal in the sand with his foot.

As we approached the vast metal factory in the desert, I could see the black, putrid smoke spewing forth into the pale blue sky. There was little wind, so the noxious column stretched up as far as I could see. 'We live like animals here,' said Syid. 'At least in the West you live like human beings.' He paused. 'Look at that factory. This country will sell its soul for hard currency. It doesn't care if its people suffer. People are ill here – but why do they keep quiet? Their voices are too hoarse from shouting.'

He squatted in the dust, staring at the factory, took off his fur hat and ran his fingers through his short, dark hair. 'This country is ruined. Hitler tried to destroy this country for five years with machinery and arms; Gorbachev has destroyed this country in five years with his tongue. He and Yeltsin are killing us.' He imitated their blank smiles and waves, their nodding and photo-opportunity poses. 'All hot air.' He spat into the dust. 'They go home and drink themselves to sleep. They're lining their own pockets; then they'll go and buy a house somewhere abroad and retire. They don't care about us, they think only of themselves. If only we had someone intelligent in charge.' He grabbed hold of a piece of wood and, knocking it, said, 'Gorbachev and Yeltsin'. Snorting with hatred, he then chucked it away.

Syid hated Gorbachev's weakness. He lauded the likes of Brezhnev, Andropov and Stalin. I was not about to argue the evils of Stalin with Syid – he was a passionate man with a violent temper that I did not want to provoke – so I tried a gentle argument: 'But you had no freedom of speech. You can now read Solzhenitsyn,' I said.

'Bollocks,' said Syid. 'Who wants to read Solzhenitsyn when there's no sausage on the table? All the old Communists now call themselves Democrats, but they're still the same people. They think only of themselves. Before, the people here helped each other, but when a man is hungry, he thinks only of himself. I believe that there'll be civil war here. I'm sure of it, but I don't quite know when.'

He gestured towards Sveta, who was now also crouching in the dust. 'They won't even serve Sveta in the shops here, because she's Russian and not Turkmenian. They say they've run out of things and then they serve the Turkmenian women behind her in the queue. Look at the Armenians and the Azerbaijanis – they hate each other. I think Gorbachev was an American spy, sent over to bring this country to its knees. There were no arms in Armenia before *perestroika*. Where did they come from? America, of course.'

He spat again into the dust. 'When Gorbachev took down the Berlin Wall he basically said, "Come in, lads, and take what you want." Working as a driver, I live on 300 roubles a month. That's why I left Tdagestan – I can't afford to live there any more. I have work here and will stay for a year in the hope that things will get better. You can't live on 300 roubles a month when sausage is 50 roubles a kilo.'

Back home Sveta held court. Her sister-in-law had arrived and she, along with Gybia and Sveta's mother, all sat round, asking about food prices in the Ukraine. Before the price rises on 2 January 1992, produce was the same price in whatever region of the country: cheese in a state shop would cost the same in Moscow as it did in Vladivostok. Sveta explained the coupon system in the Ukraine, which had forced her and Syid to leave – without residency they were not entitled to coupons and so had no access to food. 'And anyway, our hair was beginning to fall out because of the radiation, so it was much better that we left,' she said.

The four women sat around drinking tea with boiled sweets – the sugar supply had long since dried up – and compared the prices of children's pants. 'They're 25 roubles here,' said the sister-in-law. 'Really?' replied Sveta. 'They're nearly 40 roubles in the Ukraine.'

Gybia chuckled: 'What can you do? You just have to laugh. I never know how we survive, but we do. It always amazes me that any of us manage.'

The father, who had been listening to the conversation, began to weep. Silent tears rolled down his leathery, yellow cheeks. 'What are they doing to us? I can't live like this any more. All the aid from the West goes to Moscow, nothing ever gets here. What are they thinking? In Moscow, people live well; here we have nothing at all.' His voice was loaded with tragic confusion. He could not understand why, when things had been so good before – cigarettes and sausage had always been in plentiful supply – why it had all fallen apart. Words like *perestroika* and *glasnost* meant nothing to him. He had worked hard all his life and done what he was told. He would never understand capitalism or democracy. He thought that Stalin was a great man, because he fed the people and there was no crime.

Georgi is one of the victims of the modernization of the old Soviet Union. His is the generation that lived through the famine and the purges of the 1930s, through the Great Patriotic, or Second World War. They survived the Cold War, only to come out the other side to face *perestroika* in their old age, where decades of information starvation have left them unprepared. It is only the young who will benefit. The old have already been left behind.

We sat down to supper of salted fish, bread and chopped onion, taken from a large sack propped up in the corner of the papered veranda. We sat outside on the steps, waiting for the grandparents to eat – there was not enough room at the table for us all and we had nowhere else to go. We talked to a neighbour who was feeding bread to five future fur hats. He would sell his rabbits in a few weeks at 25 roubles a pelt.

The water came on again and the orange-haired grandmother began to fill the bath once more, although yesterday's water had hardly been touched, except for a few jugfuls, which had been used to flush the loo.

The whole family gathered around to watch the television. The brother-in-law, who had a weak heart and was unable to work, was still in his blue tracksuit. He sat in the same corner of the sofa bed, the bed on which Sveta and Syid would sleep for the next year. His wife Tanya, plump and twenty-three, sat beside him. Their four-year-old daughter played on the floor with an empty cigarette packet. They watched *Superman* in black and white – the colour switch had broken two years ago.

DAY 36

Sitting down to salted fish and more bread, we were given jam jars of *kvas*, a home-made, fortified ginger beer. With a cotton-wool mouth, dulled head and eyes that would barely open, let alone focus, I could not have felt less like drinking, but my protests caused offence and met with a selective deafness. There was an urgent hedonism about our drinking – we were leaving Chiliken and Syid did not want us to go. We had proved to be a welcome diversion from reality, and an excuse to drink.

The old father began frantically rattling around the flat, shaking his jaundiced cigarette holder. Then, sitting down in a corner, he burst into tears. 'There are no more cigarettes in the house,' he screamed like a petulant child. He shook and stamped his feet. He had smoked all the cigarettes that we had brought with us as presents, and now that we were going, there would be no more.

There was a loud banging at the front door and the neighbour from across the hall burst in, accusing Syid of stealing his hat. He was Turkmenian and sweated vodka. He pulled out a knife and, crouching aggressively, began to shout at Syid, doubting his parentage and his mother's profession. Syid, with the speed of those accustomed to defending themselves, socked him on the jaw and threw him down the stairs into the dust outside, following up with a flurry of kicks to the kidneys and a volley of spit. The Turkmenian, covered in blood and humiliated by his public defeat, crawled out into the street, swearing.

It was all over in seconds, but the outburst created an awkward atmosphere. The family shuffled around, embarrassed, while Syid tried to excuse and explain himself to me. 'Don't think badly of me,' he said, half closing his eyes and looking at the floor, 'He pulled a knife, and I hate it when people do that.' He looked up and stared into my eyes, searching for some sort of support. I smiled weakly and pretended that I understood.

Syid, disgusted with himself and unable to bear the atmosphere in the flat, went for a walk. I sat with Sveta on the small bed in the corner of her room, surrounded by the posters of women in black leather and maroon lipstick. We listened to crackling music on the spool tape recorder while Alissa bounced around and threw herself onto the bed, giggling.

Sveta had had Alissa when she was eighteen. The father was half Turkmenian and half Tartar. Sveta had not married him. Soon after Alissa was born, he was arrested for robbery. He spent three years in prison for stealing from an international environmental group who were researching the climatic problems of the area. Almost as soon as he left prison, he re-offended and was locked away for another three years. Sveta never sees him, although he is now out of prison and living in Chiliken. Alissa vaguely remembers her father. 'He has dark eyes, just like me,' she said, thoughtfully.

Sveta met Syid almost a year ago, when he came to work in Chiliken. Since then, they have travelled around in search of work, ending up in Chiliken because if they don't find work, at least Sveta's parents will look after them. 'Parents do that sort of thing in this country,' explained Sveta. 'They're one of the few things that can be relied on.'

Later we made the long bus journey to Nebit Dag. As we crossed the desert, Syid's mood swung from the bawdy and jovial to the intensely introspective. Sveta fell asleep, her relaxed, round face looking innocent at rest, except for the flash of hard, pink lipstick that clogged at the corners of her mouth. I sat gazing out of the window, counting oil rigs.

Sveta's sister-in-law was not at home when we arrived. We sat outside the block of flats on our luggage, shielding our faces from the blowing dust. Joth and Syid went to the market in search of cigarettes.

The sister-in-law's neighbour saw us sitting in the sand and invited us in. She was plump, with dimpled hands that she rested on her round stomach. Her small eyes were set in her fat, jolly face. She had bleached the front of her hair a yellow-blonde, but the remainder was dark, either through lack of dye or because she had been unable to reach the back of her head. Smiling broadly, she offered us a cup of coffee.

'Coffee?' said Sveta, her eyes shining. 'Where did you get that?'

'Oh, under the table, you know, like anything that's really worth anything. It was 250 roubles,' she replied, obviously pleased with her purchase.

'That's expensive.'

'Not for coffee it isn't. There hasn't been any here for so long that I can't remember when we last had some,' she retorted, justifying her seeming frivolity.

While she heated the water, the two women began to chat about prices and the availability of goods, comparing Nebit Dag with Chiliken. They were all of 150 kilometres apart, yet there were differences. 'Of course, the biggest problem of all is cigarettes,' said Sveta.

'I have some,' said the woman.

'Have you?' Sveta and I answered in unison.

'I hide them from my husband. He doesn't know I smoke, although I think he suspects I might,' she replied, giggling at her wickedness.

We drank our coffee. Sveta clasped her cup in both hands and savoured every mouthful as it sent shivers of delight down her spine. All three of us sat in silence, enjoying our caffeine and nicotine buzz.

Our ecstasy was broken by the sound of the doorbell. Gybia turned up. Unable to find us next door, she had tried the neighbour. She had come from work, cooking for 100 labourers who work on the oil rigs in the desert. Her face, normally dark skinned, was painted a pale white with foundation and powder. Her eyes and lips were thickly covered in dark colours. It all gave the impression of an eight-year-old girl who had spent the afternoon playing at her mother's dressing table. She soon joined in the nicotine and caffeine tasting.

She brought out her make-up collection. The two women gathered round. Reverently, they began to pull it apart, trying each shade on the backs of their hands, rolling the lipsticks up and down and discussing the subtleties of each colour.

'Where did you buy it all?' asked Sveta, hardly able to disguise her envy.

'Under the table, for 500 roubles, last week,' said Gybia, with a contented smile.

'500 roubles? That's not bad,' said the plump woman, putting on a mauve lipstick. 'You have all the colours you could possibly want.'

Joth and Syid returned from their unsuccessful cigarette trip, along with the plump woman's husband, who was gangly, unco-ordinated and stooped like a man irritated by his own height.

The kitchen was now completely full, so we moved into the sitting room, a dark room with ginger velour sofas. The husband was an air-traffic controller and began to talk about his future plans. 'I'm going to learn English soon to try and further my career,' he announced. I nodded in encouragement and approval.

The plump woman was making a lot of noise in the kitchen and suddenly appeared with a plastic cloth, which she placed on the low table between the ginger sofas. She brought out bowls of steaming, watery soup with lumps of fat spinning in circles on the surface. Small shots glasses of samogon were passed round and Sveta took it upon herself to make a toast.

'To our meeting,' she said. Then, leaning over towards the plump woman who had looked after us all afternoon, she asked: 'What's your name?' There was a cold silence, and I sniggered in embarrassment. Everyone turned to the plump woman.

'Ann,' she mumbled, offended.

'Oh, err, to Ann!' said Sveta with exaggerated bravado, hastily trying to rectify her mistake.

We all clinked glasses. The soup was too hot to eat quickly and the conversation no longer flowed. The sister-in-law returned and called next door to inform us of her arrival. Syid made his excuses and left his soup, samogon and the flat. The remainder of the party scalded their lips in an attempt to leave the table more quickly. Enough soup consumed so as not to re-offend the cook, we left en masse.

Next door, we were introduced to four Turkmenian men, all of whom shook Joth's hand, but ignored my arm, outstretched in friendship. Embarrassed yet again, I ran my hand through my hair to disguise my mistake. It did not go unnoticed.

'We don't shake women's hands, we just nod in their general direction,' explained one man with a long moustache. 'Oh, fair enough,' I smiled, irritated.

We sat on the floor of the furnitureless flat around a plastic sheet. This surrogate table is sacred and, according to Muslim law, it is forbidden to defile it with your feet. We drank vodka and ate an obscure, cured fish that was chewy and tasted of ash tray. I went to the bathroom to spit out the contents of my mouth – fortunately the water had just come on, so the noise disguised my sounds.

Two bottles of vodka later, we were packed into the back of a Lada and driven at speed, without due care and attention, to the train station. There, amidst a cloud of back-slapping, we were put on the train to Ashkhabad.

DAY 37

Ashkhabad is not a beautiful city. Nestling on the border with Iran, it more or less escapes the freezing snows and evil winters of Siberia, but it becomes a dust bowl in the summer, airless and choked. In mid-winter it was dull grey and cold. It conformed to the plans drawn up by the one architect who seems to have built all Soviet cities, with wide streets, flat square buildings, aggressive granite statues and patches of earth named after the leader of the revolution or some local hero.

The only thing of great beauty in Ashkhabad is its people, We walked around the market in the centre of town, my eyes starved of all but grey, blinking at the orgy of colour. Turkmenian women sat around on hessian sacks of herbs and orange spices, their dark red dresses trailing in the dust, their sleeves heavy with embroidery. In front of them, on hand-woven carpets, lay extravagantly striped trousers made from different types of silk – the women wore these loose-fitting trousers under their skirts. Some wore dark velvet coats or small waistcoats that were embroidered with gold brocade. They crouched on the ground, huddling together for protection against the circling, dust-laden wind while they sold ropes of twisted cotton or silk. Their wrists and ankles tinkled with the sound of bells as they moved.

The air lay thick with the smoke of hundreds of small fires scattered around the market. Laced in the smoke, the smell of frying meat and boiling fat tickled my nostrils. A group of women squatted in a row behind large tin bowls covered in cloths. As I approached, they lifted the cloths to show steaming dumplings and pancakes filled with grass, which they had made early that morning. I bought a grass-filled pancake. It was chewy and tepid and the green contents slithered down the back of my throat. This is what cows feel, I thought, as I munched on the watery mixture.

In one corner stood an old man, his head swathed in a dirty grey turban, his face brown and old. He wore a long robe to the floor and leant on a cleft stick. In front of him were a whole range of twisted roots and dried herbs displayed in half-open, white, cotton bags. He was the local medicine man. I walked up and explained my condition – bleeding gums, wobbly teeth, tiredness, and cracking skin around my mouth. 'That's scurvy,' he said, in a quiet voice. 'You've had nothing that is good for you to eat for a long time.' He looked through his collection of herbs and handed me a newspaper cone of what looked like dried grass clippings with faded blue flowers. He told me to gargle night and morning, mixing the herb with hot water. 'At least three glasses full,' he said with a nod. I reached to pay him. He refused. 'You are a guest in my country and it has made you ill. The least I can do is cure you,' he said smiling. He had almost no teeth.

We spent the afternoon in the station trying to organize tickets. Our train left at six in the morning. I sat talking to the woman who served thick, sweet coffee in the café at the station. It was the first time I had managed to buy a cup of coffee in the street. It was warm and sent a shiver of delight through me. The woman was small, plump and on her pension. 'Life on a pension is so boring, which is why I work here from six in the morning to six at night. It keeps me busy and also gives me a little extra money, which can't be bad.' We asked her if she knew whether we could get the train to Minack, on the Aral Sea. She did not know. She had only ever left Ashkhabad once in her life and that was two years ago. 'I received a telegram from my next-door neighbour who had moved to Tashkent, ordering me to arrive by 1 May. I panicked, thinking that someone was ill, and left in a hurry. It was so embarrassing – I left without presents and food and even without vodka. They had invited me there for a party.' She laughed.

Driving back to the hotel with a taxi driver who, for reasons best known to himself, had attached his brake pedal to a light built into his gear stick, we began to discuss the racial tensions in the area. His wife was Ukrainian and he was Russian. His relations had arrived in Ashkhabad just after the Revolution and his family had lived here ever since. 'What's so strange at the moment is that the

Turkmenians want to look like Russians. They're buying Western clothes and listening to our music. We, on the other hand, do not want to look like them,' he said, turning down his Beatles cassette in the car. 'Since *perestroika*, none of the people seem to get on in this republic. Everyone has become racist and nationalistic. We all have nationalistic problems now. We used to be a union and now we all hate each other.'

Back at the hotel, we ate at a table that had been reserved for us. 'Foreigners' had been written on it in big letters and the old boy running the restaurant hugged me as we walked in. The music, played by a live band singing mutilated Western tunes, was so loud that we had to shout to order our salted fish and bread.

The old woman who ran our floor could not contain her curiosity at our arrival. She had never met foreigners before and had endless questions as she boiled up water and made us some tea. She had seven children and was from Georgia. She could not understand why I did not have children and was convinced that I had a biological problem. She muttered something as she waved her hands over my head and caressed my stomach. 'Tonight is a full moon,' she said as she handed over the tea. 'It's a good time to have a boy. Now run along and conceive, and call him Ashkhabad,' she said with a wink.

Uzbekistan

· · · · · · · · · · · · · · · ·

DAY 39

The train to Nukus took twenty-two hours. We sat drinking thin yogurt, the only food available on the journey, as we crossed the red desert – mile upon mile of red, brown, rocky, flat nothing. The train stopped at small villages on the way and old women rushed into the carriages, selling stale cakes and hot dumplings.

At four in the morning Joth and I jumped from the train as it was leaving the station. It was cold and dark and the short platform was almost empty. As we collected our belongings, which we had thrown from the train in our panic at almost missing the stop, we were accosted by the police. Unaware as to the exact reason for their sudden interest, I exchanged smiles and trite greetings. Hauled into the office, we were made to explain the purpose of our visit, as taxi after precious taxi left the station with semi-dormant passengers nestling in the back. With puffy mouths and eyes, angry under the neon lights, we explained and re-explained what we were doing. They asked to see our passports. We refused. Somehow this stand seemed to please them and there then followed a scene of gratuitous backslapping. With a volley of shouts of 'friendship' and 'guest', they found us a taxi and, bargaining down the price for us, wished us on our way.

We drove through the blackness to Nukus, only to discover that the bus to Minack took six hours and would not be leaving for another three. We persuaded the taxi driver to take us further. Tripling his price, he went back to his house to raid his store of petrol, which he proudly showed us. We drove in the pale blue light of dawn through the frozen desert, where stunted, aggressive bushes were eerily coated in a hard frost, and large expanses of earth glistened with pinky salt that seeped to the surface. The single track was potholed and covered in black ice. Twice we skidded off the road, first to avoid a milk truck as it careered towards us in the semi-darkness, the second through driver fatigue.

After five hours, we arrived in Minack on the Aral Sea. Its bold, red, metal

Soviet signpost, with jaded hammer and sickle and dancing fish, were testimony to its fishing past and a bitter reminder of its destroyed present.

The Aral Sea has lost almost half its volume in the last thirty years. The damming of the region's two major rivers, the Syr Darya and the Amur Darya, in the 1960s for cotton and rice cultivation caused the sea to retreat up to 100 kilometres in places, leaving whole communities without any livelihood and whole fleets of fishing boats stranded in the sand.

We drove through the town along a dusty track. People along the side of the road stopped and stared at the car. 'No one drives through here any more, that's why they are looking,' said the taxi-driver. 'There's no petrol and anyway, who would want to come here?'

The town ran alongside the gritted track, decaying shacks lining the two-kilometre route. Crowds queued for yellow buses, and only the occasional motorcycle and sidecar drove past. We passed the huge, crumbling building of the central Soviet. The sickle had fallen from the insignia. We found a hotel. A rusty door swung on one hinge, the floor was flooded with water and mud. 'I think this one is closed,' said the taxi driver, 'There must be another.'

We found another hotel, but it was empty. I wandered around the brown-tiled hall, shouting. Eventually, a small woman with a floor mop and bucket in her hand checked us in. She could hardly be bothered to pick up the pen to sign the documents, but finally we were given a key. The room had no light bulbs, no running water and the bath was full of cement. She pointed to a small wooden hut in the field out the back. 'That's the toilet,' she said, puffing up the pillows as she left.

The taxi driver left. It was 11 a.m.

We had no transport and no means of getting any. A jeep parked outside the front of the hotel belonged to the men in number 12. They were scientists who had been in Minack for two weeks assessing the effects of the salt pollution on the children in the town, testing the ill and deformed children and comparing their results to the salinity in the soil. They were instantly friendly but were about to leave. They told us that there was no transport and no food anywhere. 'Well, there is, but you need ration coupons to buy anything,' explained the skinny scientist with lank, grey hair. 'I managed to buy some bread yesterday, but I brought all my food with me.' We did not have ration coupons, so the two of them clubbed together to give us a few sheets. 'It's the same all over Uzbekistan. If you don't have them, you'll starve. You can't buy anything without them.'

The only way that we could get transport, they said, was to go to the Soviet and ask for help. 'They're obliged to help foreigners,' he explained. The larger of the two offered to ferry us up there.

The head of the Soviet was a plump, complacent man. The benevolent face of Lenin looked down on us from the wall as we were refused any form of help whatsoever. 'Minack is closed to foreigners,' he proclaimed, with a smug grin. 'You'll have to leave immediately.' This was said with such irritating finality that it precluded any ability to sweet talk or any 'present'.

Nevertheless, I sat and argued *perestroika*. I explained that we were there to help. 'The people of the West must know about the huge environmental problems here and then they will help,' I said with passion.

'I don't care,' he said, shuffling papers on his desk. He paused and added in a threatening tone, 'We still have the KGB, you know.'

'They don't appear to know very much do they?' I said sarcastically.

'What do you mean?' he asked aggressively.

'Well, we're here for a start,' I said. 'And you knew nothing about that did you?' He ignored the comment and returned to his work. He refused to acknowledge us any more, keeping his gaze firmly on the desk. Muttering something highly offensive, I left.

We set off to walk along the muddy track back to the hotel. I managed to flag down a car. We chatted up the driver and offered him a ludicrous amount of money to drive us around for the next few days. We had to drive the twelve kilometres or so to see the boats stranded in the desert by the diminishing sea. He said that he would return in half an hour, after excusing himself from work.

We sat in our hotel room and waited. Out of the window we saw a police van arrive. Three of them marched upstairs and barged into our room. They sat us on the bed and questioned us for half an hour. Again, we refused to show our passports. 'You are under arrest,' they said. 'You have one hour and a half to pack your bags, you will then be escorted to the three o'clock bus and driven out of town. At the other end you will be met by the KGB, who will take you to the visa office. You are not entitled to be in Uzbekistan, let alone Minack. You have the status of illegal immigrants and will be treated as such.' With that, they left.

We had just over an hour to achieve what we had come for. We persuaded the scientist to drive us to the hospital on their way out of town. We arrived at the rotting white building just as the head doctor was leaving for lunch. He refused us entry – without the correct paperwork we were not allowed to set foot inside the hospital. He smiled as he ushered us into the back of his car to drive us back to the hotel. He obviously enjoyed the power game.

Time ticking away, we wandered behind the hotel. We walked past a block of flats that were so dilapidated that I thought no one could live there. They were surrounded by rubbish, the concrete covered in rust from dripping drains. A small girl came out to play, followed by her brother. Renat was twenty-three and worked in a fish-canning factory. They canned fish sent down from Moscow because the supply from the Aral Sea had long since dried up. He took us in to meet his family.

His parents, Amurta and Isaeyva, were sitting on the floor of the furnitureless room, drinking tea and eating bread. 'Come and have some lunch,' said Isaeyva, the mother, as she sat, hunched over in a dirty, floral dress. They had nine children and the whole family lived in the three-roomed flat. There was no water in the house: they collected it from a tap in the street. 'We haven't had water here for ten years,' she said, as she tore a strip of bread from the round, flat loaf in the middle of the floor. 'I do believe that it will return. It has to. Well, that's what they say, anyway.' The room was hot and smelt of stale pickles and sweat. Three small children lay on the ground, rolling on their backs with boredom, their faces dirty and their clothes too large and littered with holes. They wore stiff tights and no pants.

The family lived off rationing. Isaeyva brought out her ration book and showed me their name, address and the number of children in the family. 'This gives us seven kilos of flour, 100 grams of tea, two light bulbs, two bottles of vodka, eighty grams of sugar, some macaroni and two pairs of galoshes a month,' she said as she ticked them against the book. 'Well, in fact, everything is bought with coupons, it's just those things that are rationed.'

They did not appear to understand why the Aral Sea was disappearing. They saw it as some freak of nature. 'You should come here in the summer if you think this is bad,' she said. 'The sky is dark with dust and we can hardly leave the house. And, of course, we haven't been able to grow anything here for years. But

I know things will get better, because the authorities tell us they will. But until they do, our children fall ill around us.'

We walked back to the hotel to find the police waiting. Ushered into the back of the van, we were taken to the bus. Escorted on, we were shown our seats and told not to leave them until we were collected at the other end.

The bus was packed. Faces pushed up against the glass, we trundled along the single-track road back to Nukus; women stood, carrying their screaming and wriggling children, for the six-hour journey. We were squashed next to a history teacher and a fisherman. They engaged in conversation.

'At least, when we were a union, the Russians were helping to clean up this huge environmental disaster. But now we are completely incapable of sorting it out ourselves. Uzbekistan has no money and the world is already tired of listening to our problems. Someone must do something. The dust gets worse every year and nothing grows. And it's all because the Russians wanted cotton,' said the history teacher. The whole bus fell silent as he spoke.

'I last caught a fish in the Aral Sea in 1972,' interrupted the fisherman. 'Our kolhoz fishes in some fresh-water lakes in the area, but there's almost nothing there now. I know the water will come back – it has to.'

The conversation continued in this way, the people around listening and adding their own opinions. The route to Nukus was lined with wasted water, as flooded irrigation channels spewed their precious load onto empty fields. Broken or incomplete pipes poured water into the desert, leaving areas of land semi-flooded, mixing in with the flat expanses of salted earth.

Arriving back in Nukus, it was as dark as we had found it that morning. Dropping from exhaustion and hunger we planned to eat and sleep immediately. The police did not meet us at the bus station – someone had obviously forgotten to make the call. The bus emptied and the driver offered to take us to the hotel. We accepted gratefully. The bus to ourselves, we drove through the town, chatting away. We drove past the hotel.

'I've just got to drop in at the airport,' explained the driver, as we watched our sanctuary disappear. He, in fact, collected his wife, girlfriend, lover, daughter – I was not sure which. She sat in the front in silence as we drove past the hotel again. Rattling around in the large bus, we arrived at the depot and picked up another driver, who had just arrived from Samerkand. He invited all four of us to supper. By this time all we wanted to do was sleep. I almost cried with exhaustion.

We went to the house of the second driver's Russian lover, parking the bus outside. She greeted us and then, sitting us down to rice and vodka, bombarded us with questions.

'I'm his girlfriend,' she announced proudly, without us asking. 'All the long-distance drivers have girlfriends, one in every town,' she said, laughing. 'But he only does Samerkand to Nukus, so there's only me and his wife.'

The other couple were becoming restless and we did not stay long. The bus driver finally dropped us off at the hotel, where we collapsed at reception. They refused us a room. No visa. 'Are we to sleep in the street?' I shouted, standing firm, hands aggressively on hips. Eventually the old woman gave in. 'We have the KGB, you know,' she said, looking over her spectacles. 'I know,' I replied, the whole scenario sounding boringly familiar. She telephoned through, giving them our room number. Fortunately, the KGB also sleeps. 'They'll come and interview you at eight o'clock, tomorrow, in your room,' she said efficiently.

'Let them come,' I said as I wandered towards the lift.

1 a.m, and finally we had found somewhere to sleep.

DAY 40

We stole out of the hotel at 6 a.m. to avoid the KGB and persuaded a man on his way to work to drive us to the bus station. The next bus was in two hours. It was dangerous to hang around – the hotel would surely miss us and then inform the KGB. We found a taxi driver to take us to Urgench. Listening to some Western music that he insisted on collecting from home on the way, we set off once more through the frozen desert.

Three and a half hours later, we arrived in Urgench, an unremarkable, ugly town. We spent the morning taking nos, a strange form of green snuff placed under the tongue, with a shoe-repair man. The small kiosk by the train station was crowded with men, all sitting around talking, while one man worked cleaning and repairing shoes. We squashed up on the bench beside them while our shoes were being cleaned. 'These shoes are nice,' said the man as he picked them up in his blackened hands. 'Where are you from? You could never have bought those here.' My reply brought about an awed hush. 'That's in the West!' said one old man with a dark, sun-scorched face. 'Can you get boot polish there?' asked the shoe repair man. 'Without coupons?' We were offered more and more snuff. It was hard to keep it under my tongue, and it mixed with my saliva to form an acrid, green liquid that trickled down the back of my throat. The tobacco rushed through my veins, sending my heart pumping and peeling my eyelids back, making me feel wildly awake. I looked around the packed room to see everyone fidgeting slightly, enjoying their manic buzz.

We visited Kiva, passing the Lenin and Karl Marx communal farms on the way. Large women bent over open-air clay ovens cooking bread, the smoke curling in ringlets into the sky. Massive posters of Lenin surrounded by workers neck-deep in cotton, fists punching the air proclaiming 'The joy of toil', lined the route.

This legendary city, in the Khorezem Oasis, which was on the silk route to the Volga and Eastern Europe, is like a living museum. Turquoise domes and intricate mosaics house the population and provide shelter for the animals that roam the narrow streets.

We met a marriage party leaving the heart of the city. The bride, looking more exhausted than radiant, walked among the orange clay walls, followed by her entourage, her white dress trailing in the dust. The Soviets have a tradition of visiting places after marriage ceremonies – Lenin's mausoleum, the flame of the unknown soldier and Tolstoy's grave are all favourites. The groups make the pilgrimage straight from the civil wedding service, shuffle around the particular place of their choice with meaningful stares and then leave. It is hard to marry without a God and these places add some sort of sanctity to an otherwise dull signing of contracts.

The train to Sharju was packed. We walked into the carriage crammed with fifty-eight people who had spent the past three days together after leaving Moscow, filed like bodies in a morgue. The shelf-like beds were piled three high, leaving a narrow corridor between. The carriage reeked of stale air, sleep and sweated alcohol. As we walked in, the carriage fell silent and eyes followed us as we walked down to find our particular shelves. Two women sat, their legs stretched out on the plastic beds, babies at their breasts. They both had eyes glazed with fatigue and boredom. One of them started to change her baby. Laying it out on the bed, she placed some plastic sheeting around its bottom and, pulling its legs straight, she held its ankles together as she tied a piece of material tightly around its legs. When she had finished, it lay, unable to move, wrapped up like a sausage, in a small, highly portable bundle.

Opposite us was a group of soldiers drinking vodka. Sasha was out of uniform and sat swigging a half-full bottle, reading a pornographic magazine. He followed me to the small space between the carriages, to smoke. He started to talk to me about sex in the West. 'I bet you're all liberated and do it in thousands of different positions,' he said, his eyes bright with excitement. 'Some do,' I said, flicking my ash to the floor, embarrassed.

The carriage was crammed with food that people had brought for their three-day journey – eggs in plastic bags, glutinous meat balls in jam jars and hunks of home-made bread. People sat in rows on the bottom bunks, three either side of the low tables. They had become unwilling acquaintances during their travel. The distraction of our arrival was welcome, and some decided to make the most of it.

The beds around ours became full. A man walking through the train, mumbling 'vodka, vodka', under his breath, was besieged. We sat drinking out of china bowls and plastic mugs. The threatening atmosphere melted away, barriers slowly came down and, although curiosities were drained by travel, we began to talk. An Iranian from Samerkand held court. He sat, wildly gesticulating and leaning forward with excitement. 'Gorbachev is a man of pure gold!' he exclaimed. 'I love him. He is the best thing that ever happened to this country of ours. I hate the Communists, they have brought this place to its knees. They're parasites. We have useless managers, no one cares about anything, it's always someone else's problem or responsibility.' I was quite taken aback by his enthusiasm and his views – he was one of the first people we had met to air such views and in such a public place. No one argued against him. They all sat and listened, some laughing nervously.

Ilkhom cited example after example of Communist behaviour. 'You arrive at a hotel and they won't let you stay: they have rooms but they just can't be bothered to fill out the forms, until you bribe them of course. Communists! Shoot them all!' he shouted, waving his arms in the air.

The party broke up and the whole carriage descended into a symphony of snores. An old man to my left, after a bottle of vodka, was particularly sonorous. We stayed awake, our money tucked down our pants. At 2 a.m. we arrived. Ilkhom helped us off the train and insisted that we come and stay with him in Samerkand.

After beating at the door of a hotel and pleading with the night watchman, we were allowed a bed.

Turkmenia

· · · · · · · · · · · · · · · · · ·

DAY 41

A fat man in a fat car with black leather seats agreed to drive us to Repetek, back in Turkmenia. We were stopped at the border checkpoint, but the guard was so excited to meet foreigners for the first time that, after a barrage of questions about England, he waved us on. Driving through the desert, the sun shone bright but weak, reflecting off the sand. The driver dumped us in the centre of the collection of houses and left in a cloud of dust.

Repetek, a small oasis in the heart of the red desert, is connected to the outside world by the main railway, which runs through the hamlet like an umbilical cord. It is mainly populated by the Kazaks, who fled south after the Revolution to escape famine, in search of work. A man with a flat, pock-marked face and marbled jeans approached us. Albai lived in the village and said that, although we could not stay in his house because it was too small, his best friend would definitely have us to stay.

We sat in the sun on a large wooden table waiting for Albai to secure a room for the night. An old Russian woman sat wailing on her steps. She rocked backwards and forwards, clutching her knees, tears pouring down her furrowed cheeks, her headscarf slowly sliding off her head. I walked over to see if there was anything I could do and she grabbed hold of my hand, clasping it between hers. She smelt of alcohol. 'I'm a hopeless, hopeless woman,' she said staring at me with her red eyes. 'I'm a hopeless, hopeless woman,' she repeated over and over again, rocking for comfort. Suddenly she stopped and, squeezing my hand, said, 'We are all hopeless here. We live here in the desert and time has forgotten us. No one thinks about us any more. My television is broken and no one can mend it. All I want is to watch my television and drink more vodka.'

Albai shouted me over: 'You're not talking to that woman are you? We have about ten Russian families, out of a hundred, in the village and they're all like that, drunk all the time,' he said with a dismissive snort.

The village was full of women with long plaits running down their backs and brightly coloured floral printed clothes. We passed small, low houses, each sectioned off by wooden fences, with long, low tables that extended from the back door into the yard. We were introduced to Kolya and Tanya (their Kazak names, Kuben and Tlekes, they said were too complicated for us to use). They lived with their two small daughters on the outskirts of the village, overlooking the desert. By Soviet standards, their house was large, with three rooms off from a central hall. One, blocked off by a lace curtain, contained Tanya's dowry: silk mattresses piled high to the ceiling, a mother-of-pearl and carved wooden trunk packed with beaded waistcoats and hand-stitched silk dresses. It was covered in dust.

They offered us some tea and lit the wood-burning stove outside in the yard. Next to the stove, impounded in a wooden fence, were two goats that Kolya had recently brought; they also had two sheep and a few chickens. Their loo was a small hut some distance from the house, in the desert. They had no running water in the house, but a tap in the garden. We sat in a large room covered from floor to ceiling in dark carpet; a framed photograph of Michael Jackson stood in the corner next to a large wooden bed covered in silk. Tanya covered the floor with long, flat, silk cushions that she had made and laid a mat on the floor. We sat in a circle drinking tea with huge lumps of crystallised sugar floating on the surface.

Kolya, a slim, dark man with the Eastern eyes of the Kazaks, was quiet and spoke little. He showed little emotion but exuded the introspection of someone who thinks and involves himself little in the paltry goings-on in a small village. He is a truck driver for the state and his wages, since the New Year, have risen from 1,000 roubles to 1,500 roubles a month. He works around one day in every fourteen. 'I got my job through connections – that's why I hardly do anything,' he laughed.

Tanya was round and gentle and laughed often. She did not join us when we opened the vodka, but busied herself preparing for the departure of her youngest daughter. Tanya's mother, who lived in the town, had come to stay and would be taking the youngest home with her. The grandmother wore the traditional dress, with white turban swathed around her head and her hair in grey plaits. She had a long, midnight-blue, velvet coat with embroidered cuffs that hung around her fragile wrists. Her slim feet were snug in thick, coloured socks and black, shiny rubber galoshes. She sat outside staring at the desert, her feet swinging in the gap between the table and the earth. She chuckled at us, but said nothing.

We spent the afternoon in the desert collecting firewood. Kolya drove over the dunes in his state truck, with complete disregard for either machinery or the brittle bushes that covered the mounds of sand. The sun was low in the sky and the wind fresh when he took us to the top of a dune. Below, the desert seeped far into the distance, like a crumpled piece of russet silk. It met the sky miles away, merging in a thick band of misty grey. 'This is my favourite place,' said Kolya, crouching in the sand. 'I come up here and watch for hours. Quite what I'm looking for, I don't know, but it's quiet and nature here is wild and devoid of man.' We sat and watched the sun slowly disappear. 'I love my country,' said Kolya, addressing no one in particular, 'but it's being destroyed by people who do not know how much pain they're causing.' He suddenly became efficient and, clapping his hands together, stood up and ordered us to put the wood on the back of the truck.

Back at the house, Tanya was sifting flour. 'I can't believe it's so expensive – 150 roubles for a sack that lasts about a week, sometimes less. And I'm sure it's not as good as it used to be.' She sat crouched on all fours, her white scarf tight around her head, her cheeks brushed with flour. Albai's wife sat on the floor next to her, her long skirt tucked under her legs, chatting away. I sat down too. Neither of the women could understand how I could have reached my age and had no children. 'We have contraceptives in England,' I explained.

'Oh those,' replied Tanya, leaning back on her heels and wiping her nose, covering it with a fine layer of flour. 'We don't really have any of those. Some people have the coil, but they're very expensive and don't really fit.'

'There's abortion,' said Ana.

'Oh yes, there's plenty of that,' said Tanya. 'The only problem is, they can't do it here of course – we don't have a doctor or a clinic. We have to go into town. We go on a daytrip, or at least that's what we say to everyone, including our husbands. They would kill us if they knew.'

Kolya suddenly walked in. 'What was that?' he asked. Neither of the women replied. Tanya carried on sifting the flour.

Tanya then added water to the flour and kneaded it into a thick, stretchy dough, which she rolled into a thin square and cut into long, thin strips. She was making a special dish, she said, and went outside to cook on the wood-burning stove, which belched smoke into the evening sky through a long, rusty flue.

We sat down to supper. A huge bowl of pasta strips and meat was placed in the centre of the mat, we all gathered round with spoons in hand and tucked in. Kolya had found more vodka from somewhere, and a bottle of home-made wine. The news of our arrival had filtered its way through the village and a group of men arrived to ask questions about the Beatles and the price of cigarettes.

Tanya did not allow herself to get drunk. She returned to the kitchen and, unwrapping the flour that she had so painstakingly knotted in cloth a few hours before, began preparing the dough for bread the next day. Once more on all fours, she kneaded away, her fingers penetrating deep into the dough, slowly mixing in the salt, sugar and water. Ana was curled up asleep on the floor next to her, covered in a quilted coat.

Next door, Zamira, their six-year-old daughter, was completely over-excited. She bounced around to the music, showing off to the grown-up men who lay horizontal on the mattresses. Squealing with delight, she bounced on her bottom and then collapsed to the floor.

With all the alcohol finished, the visitors left. Tanya made up our bed, piling up the mattresses from her dowry, which she then covered with a patchwork quilt.

DAY 42

Tanya was up with the sun, baking her bread in the clay oven in the yard. Rolling the dough out into a flat circle, she then pressed it to the walls of the oven, digging a fork in deep to create a circular pattern. A fire of sticks and charcoal burnt at the heart of the oven. Every so often she bent over and sprinkled a palmful of water on the loaves to prevent them drying out. The pale orange light of the early dawn shone on her face as she stood, with her hands on her hips, staring at the flames. She turned to me and smiled. She then leant forward and broke a piece of clay off the rim of the rounded dome and popped it into her mouth. 'It's very tasty,' she said, laughing at my puzzled expression. 'It's full of vitamins. I used to eat it all the time when I was pregnant.'

Kolya woke up full of enthusiasm. He decided that he wanted to find the nomadic Turkmenian tribes that roam the desert. The Kazaks more or less inhabit the villages in the desert; the indigenous Turkmenians live off the desert itself. Kolya raided his petrol supply that stood in barrels next to the goat pen. Taking hold of a rubber tube, he sucked out the air and filled bucket after bucket with the stinking diesel. Three times he sucked too hard, his mouth filled with fuel and his face screwed up with revulsion as he spat and retched into the sand.

We collected a Ukrainian tractor driver who lived next door and deposited the daughter, Zamira, between us in the cabin of the truck. She squatted on all fours, holding on to the dashboard as we bounced down the track into the desert. We drove for miles towards the sun in the cloudless sky. The desert, barren and without any point of reference, appeared limitless. After about an hour, the Ukrainian suddenly hit the top of the roof and shouted to Kolya to turn left. We turned off the track and headed across the steep dunes, where our progress was continually hampered by the parched bushes and the shifting sand. Eventually, we arrived at a flattened circle of sand covered in camel droppings. They had been there and had probably left that morning, said the Ukrainian after he felt the heat from the glowing embers of the abandoned fire. Where they had gone, he could not say. We backtracked to the road and continued into the desert.

We came across a small oasis, surrounded by nothing. Four men stared as the truck approached. They were mending tractors and large pieces of metal stuck out of the sand. 'These are the desert mechanics,' said Kolya. 'They live and work here all year round. No one disturbs them. They are completely self-sufficient, with their own water and generator.' They stood against a background of old Communist posters that were pinned to the walls of the three shacks, their soul-stirring red backgrounds bleached pink in the sun, the yellow letters turned white. It was a wonder that they knew that the outside world existed at all. The four men simply watched as we jumped from the truck, regarding us with deep suspicion. 'Where are the nomads?' asked the Ukrainian. One of the men, leaning on a stick, pointed into the desert. 'Have you seen any recently?' the Ukrainian ventured. There was a long pause and I thought they would not answer. Eventually one of the men replied, saying that a group had been that morning to water their camels at the well, but they had not stayed long and would be far away by now. As to the direction? 'Allah knows where.'

Running low on petrol, Kolya decided to give up the expedition. Driving back through the desert, we began to talk about marriage. 'The Russians are terrible about their marriages,' he said disparagingly. 'They do it for a bit, get bored, and then divorce. I don't know why they bother in the first place. When we Kazaks get married, it's for life and nothing will break us up. It's all this female liberation that's destroying marriages – that's the real problem.'

On the outskirts of Repetek, we stopped at a café by the side of the road. It sold green tea served out of jam jars. A group of drunk policemen were being aggressive. They were plain-clothes policemen who collected bribes in the towns and then came out to the desert to pick fights. 'This place is always full of them,' explained Kolya. 'And as soon as you hit them back they arrest you for assaulting a police officer.'

Two of them came over to us and started to hassle about visas, trying to arrest Joth because of his camera. 'They're American spies,' they shouted. 'Arrest them.' The most obviously drunk hauled himself into the truck and tried to pull Joth out, tugging at his camera strap. Kolya kept reassuringly calm and, slipping the truck into reverse, pulled away.

Sitting in the sun that afternoon, the postmaster meandered into the garden. He was drunk and had heard through the village grapevine that we were there. He had come to talk. 'We need the Communist Party to stay alive,' he shouted, clenching his fists at his side. 'The KGB must stay. The Communist Party is the strength of this country: without it we will fall apart. The Soviet Union was a great country. The West feared us, the whole world was frightened of us. But now we are weak and the Americans are feeding us. Gorbachev is a traitor; he betrayed his country. The Communist Party will return. It has to return if we are to survive.' He marched up and down in the dust as he shouted. He continued for almost half an hour, explaining the virtues of the 'iron fist in a velvet glove' approach to government. 'We need strong rulers. Our people only understand strong govern-ment. Stalin was the best leader this country ever had: he made us great and the envy of the rest of the world.'

He began to repeat himself, grabbing hold of my shoulders and shaking me.

'The Communists must return,' he shouted, more as if to convince himself rather than me. All the while, Kolya sniggered behind his hands that covered his face. It was difficult to determine whether he was sniggering through embarrassment or genuine disapproval of what the postmaster was saying.

After Kolya had slowly ushered him away, he explained that the postmaster had been powerful under Communism. A life member of the Party, he used to fine other members who did not toe the line, reporting them to the Party officials. He was a paid and resident spy. Since the fall of Communism, he wanders around the village all day, lamenting his lost power, with a bottle of vodka in his coat pocket.

'Don't people resent him?' I asked, mildly irritated by the political broadcast that I had been forced to listen to. 'What's the point?' said Kolya, with a shrug. 'He's harmless now, and rather pathetic. Anyway, the village is too small to bear grudges. If I were rude to him, I would not receive my post.'

We went to buy train tickets for that evening. The kiosk was closed but we went to the station manager's house. He held the key to communications and was the most powerful man in the village. Kolya was duly humble as we entered. He told us not to bother him but to go next door to the cashier. She and two other old women were ensconced in a bottle of vodka, along with a group of four men. They made us sit down to exchange toasts and crunch pickled gherkins. Eventually, the old woman wove her way to the station, opened up and, after a few telephone calls, handed over two tickets. Refusing more vodka, we returned home.

Tanya had been standing at the stove almost all afternoon. It was Joth's birthday and she had cooked a Kazak feast in his honour. We sat down to a huge plate of saffron rice and camel. The meat, which had been drying on the washing line all afternoon, was sweet and tender. It was a great delicacy in the area, where camels are highly priced and only slaughtered for important occasions. The small puppy, tethered to a rope in the yard, yelped for the scraps. Its ears had been cut off to prevent it from sleeping, thereby making it a better guard dog, according to Kolya. We sat outside on the doorstep, throwing the remains of the camel at the dog. The sun had long since set, and the desert was quiet, the sky a dark blue, the stars spreading towards the horizon like a gentle sprinkling of icing sugar.

Kolya began to discuss the mafia. 'They're everywhere,' he said, throwing another piece of meat. 'Anyone who has any position at all will pay money to the mafia or the mafia will do them in. There was one woman in the village who was very honest and refused to deal with them. They shot her three months ago because she would not pay them. They control everything and everyone. People pay because they're afraid.'

At 3 a.m. we left to catch the train to Samerkand. I had developed a raging fever and could hardly walk; I felt my face burning and I was pouring sweat. We had no place on the packed train and had to wait for the next stop in two hours. We sat on the dusty floor among the cigarette butts and waited, heads lolling forward, our arms wrapped around our luggage. Finally the train emptied and, dragging ourselves to the muggy compartment, I moved the warm mattress to find that it was covered in sick. I threw it to the floor, to see two fat cockroaches run down the crack in the wall. I collapsed to the floor and started to cry. It was five in the morning, I felt horrible and there was sick all over my bed.

The ticket collector gathered me up and moved us to another compartment. Joth made my bed for me and tucked me in. I lay sweating, under Joth's instructions, dressed in full thermals and an extra blanket.

Uzbekistan

....

DAY 44

Samerkand is full of turquoise domes. The streets heave with traders buying and selling. All along the narrow alleys, small charcoal fires smoulder, heating chunks of meat and fish on long sticks; open drains, clogged with pieces of chewed flesh and old vegetables, flow either side of the road.

Walking through the city it becomes apparent that it is a strange kaleidoscope of peoples, colours and architecture. The Uzbeks, in their long, brightly coloured coats, with closely cropped hair and square embroidered hats, sit in doorways, drinking green tea out of round cups that fit snugly in both hands.

They are short people, with smooth brown skin, flat faces and Eastern eyes. The men sit around in groups, their legs neatly crossed under them, wearing loose trousers and soft, leather, knee-length boots, which they protect with black galoshes.

The Tadjiks, from just over the border, look similar except their coats are brighter and their noses stronger, making them appear more Afghan. There are also large Iranian, Jewish and Russian communities in various different quarters of the city.

The architecture is part-Arabian, part-Communist. Large concrete blocks have elaborately decorated window frames; delicately carved wood drips from the corners like lace. Wide roads lined with apartment blocks rip through the city and yet the ancient narrow streets still survive. The city is dominated by the azure domes of the Registan, and the detailed mosaic of pale yellow tigers dances up the walls, flouting Islam's laws against the depiction of live animals.

We walked through the market and talked to the traders. An old woman who made Uzbek hats boasted of her wealth. She sold each hat for 25 roubles and she made and sold between three and four a day. She was relatively rich, but was so proud of her new fortune that she made her son return home to collect a video camera that they had just bought, to show it to us.

We sat outside on the long, wide tables that looked more like low double beds, drinking green tea straight from the teapots because they had run out of glasses, and attacked a parcel of fried fish that we had bought in the market. We were surrounded by families and groups of men as they all sat, cross-legged, in a circle. One man leant over and, draining his glass of tea, handed it to me. 'Can't drink without one of these,' he said, walking off.

The market was the only place where we could buy food without coupons. We tried the shops, but did not have enough to buy anything of any significance, although we did manage to find some toothbrushes, which we had been looking for since I lost mine in Nalchik. As yet, though, we had found no toothpaste.

The coupon system seemed more protectionist than a way of controlling distribution. It meant that anyone who was not Uzbek could not buy food, so preventing the poorer Tadjiks from coming across the border and stocking up on food.

Leaving the market, we came across a tanker marked *Kvas*, a weak ginger beer. We walked through the crowd that had gathered round, to find that it was, in fact, full of genuine, strong beer. About thirty men were hanging around for milk bottles; the others were drinking, pouring the beer down their necks with barely an opportunity to breathe. I stood in the queue, collected my milk bottle from a leaving drinker and rinsed it under the tap in the street. Standing in line, I filled up my bottle at the tap of the huge lorry, paid my 3 roubles and went to sit down amongst a group of men who were seated on the rusty springs of a rotten mattress that lay in the dust.

An old man in shoddy clothes, with no teeth and a large red medal pinned to his chest, came and sat next to me. He leant over and loudly whispered into my ear: 'Girls shouldn't drink, you know.' He then collapsed into a deep smoker's laugh. 'My name is Ocherl and I was in the war. Look at my medal,' he said, puffing up his chest. Too much alcohol and lack of teeth made him hard to understand, so I smiled a lot. He pointed out all his war wounds: a bullet through the cheek, arm and leg, as well as a missing finger on his right hand. He was on a pension and, as a war veteran, he had a larger pension than most. He complained about the high prices and, chuckling to himself, said, 'But then I live on a *kolhoz*, and we have a lot of food.' He began listing what he had to eat, ticking each food product off on his fingers. The other men, sitting around on the mattress and squatting on the floor, listened and laughed at our conversation. Merrily knocking back their beer, they joined in, arguing that they had shortages and that the coupon system was ridiculous. 'I mean, look at these bits of paper. They mean nothing,' shouted a man, as he stood up waving the purple sheet in the air. To the roar of the crowd, he ripped it in half, chucking the two pieces over his shoulder.

'Can you get sugar in your country?' asked the old war veteran. 'Ah, you see, we can't get that here. We haven't had any for months. We used to, but not any more. It's the democrats, they seem to have all the sugar.'

'I had some sugar recently,' a voice piped up from the crowd. Everyone turned to look at him. 'Where from?' asked another. 'My mother queued for it,' the voice replied.

We left as they sat round, discussing sugar and its disappearance relating to the new democracy. Walking past the domes of the Registan, which glowed a pale violet in the evening light, we talked to some artists who sat, painting, in the street. It was a beautiful evening: the winter sun struggled to warm the cold air: the breeze teased the ends of my fingers, turning them pink and stiff.

We ate in a restaurant that was full of men dancing together to extremely loud music. The food, cooked outside in the street, bore no resemblance to the menu. I sat next to a man almost horizontal through vodka. 'I am part of the mafia. I deal in champagne and drugs,' he whispered loudly. 'Why don't you come back to my house and taste some,' he managed to say just before his head slid onto the table.

DAY 45

Snow cascaded out of the sky as we drove to the Urgut market about thirty kilometres outside Samerkand. The road, a stone track, was virtually impassable. We had followed the advice of one of the women in the market, who had told us to go here as it would be more interesting.

The market had almost packed up by the time we arrived, the stall owners unable to bear the intense wind and thick snow. The taxi driver came with us into the market and walked with us through the empty stalls. At the far end, there was a stall selling meat kebabs; we joined the queue made up of stall holders and settled down on the floor near the fire in a small hut to eat. Rows of old women tore at the tough meat with their toothless gums. We had to eat the charred lumps quickly before the fat congealed and coated the roof of our mouths making the whole thing inedible.

We met a fat woman who invited us back to her house to view her coats that she sold in the market. She lived in a large house with an enclosed courtyard. We walked into a long room, with matting on the floor. Her dowry was piled high at one end of the room, the silk mattresses and pearl boxes were the same as Tanya's. One of her plump sons went to collect the striped, quilted coats that we wanted to see. She laid out coat after coat on the floor, her overweight husband, his stomach hanging over his trousers, sat cross-legged in the corner, witnessing her hard sell. Another fat son came to watch, inquisitive at the arrival of strangers in the house, until he was sent to another room to find some leather boots. Their wives looked on from a smaller house across the courtyard that was covered in dormant vines. They giggled as they pressed their over-made-up faces through the grill that shielded them from the gaze of the outside world.

After the bargain had been struck, the wife selling us the coat off her husband's back, we sat down to tea. A tray brimming with dried fruit, jam and nuts was placed in the middle of the floor. 'These delicacies are from our garden,' said the wife, as her dimpled hand sifted its way through the nuts. The whole family worked in the market selling various items of Uzbek clothing. They were obviously rich and exuded a fat complacency. The two wives were not invited into the room where we sat and waved goodbye as we left, their fingers forced through the narrow grill.

Later that day we wandered around the Jewish quarter of the city. It had the same buildings, narrow passages and open drains as in the centre of Samerkand but somehow there was more of a Western feel to the area. As we walked along the streets we were constantly greeted and welcomed. 'Hi. Are you Jewish?' There was a definite camaraderie. We went to the synagogue that was 150 years old and spoke to the secular leader. He was an old man with a long, white beard, who spoke in Tadjik and Russian. 'The young people are now coming to worship here,'

Dawn, Krasnovodsk, Turkmenia

Russian women, Repetek, Turkmenia

Driftwood, Turkmenia

Syid and Sveta, Chiliken, Turkmenia

Trader, *Ashkhabad*

OPPOSITE Kiva, *Uzbekistan*

Tanya, Kirghizstan

Ilkhom, Samerkand

Canning factory, Samerkand

Blacksmith, Tadjikistan

Headmaster, Tadjikistan

Zena, woman prisoner, Alma-Ata, Kazakhstan

School choir, Tadjikistan

he explained. 'Perestroika has dissolved their fear. Before, they were afraid, and only the old, who had nothing left to lose, would come. The main problem was that the state would not give them the day off. Friday and Saturday are official working days in the Soviet week. But now, since perestroika, more and more Jews are owning their own businesses, we can do that now you see, open co-operatives and start up private companies, so they can give themselves days off to come and worship.'

He explained that the Jewish community in the city had diminished from 15,000 to 10,000 since perestroika and the relaxing of the emigration laws. We sat in the synagogue, a small simple building, with our heads covered in handkerchiefs. Outside in the courtyard, a caretaker was cleaning away some of the snow and polishing the donation box. The whole complex was financed through the will of the people. The leader, voted in by the community eighteen months ago, had organized the renovation of the synagogue and the carved wooden interior still emanated the sweet scent of new wood.

We walked through the streets to the club house where a leaving ceremony was taking place for two Jewish exchange students who had come over on a two-month visit from a kibbutz in northern Israel. They had come to teach Hebrew and the Jewish traditions to the younger children and would be replaced by two more students who were arriving tomorrow.

The small hall was packed with children, all with Uzbek hats on the back of their heads. Speaking through interpreters, the students were acting out an entertainment for the children. At the end of the play, all the children were invited to come to the front and sign their names on a cardboard 'Wailing Wall' to take back to Israel. 'Do we have to write our surnames?' shouted one child from the back of the hall. This question sent a wave of concern rippling through the crowd. 'We'll only do it if we don't have to write our names in full,' said another. Fear still loomed. 'No, no. Surnames are not essential,' replied Jacob, the exchange student from the front of the stage. They all swarmed forward.

Outside, the older students were smoking. 'Most people who remain here and have not gone to Israel, want to be here,' explained one student as he lit a cigarette. 'Those who weren't afraid have already gone. No one wants to go to Israel any more because of all the problems that the immigrants are having. We will wait now for the US Embassy to open in Tashkent and then everyone will fill out their application forms. Many of us already have relations there from the last exodus in

1973. It is now so difficult to go to Moscow. We can't wait for James Baker to open the embassy. He's coming the day after tomorrow, isn't he?'

A well-dressed young Jewish boy escorted me out of the area. He worked as a clerk for a computer company but was setting up a joint venture with some American friends, making wigs to sell to orthodox Jews in Germany and the US. He had already been to America once before and was desperate to return. 'I've already filled out my application form and I can't wait for the embassy.' Sasha said with a smile.

We walked along the streets surrounded by high white walls and passed a hospital. I could just see the eyes of a young Uzbek women straining to see through the grill on the door. 'That's the hospital for French diseases,' said Sasha. 'That's sexually transmitted diseases,' he said with a laugh. 'We may have an AIDS problem here, but no one knows about it. I doubt very much that it's through homosexuality or sex. Homosexuality is illegal in this country, so therefore through the logic of the state, if it is illegal then it does not exist. But of course it does, it just goes underground, like everything else. You're much more likely to catch AIDS through dirty needles in the hospital, especially now, when we can't get any supplies from Eastern Europe. Although there's a drug problem here, the hard stuff like Gef, that bleaches your trousers, that's only found in Moscow and St Petersburg. Everyone smokes grass here, it's part of the culture. We supply the rest of the Soviet Union, or whatever they call it now.'

I asked him how the various races and religions get on in the city. 'Jew and Muslim live side by side here. It doesn't really matter what religion you are here, it's only if you are black that you have a problem here.' He elaborated, saying that most Soviets had never seen foreigners, let alone black people. 'I think that it's more through fear than anything personal,' he said as he walked onto the trolley bus to take him to the new Jewish quarter in the city.

Tadjikistan

· · · · · · · · · · · · · · · ·

DAY 46

Leaving early, we drove through the mountains to Tadjikistan. Our driver, an Iranian driving instructor, wore a dark fur hat that developed a sort of permanence on his head so that when finally he took it off, it was rather a shock to find that he was completely bald.

We drove across the border between Uzbekistan and Tadjikistan, a lamely hanging red-and-white striped bar marking the crossing. We carried on higher and higher through the foothills and into the mountains. The scenery was spectacularly beautiful: mountains the texture of crumpled silk tore into the pale aquamarine sky; sheer faces of ginger rock glowed softly in the sun. We drove through hamlets of low, wattle-and-daub houses, with people brushing snow off the flat roofs. All along the route, horsemen trotted along, their horses covered in multicoloured rugs, bearing heavy saddles with high bridges, and glinting silver buckles. The men wore the brighter, long, quilted coats that we had seen in Samerkand. The women, depending on their age, wore either white, if they were old, or dark red scarves on their heads, and their hair, in thirty or forty plaits, danced down their backs. We drove over wooden bridges that spanned deep gorges with clear, fast-flowing streams below. On the road, old men in blue-and-white striped caps stood sprinkling black salted earth from the small piles that lined the road. As we passed, they leant on their spades and turned to wave us on.

'They hardly ever see cars here,' said the Iranian driving instructor. It was true. We had been the only car on the road since early that morning. 'Firstly they are very poor, the poorest in the whole country, and anyway, there hasn't been any petrol here for months, because the Russians won't give them any. The Tadjiks have nothing to give them in return.'

Through the bright light of the sun reflecting on the snow, two small boys came galloping out of the drifts. Racing each other, they yelped, their feet stiffly bouncing in the air. The horses' hooves softly thudding in the snow, they sped past, waving one hand in the air as they left.

After five hours, we arrived in Beshkand, a small village clinging to the side of the mountain. The houses, built high on stilts with steps leading up to the door, fell down the slope; a small stream divided the village in half. We stopped to ask two small boys, playing with bicycle wheels, the way to the head man. They told us to go to the school but, cowering away, they refused to get into the car and direct us.

As soon as we approached the school, another ugly Soviet concrete building, the headmaster rushed out to meet us and ushered us upstairs to his office. The English teacher was immediately ushered in to talk to us. 'Hello, my dears,' said a fat, sweaty man as he walked into the room. He had studied English in Leninabad, but had never spoken to foreigners before. The headmaster, keen to test his teacher, made him talk in English. 'Hello, what is your name?' I asked. He stared back blankly and then suddenly replied, 'Very well, thank you.' The headmaster leant forward on his seat. 'Well? Well?' he said, bouncing around. 'Say some more.' The situation became more intense and more embarrassing as every question I asked was greeted with a blank look or a non sequitur. 'I find it hard to understand your accent,' the fat man finally admitted in Russian. 'It must be because I am from London,' I said. 'Yes, yes, that's it,' he said. 'You are English.'

This trial over, we were allowed to see the rest of the village. As we walked out into the snow, the whole of the village lined up along the road to watch us. The rows of striped, padded coats fell silent as we passed. There were no women to be seen and no one ventured near us. A man with a smooth, dark face and a long moustache rushed up to me. 'Hi, I'm a democrat,' he said, a naïve enthusiasm smiling in his eyes. 'I was elected three months ago, and I'm the only democrat in the village,' he added, tugging at my hands. 'That's great,' I replied, not quite knowing what else to say. He then turned and ran after the small yellow bus that had just spattered the bystanders in slush as they stood and stared from the curb.

We moved on, the rest of the village following at a safe distance. Down the hill, in the centre of the village, a woman shyly let us into her house. Walking through a shady courtyard cleared of snow and climbing up some steep steps, we came into a huge, bare room with a carpet on the wall. She apologized that she was cleaning and continued her work. Bending from the hip, she carried on sweeping the floor with a bundle of sticks bound together with rope. She could not buy anything in the shops: it was all too expensive. 'Anyway, we can produce what we want here. It's in the town, where they have no land, that they live badly.' There was a murmur of agreement from the crowd outside, who stood in silence, listening to our conversation.

Leaving the house, we passed two girls in the street laden with heavy churns full of water that sloshed over the sides as they walked along. By the communal tap, a group of women had gathered and were chatting amongst themselves. They turned their backs and lowered their eyes as the entourage walked by.

Returning to the school for lunch, we sat down with the headmaster, Abdul, to eat sour cream, bread and semidried grapes. 'We're now teaching our children Persian,' he announced. 'We started in the second grade in September, and we now don't teach Russian until the third grade. Our natural links are with Iran and Afghanistan. After all, we're Muslim; we are a little Iran. We have always been part of Iran until the Revolution came and divided us. And we shall go back to Iran. We are all one race, one religion and one language. Iran will come to our rescue now that we no longer belong to Russia. We are all learning Persian and soon no one will speak Russian.' He gave a huge smile.

'Russia is dead, but Communism must live on. Gorbachev and perestroika have destroyed us, but we will become Communists again. Eighty per cent of the village is still Communist. I am still a member of the Party. We need the discipline and the structure and, of course, we need the secret police.' He sat, surrounded by faded slogans on the greying wall, drinking green tea. 'Now Stalin, he was a wonderful man, as was Brezhnev. Khrushchev was a fool.'

'Stalin was an animal,' I replied with force.

'What do you mean?' he replied angrily. 'We had food to eat and petrol to run our cars, and everyone was one big family. There was no racism. We could travel to buy food in Uzbekistan. Now the coupons stop us. We have ration cards for basic foodstuffs – we never had that under Stalin.'

We went to the gym to watch some gauche girls dancing while the plump English teacher bobbed around in accompaniment, playing a small guitar. They whirled around in their long, dark red frocks. Then, easing down onto their knees and shaking their shoulders, they slowly leant down, their heads touching the floor. Moving from side to side they twisted their fingers in the air and spun round, their long black plaits hitting them in the face with the momentum.

I left and wandered through the snow, coming across a blacksmith just off the main road. Inside a darkened room, he was surrounded by men who occasionally left to smoke a joint in the snow. Then they would return to sit, staring at the flame. The blacksmith stood smelting metal, making knives and nails for the village. The room became progressively more and more packed as they all sat around, watching him. His strong face was illuminated in the darkness by the glow of the metal. His dark skin contrasted with the blue-and-white of the regulation, padded-cloth labourer's hat, dished out by the state.

On leaving the village and driving back through the mountains, we came across the weekly livestock market. About 120 men were standing around talking, while twelve fat sheep and some cattle were tweaked and paraded about by their proud owners. A man with a gentle face and long eyelashes, whose lips shone in the sun, purred as he stroked the soft velvet nose of his black ram. 'Is he your friend?' I asked. 'My very best friend,' he replied with a smile, still stroking the animal's nose. 'Then why are you selling him?' I asked. 'I've reared him from a small lamb and now I can no longer afford to keep him. I'll sell him for 2,000 roubles and then we'll live a little better.' He also had two ewes with ginger fleeces. He was less attached to them, but stood picking the earth out of their long shaggy coats as buyers walked past, checking teeth and chatting to each other. There was little bargaining going on: it appeared to be more of a social event than anything cut-throat. As I stood talking to the man with the ram, a curious crowd gathered round. They all stood and listened. The black ram, sensing that he was the centre of attention, moved away from his master and shoved his nose between my legs. 'I think he loves you,' said his owner with a giggle. The rest of the crowd collapsed into roars of laughter and gathered round, giving me hearty slaps on the back.

We were escorted back to the car by a small group of boys shouting 'Hello English!' and sniggering. We drove back to Samerkand, passing a row of almost 200 men leaning against a wall alongside the road. 'Someone important has died,' explained our Iranian taxi driver. 'They will all sit there until the sun goes down.'

'Why are there no women there?' I asked. 'Women aren't allowed,' he replied. 'They stay at home and cook the food.'

As we drove back across the border, our driver began to eulogize Uzbekistan.

'You see what animals they are in Tadjikistan. You saw how afraid of you they were. Uzbekistan will be great because we have all that we need to be great – oil, gold and, of course, white gold, or cotton. The Russians love our cotton. The Tadjiks have nothing and they will continue to have nothing and live badly as they always have done. They are pathetic, backward, ugly people. We, on the other hand, will be great.' He turned to look at me, a smug smile on his lips. 'Toyota is building a car factory in Samerkand, you know.'

Uzbekistan
· · · · · · · · · · · · · · ·

DAY 47

Ilkhom was a huge man with a wide, flat face, thick, black hair and a body that he did not quite know how to control. He flopped and slumped and gesticulated wildly. He had a naïve enthusiasm about him and a generosity that went beyond the bounds of normal behaviour. We had met him in the third-class carriage on the train from Urgench to Sharju and he was so excited that we had taken him up on his invitation to come and stay that he could not contain himself. He constantly broke into a smile or laugh and spontaneously hugged us or slapped us on the back. He had a burning desire to show us his home and where he lived to prove that perestroika could work. 'I want to spit on Communism, to laugh at the hardliners and give my family the best life possible,' he would say.

His family were third- or fourth-generation Iranians. They all lived together in an enclosed area of the Iranian quarter of Samerkand. His father, with the four sons, all had houses around an enclosed courtyard. Each of the wives had a small kitchen surrounded by glass. They faced each other while they cooked, like a row of battery hens. In the middle of the yard was a small patch of land with six apple trees, and on one side, a few goats and two cows stood tethered in a small pen. Outside the yard in the street, more sheep stood lazily munching hay in a pen next to the open-air loo. Water came from a tap in the middle of the yard and the family washed at the communal baths about twenty minutes away.

We were never introduced to Ilkhom's wife, who remained in the kitchen throughout our stay. She never spoke to us, save for a few curious questions that Ilkhom translated into Russian for me to answer. Small and dark, with long black hair, she came from a village outside Samerkand and could not speak Russian. She went quietly about her duties and was known simply as 'my wife'.

The whole family, the father and the four sons, worked in the canning factory over the road. It canned tomatoes, carrots and caviar.

But Ilkhom stole for a living. Not from the people, he insisted, but from the state. 'My father taught me never to steal from people, but you can steal from the state because they rob people of everything anyway and what does it matter, they'll never notice.' He illustrated his point by stealing a vase from his table and running away with it. 'This I would never do,' he said, with such pride that I could not fail to believe him.

He was in charge of shipping produce to Vladivostok. 'Who would notice if a shipment went missing?' he asked with a smile. He very rarely turned up for work. He had the whole process down to a fine art. Cultivating a contact at the factory, he would be warned when the inspectors were turning up and only then would he bother to clock in. 'My official wage is 300 roubles a month. Only an animal could live on that,' he said with disgust.

We spent the afternoon drinking vodka, squashed around the table in the sitting room, the wife waiting on us. Ilkhom loved Gorbachev with the passion of a slave released from his chains. 'Gorbachev is gold dust; he is marvellous. He has finally stopped the evils of Communism. He is the best person in the world. I mean, if he did not exist, then you wouldn't be here.' We toasted our arrival and hugged each other.

'Look at the way we live here. It's ridiculous. We have money to build a beautiful house but here people are afraid. If we build a bathroom and have running water, then someone will say, "Where did they get the money from?" They'll find out where you work and realize that you could never afford all that on your salary, so then you would immediately be sent to prison.' He laughed, imitated his throat being slit, and toasted Gorbachev once more.

His elder brother sat down at the table. His eyes half-closed and glazed over, he immediately brought out a whole sachetful of grass and began rolling a joint. He had been in prison for four years for attempted murder. 'I was drunk and he was a Communist. So I stabbed him,' he said, laughing. Ilkhom laughed louder still and slapped his brother on the back. 'Oh God, prison,' said the brother, lolling on the table. 'All they give you is black bread and water. At least in the West they let you watch television. Or at least, that's what I've heard.'

We left the house for a tour of the factory, Ilkhom leading the way. While we walked through the narrow, dark streets to the main road, people stood aside to clear the way. They bowed, placing their hands on their hearts as Ilkhom walked past, greeting him with a frightened respect. He did not seem to notice. He generated such fear and respect in the other Iranians on the street that I could not help wondering, given the size of the family's house and the new television set in the sitting room, what Ilkhom really did for a living.

We walked straight past the security guards into the factory. They, too, greeted Ilkhom with a strange respect. We were introduced to another brother, who was drinking vodka by himself in a small hut near the store house. The store itself, piled high with rusty cans, was guarded by an old, simple woman with no teeth. She squealed like a small child when Ilkhom walked in. She knew him and extended a gnarled hand before returning, giggling, to her small office in the corner of the room.

The factory was falling to pieces. 'Look at this,' shouted Ilkhom, surrounded by steam escaping from broken pipes. 'What sort of caretaker is this? This is Communism for you.' We walked along the cracked concrete paths that surrounded the factory, clouds of escaping gas belching forth and blurring our vision. The smell scratched my nostrils and made my eyes water. 'What gas is this?' I asked. 'No one knows,' said Ilkhom. 'All I know is that my children can't breathe in the summer and everyone has bad lungs.' A sign saying, 'Thank you for toil' lay plaintively across the path. Ilkhom kicked it as we walked by.

Inside the factory, four women stood washing glass jars, sent from Russia, in water with a grey film floating on the surface. They then loaded the jars onto the spikes of a machine, which sent them on to another room. Dressed in boots, with white scarves tight around their heads, they stared at us.

In the next-door room, the air was full of steam. A long, oily conveyor belt was transporting rotting carrots through a giant peeler to huge vats to be boiled. It spilt half its load onto the floor before it reached the vats. In the room just off the main factory, a mountain of filthy carrots stood, waiting to be loaded onto the conveyor belt. There was a smell of decomposition and a rotting slime covered the floor. Back in the main factory, women in stained overalls stood smoking cigarettes and shaking the containers of boiled carrots. They then wheeled the vats of steaming vegetables across the floor, their faces dulled and wet with steam, their hair dirty, their movements mechanical. The floor was covered with water and broken glass as the women minding the jars lost their concentration. Light poured in through the skylights in the roof of the factory, picking out the congealed oil that covered the forty-year-old machinery.

'Stalin created this factory with machinery from Moscow,' said Ilkhom. Further along the line, a woman sat at the conveyor belt with a jar of carrots and a large spoon in her hand. She spent the day topping up the jars which had not been correctly filled by the machines. We continued into another room full of machinery half in and out of boxes, covered in dust. 'This was brought from the West or Czechoslovakia, but no one can understand the instructions. So it just stays here – another waste of money,' explained Ilkhom.

Outside, a billboard boasted Communist slogans. 'I asked the manager to paint those over,' said Ilkhom, 'but now I think they serve as a good reminder of what Communism stands for: a waste of money and human beings. No one cares in that factory, so they do their job and go home and just get drunk. The food they produce is disgusting, but no one cares. They get paid just the same.'

High on one of the walls that surrounded the factory ran the slogan in both Russian and Uzbek: 'Study, study, and study'. 'Another erudite quotation from our father Lenin,' said Ilkhom as he goose-stepped past. 'What does that mean? Nothing. Study? What for? To work here?' He began to laugh in a manic, exhausted way, jaded tears rolling down his cheeks. 'It's all rubbish.'

We left the factory and walked back home, greeted once more by the same bows and hands placed on hearts as when we arrived. 'Look at this road!' exclaimed Ilkhom. 'Imagine what it's like in the summer.' He imitated how he would cross the road in the summer. Choking and spluttering, he covered his eyes and mouth and, crashing into the wall on the other side, he collapsed in a heap. 'That's how we cross in the summer. There's so much dust everywhere that you just can't breathe.'

Back in the courtyard, each wife was in her own kitchen. The grandmother's stove was not surrounded by glass and she stood outside in the cold, chopping up vegetables on a small bench. Ilkhom's wife did not join us when we sat down to eat, but ate with the other women in another room off the courtyard. The grandmother and daughter-in-law came to join us for tea, after we had eaten. They both had heavily painted eyebrows. A thick, black line of kohl joined them together in a line that extended down the face to the bridge of the nose and curved back up again to join the other eyebrow. This made them both look strangely sinister and bird-like, the heavy line emphasizing the brow and the length of their noses. It was a sign of great beauty. Their hands were dyed with henna; their finger nails and toe nails shone a rusty brown at the tips, as did those of the children.

I was as fascinated by these women as they were with me and we sat and stared at each other. They asked me questions, using Ilkhom as a translator; none of them could speak Russian. They touched my hair and my skin because it was paler than theirs and asked if women drank and smoked where I came from. They wore long, heavily embroidered clothes and sandals, and their hair was bound up in scarves. They had heard that it was important to be thin in the West, but the wife's mother had burst into tears when she had seen that her daughter had lost weight. 'When I was married I was fat,' said the wife. 'My mother tried to take me away from Ilkhom when she came and saw me. Only poor people are thin here.'

Ilkhom soon became bored of female conversation and refused to translate any more. He ostentatiously turned on the new television and watched the news. A young entrepreneur was donating money for a statue to be build in honour of Gorbachev. Ilkhom was beside himself with excitement. 'What a brilliant man he must be. That's what we all should be doing.' He rushed into the next-door room and brought back a garish piece of crystal. 'How much would this be in England?' he asked, moving it so that it glistened in the light. 'I have no idea,' I replied. 'I have a lot of it,' he explained, taking me next door to a room that I had not realized existed. It was full at one end with his wife's dowry – piles of mattresses and two intricate boxes. The shelves were stacked with crystal and golden, hand-painted teapots. This was obviously Ilkhom's warehouse. Quite where he collected all the goods from was anybody's guess. 'Here and there,' was how he explained it away. He was planning to sell it all in time for his five-year-old son's circumcision, which would take place in May. 'A master will come to take off the foreskin and there will be a party lasting three days, with relations and friends from all over the country. We will drink and dance,' he explained excitedly. 'So, to make it brilliant, I must sell all this crystal. We're also going to renovate this room especially for it.' He had already started and a collection of semi-assembled furniture lay spewing out from cardboard boxes. 'All this is for my son's circumcision. It'll be the best party my family has seen in their lives.'

DAY 48

Ilkhom took us on a guided tour of the Iranian quarter. He wanted us to see the crumbling buildings and squalid housing to demonstrate the horror of Communism. Everywhere we went, he would shout, 'Take a look at Communism. It treats people like animals.'

We walked into a hostel for factory workers. Sixteen families, each with eight or nine children, lived along one corridor. They each lived in one room and shared the kitchen and bathroom. The corridor was dark and smelt of drains; the people were dirty; the children naked. The women stared blankly: they had not had the luxury of privacy for so long I doubt they knew how to be on their own any more.

Ilkhom showed us the school where he had grown up. 'Even as a child, I was not a Communist,' he said. 'I was extrovert, happy and full of life, running around this playground laughing.' He bounced around, pretending to be a child. 'There was one rocking horse in the playground for us to play on. I rushed up laughing to the queue and I remember the teacher pushing me to one side. "You," she said. "You are not allowed to play on the horse." So I ran off and then, a few minutes later, with a sombre expression and my hands behind my back, I returned.' He imitated a child's walk, his feet slightly turned in, as he walked once more to the steps, reliving the whole experience. 'And, of course, she then let me play on the horse. You see, I now give my son everything because I was not allowed anything at school.' Of his daughter, he said nothing.

Back home, the wife was still in the kitchen, preparing the supper. It was her birthday and her sister had arrived from the country to see her. The sister sat in silence in the room, watching the television. Ilkhom did not talk to her. Instead, he turned to Joth and said, 'The problem with Communism is that it elevated women. It made them above men. Women are there to be loved and to keep home. Communism put women above men. My wife is a Communist but I am educating her not to be. We shall soon put women back in their place.'

Ilkhom and I had a difficult relationship. He did not quite know how to treat me. He naturally bonded with Joth and would never address any statement or question to me directly. He used me ostensibly as a translator, ignoring most of my questions unless I added 'he asks' at the end. He always carried Joth's bags and never made any move towards mine. The concept of female equality was alien to him: he associated it with Communism and the disturbance of Islamic culture and the natural order of things. He loved his plump son and ignored his dowdy daughter. He loved his wife, but never spoke to her. His was a strange form of chauvinism: he just ignored women, not out of malice, but, as he perceived it, propriety.

After supper we went to the grandparents' quarters. They were sitting, covered in a rug, around a low table on the floor. I was invited to put my feet under the rug. It was deliciously warm. Resting my toes on the wooden bars of the table, my legs were warmed by glowing embers from a fire that had been lit about a foot below, in a grate under the floorboards.

We sat watching the Soviet version of 'Blind Date', called 'Love at First Sight'. The grandfather suddenly stood up in disgust. 'We like our women clean, not like those dirty whores,' he shouted, and left the room. The youngest of his daughters sat entranced and giggled all the way through.

Walking to the train station, we passed through a housing estate. In the half-light I could see block upon block of crumbling flats. We came across a group of about twenty men, all loitering in a doorway. They stood comparing two pigeons. They handled them with firm familiarity, discussing feet, wingspans and prices. Ilkhom approached them with jovial familiarity. He showed us off like prize bulls in a show ground. 'They're from England,' he boasted. 'No,' they all muttered in unison. Their fascination was embarrassing. They each compared how long they had learnt English at school, but none of them was bold enough to speak. They were waiting for a friend to come back with some beer, which they had heard was on sale in another part of town. We stood in the dark, waiting for the friend to return. They shuffled their feet and stared at the ground; a crowd had begun to gather around us. The message was passed around that two English people were outside. They had all come to stare. No one spoke except to ask the price of things in the West and then they marvelled at how expensive it all was. We left after half an hour, promising to return.

The station was packed. We tried to enlist the help of the police in buying tickets. They took us into a cell and dragged in Ilkhom, who had been hiding in the shadows outside. This was the first time we had seen Ilkhom out of control of a situation. He nervously hopped from one foot to another as he lied about how we met and why we were staying in his house. They took his passport to register that he had had contact with foreigners and then, with the condescending smiles of petty bureaucrats, said they would only help us if we paid them triple the price of the fare.

Outside the station we met the same driver who had taken us to Tadjikistan. He was frightened of Ilkhom and drove us back to the house for free. While we waited for the train, the grandmother came and painted my eyebrows with kohl. Taking a fine paintbrush and a small brass container of kohl, she covered my eyebrows and painted a V shape down my nose. It made me look evil, but to wash it off immediately would have been rude.

Returning to the station, the police still refused to help us unless we bribed them. Then Ilkhom remembered that he had a contact from school who was the station manager and enlisted his help. 'I used to hit him at school, so he is frightened of me and will definitely help,' said Ilkhom with a giggle. We sat in the bicycle shed in the pouring rain waiting for the tickets to arrive. He charged us twice the amount of money that was written on the ticket and Ilkhom was furious. As the train drew into the station, the manager tried to stop us getting aboard. Shouting for visas and our passports, he began to yell for the police. We ran onto the train and, as it drew out of the station, I could see Ilkhom punching the manager on the platform as the rain poured down.

DAY 49

It was 6 a.m. and Sveta's phone did not work. 'All the engineers have left town for better jobs,' said an old man who was standing in line with me. 'Nothing works here any more.' Three hours later we managed to get through and arranged to meet Sveta near the market. 'I'm twenty-five years old, and I'll be wearing a grey coat and grey boots,' she explained. From this description we were supposed to be able to find her easily in a crowd, but of course, we did not and she approached us unawares.

We walked back to her house in virtual silence. Suddenly she turned to me and said, 'God, I hate these people.' 'Who is that, then?' I asked, somewhat taken aback. 'The Uzbeks,' she replied. 'A friend of mine was raped last week by an Uzbek. It was ten o'clock in the morning and he dragged her at knife-point to her house just by the market. She attempted to report the crime to the Uzbek police but they refused to do anything, telling her that if she did not shut up about it they would rape her as well. They said that because she was Russian, she must be lying.' I was totally shocked by the story, which she had told within five minutes of meeting us. Her hatred for the Uzbeks was pathological. She snarled as she walked along. She recounted the story with such passion that it made me wonder whether the victim was not a 'friend', but herself.

'Is she getting some form of counselling to help her through all this?' I asked rather naïvely.

'Counselling,' snorted Sveta. 'No. She has an appointment next week with a doctor to see if she has caught any sexually transmitted diseases, and that's all.'

We arrived at Sveta's house, a three-roomed place with a kitchen and an outside bathroom that was kept warm by four constantly lit gas burners. Sveta was the junior chess champion of Uzbekistan and now taught English at the local primary school for 600 roubles a month. She lived by herself in this house that she had been born in. Her parents, both chess teachers for the state, had moved to a flat about fifteen minutes' walk away when she got married. Sveta had married when she was twenty and divorced when she was twenty-three. She had a grey, lifeless face, toneless skin, grey hair and grey eyes. She had an amazing ability to stare for hours at a time at the wall, smoking cigarettes with no thought apparently going through her mind.

Sveta made us breakfast of black bread, cheese and tea — coffee was too expensive. We sat down to smoke and talk. She leant forward, resting her heavy head in her hands, and took a long drag of her cigarette. 'I hate this country. But I can't leave it. The whole Soviet registration system means that I can never leave. I'm stuck here.' She gazed at the table. Her ash fell on the floor, but she did not move to pick it up. 'I have a grandmother in the Ukraine, but she hates me because my birth prevented my mother from being a great chess champion. So I could never go there. All I want to do is to leave this place, go abroad, go to England,' she said, tears of frustration stinging her eyes. 'But you know, my salary won't even buy me a train ticket to Moscow to get the visa.'

'Why d'you think England would be so marvellous?' I asked, trying to shatter some of her illusions. 'We have poor and unhappy people there as well.'

'It's the west, isn't it,' she replied, with a wry laugh. 'And you have a queen and the aristocracy and class. We don't have any classes here.'

Sveta was fascinated by the English class system. She made us explain gentlemen's clubs and manners. She made us lay the table correctly and talk her through each course, using the right forks and spoons, telling her where to put your hands when eating. It was the first time that I had seen any light in her face. Most of the time she remained dulled and disinterested, and rarely laughed. She had been crushed by a system that she had neither the energy nor the inclination to change.

Sveta's mother arrived to stroke her cats, which she had had to leave behind when they moved to their new flat. Short and plump with reddish hair, she taught chess to small children. 'If I don't do my job properly, then my husband will have no one to teach,' she explained with a laugh. Her husband was a chess master and taught the Soviet champions. She sat with a fat, white cat on her lap and talked about Kasparov, whom she knew through chess circles. 'He has the most beautiful blue eyes, but he never looks good in newspapers because you can't see them.' She spoke with such fervour that I suspected she was rather in love with him, and imagined she probably had some sort of scrapbook full of newspaper cuttings, which she looked at when alone.

We sat down to foul meat dumplings that we forced down out of politeness. Gybia, a free-spirited girl of Chinese origin, turned up. She tore into the place, hugged us all and sat down. Almost immediately, she proudly showed off a large bag of cheap-smelling make-up. 'This is what I need for today,' she said, touching up her dark pink lipstick. Sveta, not to be outdone by Gybia's ostentatiousness, rushed next door to bring back a huge, black, shiny case, which she opened to reveal a monstrous butterfly of eye shadows. 'You don't wear enough make-up,' she said to me, putting on a pale turquoise above her eyes with her finger. 'You should make more of an effort.' I did, in fact, look slightly strange. My eyebrows were still dyed black after the Iranian kohl of last night, which had refused to come off despite countless shampoos.

Gybia demanded vodka. 'We have the food, but where's the drink?' she laughed.

Sveta replied that she only drank when she was alone or depressed, but lethargically pulled herself out of the chair and found a bottle of vodka in the fridge. Gybia and Sveta had studied English together at the Pedagogical Institute in Tashkent. Gybia now taught at the Institute of Road Construction, which she found terminally amusing, as, indeed, did we. After numerous toasts, we finally resorted to toasting the 'Institute of Road Construction' and collapsed in our chairs with laughter.

Gybia hated the Uzbeks as much as Sveta. 'I spend my whole day teaching stupid Uzbeks. They sit there with their mouths open and stare at me. They don't want to learn English and all they can say is that they should teach me Uzbek. They're all fools — they're from the villages, you see.' Sveta agreed vehemently and went on to tell Gybia about the rape of her friend. 'They're animals, these people,' said Gybia, slightly less surprised about the story than I. 'I can't believe that they think they'll ever be an independent country.' She flicked her cigarette aggressively, as if to emphasize her point.

The conversation drifted slowly towards sex, contraception and abortion. 'There are no contraceptives here,' said Gybia, leaning forward in her chair. 'There are some condoms, but never in the shops. They can only be found on the black market and they're very expensive. I could never afford them. We do have the coil, but that's also very expensive — 50 roubles for a Japanese one and if it's not Japanese then, well, don't bother. The Soviet ones don't work. I know, my mother is a gynaecologist.'

'So we all have abortions,' said Sveta, reaching for another cigarette. 'I've had three so far.'

'I have only had one,' replied Gybia.

'Really?' exclaimed Sveta, with genuine amazement. 'How come?'

'Luck I suppose,' came the reply.

'My ex-mother-in-law has had seventeen. I know loads of girlfriends who have eight or nine already. There are two different types,' explained Sveta. 'The first is when they vacuum you out, the second is when they induce labour. The second is the worst, obviously.'

'Do people counsel you afterwards?' I asked.

She looked puzzled. 'What for?'

'Well, in case you have any emotional problems,' I said, rather weakly.

'Why should you have any of those? It's only an abortion. It happens all the time. No one gets upset by them,' she replied, irritated.

Gybia left to telephone her Uzbek husband, whom she married three months ago. She was checking to see if it was safe to return home. She was in the process of divorcing him. He was the youngest member of the family, which meant that she was the least important person in the house, expected to cook and clean and run the home for everyone else. He had no job, no flat and drank too much. 'I have not been educated to become a servant,' she announced defiantly as she walked into the other room to telephone. 'Such cultural problems exist everywhere in this country. He is a Muslim and I'm not. The situation is made worse by such international marriages.' I wondered why she had married him.

He was not at home, which meant that Gybia prepared herself to leave. She asked Joth to walk her to the bus. Sveta handed him a knife, which he refused to take. After a long argument, he gave in and put the blade in his pocket. 'The streets are full of Uzbeks,' said Sveta.

DAY 50

We went to the Union of Writers to meet Suyima Gunieva, a celebrated literary critic and an authority on the writings of the Persian lyric poet, Alishir Navoi. She came to meet us in the Union of Writers, a rather beautiful building with wooden panelling on the walls. Posters bewailing the disappearance of the Aral Sea littered the stairs and slim men in dark suits muttered in dulcet tones along the poorly lit corridors.

Suyima was a tiny woman, coming up to just below my armpit. She had dark red hair with blondish streaks and bright pink lipstick and must have been in her early sixties. She immediately linked arms with me and began to explain the historical significance of every building in the street as we walked to her house. 'That's the Ministry of Foreign Affairs, but I think that they'll sell it to the USA or Turkey as an embassy – they'll do anything for hard currency.'

We arrived at her flat, where her daughter was cooking lunch. The windows were blocked off from the sun with huge sheets of yellowing paper. We sat down in her sitting room, packed from floor to ceiling with books and, with a naughty laugh, Suyima brought out a bottle of vodka.

Settling down, placing her plump wrists on the table, she began to talk about the rise of Muslim Fundamentalism and the ramifications of closer links with Iran. 'I don't believe that Fundamentalism will take off here. The women are veiling themselves again, but they're flirting with religion. They think that if they wear a veil, it makes them special, interesting or exotic. I dislike Fundamentalism,' she said, reaching forward for another slug of vodka. 'I see no reason to cover your face. When I went to Iran, years ago, under the Shah, I went to liberate the women. I thought: poor things, they've no idea what freedom is. When I arrived, I found them liberated enough already. Now they cover their faces. I don't think that we'll ever really do that again.'

She explained that the rise of Fundamentalism was a reaction to years of oppression. 'It's a sort of status symbol, like the Russians wearing Orthodox crosses – people are now allowed to, so they do,' she said. She sees the secularism of Soviet society as more important to its people than the growth of religion.

She moved on to talk about the implications of the break-up of the Union. 'Can you imagine being old in this country at the moment? They've seen everything from war, famine and purges to starvation and now, once again, they can't afford to feed themselves. What is independence, anyway? It's like giving a chocolate cake to a starving man: he gorges himself and is sick,' she said angrily.

So far independence to her meant rising prices, rising tension between Uzbeks and Russians and the shrinking of her country. 'Before, my country was huge. I could travel to St Petersburg and Moscow if I wanted to. Now I need a visa.' She studied at university in St Petersburg for five years, where her daughter was born. She truly loves the city. But now she was finding it hard to get books. 'I'm nothing without the Lenin Library in Moscow. I can't do my research: there's nothing here.

'The only difference independence has made is that we can now speak Uzbek without any reprisals. Before it was illegal to speak Uzbek if any Russian was present. For example, I can remember having to deliver a lecture in Russian at the university here because the Russian cleaner walked into the classroom. The whole class was full of Uzbeks but we had to speak Russian so that he could understand if he wanted to listen. Ridiculous!' She laughed. 'The big argument at the moment is what script to take – Arabic, Cyrilic or Latin. God knows which one will win.'

Talking about her life as an intellectual before *perestroika*, she said that she had avoided attending meetings that would have given her any trouble. 'I never really had problems with the police. I didn't attend meetings – there wasn't really much point.' Unlike most of her intellectual friends, her biggest problem had been trying to get hold of materials and books and, of course, the lack of computers impeded her work. 'If only I had a computer I could do so much more, but that's another dream.' She occasionally gets manuscripts from the West and she marvels at the research facilities. 'We just don't have the resources.'

We walked out onto her papered-over veranda. 'We get too much sun here,' she moaned. 'I hate the dust in the summer, it makes it hard to breathe.' With that she took out a cigarette. I looked mildly surprised. I had never seen a woman smoking in any of the southern republics. She looked at me and laughed, 'Now that's progress.'

Walking through the market to buy flowers for Sveta, we were the only customers. The Soviets have a complete fixation for flowers. In the markets in all the republics, no matter the weather, they are always on sale: they stand in snug, glass cases, protected against the snow in Moscow, in baskets under umbrellas in Kiev and here they were in large buckets. The Russians give flowers for any occasion they can think of. We walked through the rows of stalls, where sellers were charging a third of Sveta's monthly wage for a bunch of roses. Pale blue carnations were going for 100 roubles.

We returned to Sveta's laden with flowers in the hope of making her smile. She barely reacted as she sat in the kitchen, surrounded by magazine clippings of Western women. Her lips curled slightly as she set about putting the bunches into vases. 'I feel that it's my birthday,' she eventually said after about ten minutes. She settled down again to sit in her favourite chair and stare at her favourite patch of wall.

A little later, Volodya turned up. A friend of Sveta's from school, he was a young, bright banker who had just begun to make it big. But he was tired of his own countrymen. 'Sausage psychology!' he spat. 'All they ever talk about is the price of food. Don't they have anything interesting to talk about?' He was one of the first people, apart from the mafia and the black marketeers, to take advantage of *perestroika* and had an energy about him and a zest that was unknown in most of the people I had met. He was the antithesis of Sveta, who sat, getting progressively more drunk. Rocking backwards and forwards in her chair, she mumbled 'I'm drunk,' and listened to soulful Russian music from a small tape recorder that she pressed to her ear, her eyes half open, her vision blurred.

Volodya ignored her and carried on his animated conversation, explaining the rules of business in Tashkent. 'It costs 10,000 roubles to open up a shop in Tashkent at the moment. That includes bribes to the city council and protection money to prevent the place being firebombed by the mafia,' he said in a nonchalant tone.

He excitedly brought out his new business cards, which were bound up in a brown paper package. 'Hot off the press,' he announced. 'Don't they look great? All we have to do is get our acts together here and there's real money to be made. We have oil and plenty of raw materials. They are our ticket to hard currency.'

The only time he spoke to Sveta was to say that he had seen her ex-husband. 'He was wearing a leather jacket, like a mafia boss. He's rich and a black marketeer. Can you believe it? He came up to me and patronizingly paid for my ice cream.' Sveta could not have been less interested. She turned up the music on the tape recorder and rocked backwards and forwards some more.

Volodya left and Sveta turned to us both and said: 'I'm so bored of him. He's always asking me to have sex with him. D'you have friends who fuck for money? I do. Most of my girlfriends do because they can't afford to live off what they earn. Who can eat on 600 roubles a month? If you want French perfumes, nice clothes, good food and make-up, you just have to become a prostitute. There's this one Uzbek, who keeps offering me lots of money to sleep with him. I nearly did last week, but I don't think I could have looked at myself in the mirror in the morning. Or then again, maybe I could.' She was talking more to herself than either of us.

DAY 51

Sveta was too hung over to move. Leaving her chain-smoking in the kitchen, we set off to see Nasseba Abdylaeva, princess of Uzbek films and music. Running through the maze of the enormous film studios, corridors and sets, we missed her by five minutes: she had returned to her family in Samerkand, on holiday.

Tired and angry, we walked along the street, trying to find a taxi out of the area. We walked past the actors' union and bumped into a film producer who reeked of alcohol. He invited us for a drink. It was the last thing we felt like, but it would have been rude to refuse. Walking into a small, dark bar, he ordered fifty grams of spirit each. Twice as strong as vodka, I retched as I knocked it back. The producer then began to explain the film industry to us. 'We make about thirty-five films a year, but we can't export any because the type of film we use can't be shown abroad. It doesn't fit on anyone else's machinery,' he explained, beckoning the barman over and ordering more spirit, despite our protests.

'It costs us 25,000 roubles for ten minutes of Kodak film, so there's no way we could ever make a feature film on Kodak. Also, actresses at the moment have ideas above their station. They've heard how much money people make in Hollywood and are now demanding ridiculous amounts for films. It's a complete nightmare,' he said, downing his drink.

He escorted us back to the actors' union, a drab concrete building with a hall lined in jaded, black-and-white photographs of actors and actresses naïvely pouting at the lens, their make-up unprofessional, their clothes unfashionable. The studios were not working as it was winter and the light and weather too poor. He showed us a small theatre, where they put on more off-beat productions, but that, too, was closed. As we walked out of the union our escort met up with other film people and bade us goodbye, luring his new victims into the bar.

We roamed the streets of Tashkent searching for Sveta's school, where she had arranged to meet us. We ran into a large woman who asked us where we were from. 'England,' she said excitedly. 'I can speak some English,' she boasted. Puffing up her chest, she shouted at the top of her voice, 'I fuck you all!' I looked at her with a straight face. Did she realize exactly what she had just said? She looked back, grinning broadly. I looked at Joth and we both began to laugh. She and her drunk husband beckoned us into their car and drove us the 200 yards to the school.

We were told that Sveta had not turned up for work and that another teacher was taking her class. We were shown into a room where an over-excited and effeminate English teacher was telling a class of keen seven-year-olds, in navy blue uniforms with red neckties, about the joys of English pronunciation. Sitting on small stools, we listened to explanations of the difference between 'cap' and 'cape' and then left to a tirade of zealous 'goodbyes' and a round of applause.

Back at the house, we found Sveta very much as we had left her. She had not gone to school because her hangover had been too intense, and neither would she go tomorrow, as she had some private business to attend to. When pressed she replied, 'It's very private, and that's all I am saying.' She said that she could not be bothered to tell the school of her plans. 'They don't care and neither do I,' she said lethargically.

We caught a tiny bubble car, driven by a Tartar, to the station. The experience of three of us in the back of the car, our luggage at our feet and our chins on our knees, was quite hilarious. The Tartar became totally carried away by the joke and stopped at the station with us, buying us vodka and lemonade. He then walked us to the train, gave us both huge hugs, and refused to take any money.

Sveta managed to wave and smile as the train drew out of the station. I watched her on the platform in her grey coat and grey boots, her head slightly bowed. At twenty-five years old, I thought, her life had stopped before it had ever really begun.

On the train, Joth and I decided to drink the Tartar's vodka. After all, it was far too heavy to carry. We had just finished our third glass when a uniformed guard walked into our compartment and, taking hold of my shoulder, said: 'You. Come with me.' I was taken to the end of the carriage, to a small room where three other uniformed guards sat on a bed. 'As a foreigner,' shouted one of the guards, 'you must pay five times the official price for a train ticket.' I refused. Standing next to me was an Angolan student, who was also being asked for money. He was protesting wildly, saying that he lived here, that he was a student and not a tourist and that, anyway, he did not have the money. 'Then prepare to be thrown off at the next station,' screamed the fattest guard with pure venom in his voice, pushing him out of the carriage.

Turning to me, they asked me to sit down between them. Remembering my basic psychology, I remained standing, hands on hips.

'Hurry up and pay your money,' yelled one of the guards. 'You're foreign and rich. Do you have any money on you now?'

Very quietly and slowly, I asked them to explain just exactly why I needed to pay.

'You are foreign,' was the reply.

I suggested that the money would go into their pockets. This brought about feigned horror and consternation. 'It's a new rule,' they shouted in unison, shoving a piece of yellowed paper in my hand. I did not read it. 'Since when?' I asked. 'Recently' replied one guard. I insisted that I had never heard of such a rule and began to list every single train journey that we had made, checking them off on my fingers. By the time I reached Tashkent, they were beaten.

'I am therefore not paying,' I said.

'Well go then,' they muttered reluctantly.

I walked back to the compartment, shaking. The train stopped and I wondered if the Angolan had managed to avoid his fate.

We spent the whole of the next day on the train. More and more people began to knock on our compartment door, wanting to talk to us or offering us drink. I lay half asleep on the bed, dulled by the heavy heat of the sealed carriage, when a furtive knock on the door stirred me. A frightened man in a blue tracksuit hurried in and closed the door behind him, checking that he was not being followed.

'Someone tells me that you're writing about us?' he asked.

'That's true,' I replied, still slightly confused about the arrival of this man in the compartment. He began to shake as, in a low whisper, he told me about his son. He would not give me his name but said that he came from a region to the east in Siberia. He said that his son had been so badly attacked by the officers in the army during his national service that he could no longer walk. He, the father, who worked as a tractor driver on a collective farm, had spent all his savings travelling backwards and forwards to the authorities in Marghilan, trying to get his son transferred. The request had been refused, so he had smuggled him out, carrying him onto the train. He would not let me see his son, four compartments down, saying that it was too dangerous.

'This is not the first time this has happened. Did you not hear about the soldiers who could not stand it any more and murdered all their officers in a camp in Siberia last year?' he whispered, mincing his hands together. I had not. With that he got up. As he left the compartment, he grabbed hold of both my hands and said: 'Write the truth about us, write the truth. Tell people how we live and how we suffer. Tell them what you see.'

Kazakhstan

· · · · · · · · · · · · · · · ·

DAY 53

The bathing complex in Alma-Ata, built under Brezhnev, is one of the largest and most sumptuous in the whole of the Soviet Union, with a choice of four different bath systems, including Turkish and Swedish.

Joth and I walked into the huge marble hall and were directed to different sections. Although Kazakhstan's population is almost half Kazak/half Russian, Muslim propriety still prevails, precluding mixed baths. Stripping off naked in the communal changing rooms of the Eastern bath section, I was handed a white sheet by a squat old woman with plenty of facial hair. Rather embarrassed, I clutched my sheet to my chest as I wandered into the marbled area of the baths.

The pink marble floors were heated from below to various degrees of scalding. There, on the central marble circle, a fat, naked woman was being massaged by an even larger woman in a huge white bra and pants. The light from the domed skylight poured into the room, dancing on the fleshy shoulders of the masseuse. Naked women of all different shapes, sizes and nationalities stood under the communal showers having their weekly wash. Many Soviet households do not have bathing facilities, so people are forced to come to the banya to wash. With the precision of surgeons, they soaped, soaped and re-soaped, mesmerized by their disinfecting catharsis. The whole area was silent except for the noise of water touching skin and falling onto marble and the sniggers of two pubescent girls as they gossiped about boys from the floor of the 60°C alcove.

I spread out my sheet on the marble floor and lying flat on my back, I stared at the peachy ceiling, feeling the intense heat warming the very marrow of my bones and burning my buttocks. As I began to expand into the marble, a slim woman came up and asked me if I wanted a massage. I was taken centre stage, onto the round platform in the middle of the room and, flicking my sheet across my puce bottom, I lay down. She began to massage my face, finding muscles that

I never knew existed. She covered it in oil and rubbed her fingers around my eye sockets; she slapped my neck and karate-chopped my cheeks. She then covered my face in a weird, carrot-smelling cream that went up my nose. 'Keep that on for twenty minutes,' she said, and left.

The fat woman with the large white bra took over. She laid me out on the marble like some laboratory rat and began pummelling. Ignoring my pathetic squeals, she carried on chatting to her friend about the lack of milk in the shops. 'There's been nothing here for three months. I mean, how can you raise a family without milk. I have nothing to give the baby.' She suddenly stopped, her fists firmly embedded in my stomach. 'Does that hurt?' she asked, looking at me for the first time. 'Of course it does,' I managed to whisper. She felt around some more, her knuckles digging into my flesh. I whimpered. She would not give up. 'You have something wrong with your ovaries,' she announced to the whole banya. 'You've been sitting on cold steps and not keeping your back warm, haven't you?'

'No, no,' I squeaked, hardly able to breathe.

'What d'you mean, no. I can feel that you have.' She dug in deeper. I agreed immediately that I was foolish and that whatever she said was right and that I would go and see a gynaecologist as soon as possible. Satisfied with the reply, she moved on. Flipping me over, she began to elbow my bottom. The sharp points finding the heart of the muscle, she moved them in a circular motion. After slapping my back and squeezing my toes, she finally collapsed into a heap on the marble and ordered me to take a shower. By the time I had finished hosing myself down, she was gently snoring, laid out on the shiny surface like a beached whale. I quietly put the money next to her and left. Out in the street, my body shook and ached all over. I walked back to the hotel, mildly concerned about my reproductive organs.

That evening we went to have supper with Myra and Sultanat, two Kazak sisters whose telephone numbers we had been given by friends in Moscow. They were both small, with flat faces and slightly Mongolian-looking eyes. Myra worked for the Music Institute and Sultanat was a journalist. Sultanat had just come back from a trip to Berlin and was completely obsessed with the West. We sat down to saffron rice and pickles in a circle on the floor.

Myra lived alone in the flat with her daughter. Her husband did not work in Alma-Ata: he had set up his own business in his home town, some distance from the capital. He had not had enough *blat*, protection or connections, to combat the mafia in Alma-Ata, but he did in his home town. He saw his wife about twice a month. 'The mafia is so strong here,' explained Myra. 'We all have to have protection in order to function. My cousin Asia is a budding young actress. She was spotted at school, but she'll only become great if she has the right connections. No matter how beautiful she is, or how talented, if no one supports her and pulls the right strings and pays the right people, she'll get nowhere. The mafia control the film industry.'

She explained that the whole rationing system now in place in Kazakhstan has been brought about because the mafia had taken control of the food supply. 'We have sugar, but it's in the hands of the mafia, which is why it has to be rationed. You just can't buy it on the black market.' She said that it was entirely due to her father and connections that she had found a place at university, that she had gone to a good school and managed to defend her dissertation at St Petersburg University. 'No matter how intelligent you are, you have to have protection to have a place at university. Your position in life here depends utterly on who your friends are and if they're prepared to help you. Friends and contacts are much more important than money. Otherwise, who would you bribe? You'd end up wasting money bribing the wrong person!' She laughed. 'This place is crazy, isn't it? Since *perestroika* there are no more rules and everyone is on the make.'

After supper Myra and Sultanat sat singing songs and playing the guitar. They both had wonderful voices and loved singing. In her youth, Myra had wanted to be a pop star, but her father had decided against it. She had worked for the KGB as a student, translating documents from Russian into English for extra money. Her father had also warned her against getting too involved with the organization, so when they tried to recruit her after university, she refused. She was a strange mixture of hedonism and self-discipline. She had adopted the mores of female liberation, taking full advantage of her husband's absence, yet at the same time she supported the Muslim Fundamentalist revival. 'They teach us so many of the essential rituals for life,' she insisted. She was fervently nationalistic and had a keen interest in the Kazak Nationalist Party, Alash. They had been banned from selling their newspaper, *Istina*, or 'Absolute Truth' in Alma-Ata, but they still managed to sell it at the station, which is where all the country people, their main supporters, gathered.

The group, formed three years ago, was banned by President Nazerbaiev and now operates out of Moscow. They believe in the revival of the Kazak language and culture and want all the Russians who will not learn Kazak to leave the country. The fifty per cent split in nationalities makes them politically very dangerous. 'I don't hate the Russians,' said Myra. 'I just think that if they live in our country, they should speak our language.'

(A fortnight later, I spoke on the telephone to Myra and she told me that the three leaders of Alash were standing trial in Alma-Ata for attacking the leader of the main Muslim mosque. Many believed that this was, in fact, a KGB plot to discredit Alash after their public criticism of the Muslim leader, calling him a KGB mole and questioning his faith. Myra could not elaborate and our conversation was interrupted three times by tapping on the line. 'I can't tell you any more,' Myra said. 'The KGB have been listening to my phone for three days now.')

Kirghizstan

....

DAY 54

Myra came to collect us from the hotel at around midday. She was so inebriated that she could hardly stand and continually forgot what she was doing. She had been drinking vodka with a contact, trying to persuade him with all her charm to let Joth and I visit a female prison. Two bottles of vodka later and after much pouting of lips, she had succeeded. We were to go in three days' time.

We managed to persuade a driver to take us to Issyk-Kul in Kirghizstan. Myra sat in the front, loudly singing Beatles songs for the first half hour of the journey and fell fast asleep for the six remaining hours. We passed through the vast, empty steppes to the south of Alma-Ata, dotted with horsemen standing guard over hundreds of sheep and goats, and climbed slowly through the mountain passes into Kirghizstan.

It was already dark by the time we arrived at Nyrila's house. She was a close friend of Myra's; they had worked in the pioneer camps together in the summer around the lake, singing and looking after the children. We had not been able to telephone her to warn her of our arrival, but she rushed out to meet us all the same.

Nyrila was a Russian teacher at the local school, but had given up her job eight months ago to look after her paralysed sister and her old mother. She herself was not married and, at thirty-two and living in the same village in which she had been born, was unlikely to find a husband. She said that Tanya, her elder sister, was lying inside. Something had gone wrong with the birth of her fifth baby, rendering half her body paralysed. They lived six to eight hours by bus from the capital, Bishkek, where doctors would be able to help her. But she could not travel by bus and could not afford a taxi. She did not have the connections to enable her to see a doctor, or to gain entrance to a hotel, while waiting to find a doctor to see her. 'They won't let simple country people like her into hotels,' explained Myra. 'There are never rooms for people like her.'

When we walked into the two-roomed house, Tanya was lying on the only bed, gazing at the ceiling with her black eyes. She was thirty-eight but looked older; her impassive face and lack of teeth were testimony to her suffering. She lay, waiting for some miracle to help her. 'She's slowly improving,' whispered Nyrila as we walked into the dark, airless room. 'I help her out of bed in the morning and she can now walk a few paces.' Over in the far corner, a small, black-and-white television crackled showing a poorly dubbed repeat of the American soap 'Santa Barbara'. Nyrila handed her the baby. She showed no animosity towards the enormous bundle that had paralysed her, but sat calmly breastfeeding it with a docile maternal duty.

The family relies entirely on the state. With the birth of her fifth baby, Tanya became a heroic mother, which means that she is paid for her ability to reproduce. It is this small handout that keeps the whole family, including grandmother and Nyrila, alive. It is a bitter irony.

There was a red star on their front gate which indicates that their father, who died ten years ago, fought in the Great Patriotic War. The family still receives a sack of grain and barley once a month from the collective farm for his efforts. Tanya's husband no longer comes to visit: he lives at the other end of the village with the two elder children, hunts in the mountains, drinks and beats her. 'She is no longer useful to him: she can't work any more, which is why she is here. Why should he come to visit her?' explained Nyrila.

We sat down in a room that had obviously not been used in a long while, for the air was damp and undisturbed. The mattresses from Nyrila's redundant dowry lay piled along one side of the room. On the wall hung a patchwork sheet in different shades of maroon. It was covered in severe, formal, black-and-white family photographs that had been touched up with coloured inks.

It was late, but Nyrila set about cooking us supper. Tanya moved slowly from the bed with the help of the round, jolly grandmother and was placed on the only chair in the house. She sat bolt upright, the large baby on her lap, her son and daughter sitting on their knees either side of her. The two children sat and stared at us. Our fair hair and skin intrigued them. They had smooth, soft, grubby, flat faces, broad grins and Chinese-looking eyes. The little girl's hair was squeezed into two tight plaits that stuck out at right angles to her head.

In the kitchen, Nyrila stocked up the coal-burning stove, controlling the heat by removing metal rings from around the plate. She collected water from the tap outside near the road and ground some flour between two stones. Mixing the flour and water together, she made large strips of pasta and mixed them with some meat, which she had found in the small room off the kitchen where she froze food in the winter. In summer they could not keep anything cold. This whole process took her around four hours and it was nearly 2 a.m. when we sat down on the floor to eat.

The grandmother was already asleep on the floor next door, curled up in the corner, snoring loudly. She slept fully clothed because there was a shortage of blankets. When we finally went to bed, Joth and I, as guests, were given a mattress in the room that we had eaten in. We curled up together for warmth. The others, the three women, the three children and Myra, all slept on top of each other in the other room, partitioned off by a curtain.

DAY 55

We sat down to milky tea with a spoon of salt and home-made bread. Salted tea is a traditional Kirghiz drink, probably stemming from the fact that the water in Lake Issyk-Kul is slightly salty. Nyrila then served the bozo, a home-made brew made from fermented yeast. Heavy and glutinous, it becomes progressively more alcoholic as the day goes on. Traditionally given to horsemen before they spent the day in the mountains, it lines the stomach and a couple of glasses in the morning will stave off hunger until nightfall. 'It's for children in the morning and adults at night,' said Nyrila, as she gave a small cupful to the baby. 'This will also help him sleep, which means that Tanya can rest while we go out.'

We left the house, walking along the road and across the steppes towards the lake. Profoundly beautiful, it has been sacred to the Kirghiz for hundreds of years. It was made famous by the writings of the Kirghiz author, Chingiz Aitmatov, and it is said to have magical powers. However, as we arrived, it became obvious that its shores had been ruined by Soviet holidaymakers. Gaudy red metal signs and rusty roundabouts cluttered up the beaches and crumbling tables lay half-buried in the sand. Its turquoise and crystal waters were on the retreat, and no one seemed to know why. 'The Soviets are stealing our water,' said Nyrila, as she walked along the beach. 'Last year, the water was much further up the beach. They take the water for irrigating cotton that we never see, to water crops that we never eat and meanwhile our beautiful lake grows smaller.'

Each republic seemed to have built its own monstrous hotel near the lake for its summering citizens. There was one particularly hideous hotel, a giant pyramid that tore into the sky and irritated its surroundings. It had been ten years in construction, but remained unfinished. 'The foundations are cracked so there's now talk of pulling it down and starting again. I haven't seen anyone working there for years,' said Nyrila. We walked past a huge communal dining room attached to the Uzbek Hotel. 'They have discos in there during the summer,' she said, her face lighting up. 'It's great here in the summer.'

Leaving the lake, we walked back across the dry grasslands. Asphyxiated by snow all winter, the grass was just beginning to poke through and enjoy the first sun after the thaw. We went to visit one of Nyrila's brothers, who lived in a caravan at one end of the village. He was making bread on an open-air fire when we arrived. His wife was away in a clinic in another village. 'No one knows what's wrong with her. They say that it's a woman's problem, which in my book means that she has gone for an abortion. My brother doesn't know,' whispered Nyrila.

Meanwhile, much to her amusement, her brother flailed around outside, making bread for the three little children who were playing with the flames, and chewing lumps of tar that they had peeled off the road. 'We can't get chewing gum here,' said Nyrila, 'so we chew tar. I always used to do it as a child.'

Her brother was renting the caravan from the kolhoz because he had just been given a small patch of land that he was in the process of preparing for the spring. We sat in one of the two rooms. The eldest daughter, aged thirteen, prepared the water and the cups – she had naturally taken over the maternal role in her mother's absence. We also had a few strips of the newly baked bread. Nyrila laughed as her brother brought it to the table. 'What's so funny?' he asked, slightly hurt. 'It's absolutely fine. If I lived in a town I would not be able to feed my children, but as I live on the land I can make bread, cook for them and look after them if they're ill.' Myra agreed. She said that her husband would never be able to look after the family in her absence.

We then walked about three miles, across the steppes, to the foot of the mountains to met Nyrila's eldest brother, Victor. He was on the verge of becoming a rich man. He had recently left the *kolhoz* and was setting up his own, private, horse farm, selling the flesh for meat, the mare's milk as alcohol and their skins for leather. He shared his four-roomed house with another family: Victor, his wife and their four children had two rooms; their neighbours, with six children and a grandmother, had the other two.

Victor's family were all in the village that afternoon but the other children were playing in the yard when we arrived. While Victor and Nyrila chatted, I spoke to the neighbour. He had the same Mongoloid features of the Kirghiz, yet his eyes were a pale watery blue and so were those of his six children. 'They're the colour of Lake Baykal,' he said with a smile. 'The Kirghiz were originally from Siberia, but we moved here after many battles and mixed our blood with that of the Mongols. Our eyes became brown and we inherited a smaller lake, Issyk-Kul.' We stood together and looked across from the foot of the mountains, over the barren steppes at the lake shimmering flirtatiously below. 'It's not so bad,' I said. 'It's beautiful,' he murmured, his nostrils twitching slightly as he inhaled the sweet and chilly air of the late afternoon.

I went into the small kitchen to eat curd with Victor. We squatted on wooden logs or sat on the floor round a low, wooden table. Victor removed his fur hat to reveal a velvet skull – he shaves his hair every winter. His face was smooth and his skin, the colour of warm walnut, smelt of milk and hay. He had a long moustache that fell off the curls of his mouth; his dark, half-moon eyes laughed at the corners. He was a passionate horseman and told stories while he stroked a small lamb that lay in a cardboard box by the stove. He had learnt to ride at five and had spent his whole life in the saddle.

As dusk was drawing in across the mountains, Victor led me outside the house and, taking my hand, pointed far into the horizon. 'Can you see the horses coming?' he asked, staring into the distance. I could not see anything. He pointed again, and eventually I could distinguish a dust cloud through the haze of the early evening. Victor saddled up two horses. The horses were skittish and danced around as the heavy, padded saddles were placed on their backs. Victor, in his knee-length boots, loose trousers and thick sheepskin jacket, looked proud astride his horse. 'Gengis Khan!' I shouted at him as I mounted my horse. 'Emperor of all men,' he replied and, spurring his horse on, set off into the steppe, yelping, calling in the horses.

At the sound of his cries, 200 wild horses came pouring over the steppes. Victor, standing high in his stirrups, lured them in. His horse, overcome with excitement, foamed at the mouth and snorted. I rode beside Victor trying to keep pace, my knees tense at my horse's sides, the heat from its back warming my thighs. Smiling broadly, I joined in the shouting. Laughing and weaving my horse through the rocky ground, we gathered in the horses. They galloped in circles around us, foals at their mother's sides struggling to keep up. The horses were a multitude of colours, their coats thick to protect them against the elements. This was a scene that had not changed for thousands of years and tears of excitement trickled down my cheeks. As the last of the sun's rays dribbled behind the mountains, Victor rounded up the remainder of the horses and guided them to a wooden pen, full of soft hay. They continued to spiral round inside the enclosure, irritated by their captivity but delighted by their food.

Still quivering with excitement, I dismounted and handed my horse over to one of the small children, who leaped into the saddle and, with the stirrups bouncing at his feet, trotted the horse over to the trough for a drink. Victor and I sat down at the table inside the house and drank some more curd. It was warm and a thin layer of skin, taut on the surface, slid down my throat. Victor hugged us goodbye and gave us a small churn of milk. We made the three-mile trek back across the steppe to Nyrila's house, a journey she made twice a day to collect yogurt from her brother. Back at the house, Tanya was still lying on the bed. The grandmother was looking after the children.

We packed our bags and stood by the side of the road, trying to flag down cars to take us back to Alma-Ata. No one stopped. After three hours we returned to the house and asked if we could spend one more night with them and leave at six the next morning. There was nothing to eat. We sat drinking more *bozo*, more alcoholic than it had been that morning, after a day fermenting on the stove. We ate some bread and drank tea. Nyrila had given us all she had the day before and was embarrassed that she had nothing left. She found some sweets, which she put in the tea. This stroke of luck made her happier.

Kazakhstan

· · · · · · · · · · · · · · ·

DAY 56

Setting off early in the morning, we finally arrived in Alma-Ata, having travelled via Bishkek. We were on time for Myra's cousin's wedding.

It took place in a rented hall in the centre of town. The hall consisted of two rooms; the first had a small table set up to one side and a band organized in the corner; the other was laid with a banquet for about 150 people, all paid for by the bridegroom. The guests of the bride lined the edges of the hall, while the guests of the groom were all cooking the food. 'People prefer to do their own food for weddings,' explained Myra, 'as restaurants provide such filth.'

The bride's guests were dressed with extraordinary ostentatiousness. Red was the order of the day, and the colour predominated. The women all wore ill-fitting, calf-length dresses in shiny materials that rucked and gathered sweat under the armpits. One woman, dressed in a pale-green, nylon, sleeveless dress with dark circles under her arms, high silver sandals and a frizzy perm, caught my eye as she and her large bottom moved independently across the room.

The guests grew bored as the couple were late and any newcomer was greeted with a hundred pairs of quizzical eyes. The woman assigned by the state to register the happy couple was leaning with her elbows on a table, the large, gold medallion around her neck swinging backwards and forwards like a pendulum. Then the compere arrived to warm up the crowd before the appearance of the couple. Microphone in hand, to the accompaniment of an unnecessarily loud band, he instructed the guests how to sing the entrance song for the bride and groom. He sang one line and the crowd followed with a 'Jah, Jah, Jah!' Telling them when to clap, he sang along in Kazak. After a few rehearsals, it became obvious that we needed team leaders from each of the parties. The woman in the green nylon dress was voted in for the bride and Myra for the groom.

One rehearsal later and the couple appeared at the bottom of the stairs. The band played and the guests sang. The groom, in a grey, shiny suit, smiled gauchely; the bride, dressed in traditional Kazak robes of red velvet with a red-and-white pointed hat and tight waistcoat, stared, embarrassed at the floor. The service was over in a matter of minutes, each oath punctuated with a burst from the band. Sweets and crisp, one-rouble notes were thrown into the air and small children skidded around on their knees, pushing each other out of the way as they cleaned up. After the service, the crowd sang a traditional song of congratulations, led once more by the compere. The bride, nudged by her bridesmaid, bowed at the appropriate moment.

We moved through into the other room and there was a mad scramble for seats as everyone jostled to sit next to the bride and groom, who had the place of honour at the end of the table, enshrined with a white veil. Myra and I sneaked outside to have a cigarette. 'Kazak women can't smoke,' she whispered as she inhaled. 'It's just not proper.' We danced around in the snow outside to disperse the smell and came back inside.

Numerous toasts were made to the couple, encouraged by the compere who pranced up and down between the tables, not letting the microphone out of his grasp. The guests tucked into horse meat, intestines and tongue, and knocked back vodka and wine. As the afternoon wore on, the party became more rowdy and uncontrolled. The compere took it upon himself to organize the public humiliation of Joth and I. I was forced to make a drunken, slurred speech to the health of the bride and groom whom I had, of course, never met. I acquitted myself without too much disgrace, my lack of coherency being attributed to my foreignness. Joth, on the other hand, was made to sing. He bravely took hold of the microphone and belted out a quick tune. His face flushed with alcohol and embarrassment, he skipped a couple of verses to limit the length of the ordeal, before collapsing into his chair. The whole hall exploded with applause. He turned to me with little red eyes and asked; 'What did I just sing? I can't remember a word.' Suddenly the bride's father appeared and handed him a crisp, 50-rouble note. 'It's always tradition to pay the entertainment,' he said with a smile. Joth was not sure whether this was, in fact, a compliment.

After more vodka, the dancing began. I was dragged onto the floor and forced to dance with the groom. We wandered round and round together in a small circle, his clammy hands loosely gripping my waist, fixed embarrassed smiles on our faces. I looked at the floor to avoid staring at the spot that nestled in his moustache, which I presumed came from a bad case of pre-wedding nerves.

The music stopped and the prizes for dancing ability were announced. Great Aunt Anya won a yellow plastic bowl for her prowess on the dance floor; two little boys won handkerchiefs, which they immediately wiped all over their faces; Joth and I won a record and some earrings, and the bride and groom were subtly given a towelling baby jacket. As each of us went up to the table to receive our prizes, we were greeted with a fanfare from the band.

The dancing continued well into the night; the music, obscure arrangements of Western songs with Russian lyrics, was designed to please all ages and none. As we left, I was accosted by the drunken brother of the bride, who offered 100 camels for my hand in marriage. Joth bargained him up to 1,000 and we left by the back door.

DAY 57

Collecting Myra's contact, Sereg, the chief of the anti-organized crime squad in Alma-Ata, we went to the women's prison about three-quarters of an hour's drive outside the town. Myra and Sereg had been at school together and although they had not been close friends, Myra had since cultivated him as a contact, saying that it was important for her to have friends in the police force to help her out when necessary.

Sereg explained that the prison system was in disarray. 'Since the break-up of the Union, it's been hard to know what to do with the prisoners. Many of the women in this prison come from different republics and now Kazakhstan can no longer afford to keep them. In fact, we don't want prisoners from other places in our prisons, whether we could afford them or not.' His round, pockmarked face turned towards, us, his elbow hooked over the back of the seat, and the alcohol on his breath filled the car. 'An agreement has recently been signed between the republics, saying that all the women should go home, but I'm not quite sure when that will be. Not soon enough for most people, I'm sure,' he said with a laugh.

The prison was surrounded by a small town that had been built to house the prison workers and guards. There was a strange feeling of unease on the narrow streets: it seemed that the people begrudged the prison, even though it was their livelihood.

We were to spend the night in the small hostel just inside the prison walls, which was reserved for visiting husbands and families of the inmates. Ushered inside the building, we were made to sit at a small table and wait until the head of the prison, unaware of our arrival, had left. The deputy head, a friend of Sereg's, then joined us.

Buluta was a quiet man and, intimidated by Sereg, would not speak until he had the nod of approval from him. Sereg brought out two bottles of vodka and began to drink, but Buluta did not join us. The alcohol loosened Sereg's tongue and he began to chat about the problems in the Chyi Valley, just to the northeast of Alma-Ata. 'Two hundred million hectares of opium are growing there in the valley and the Western mafia, posing as foreign journalists, are now setting up their initial contacts, preparing to open the whole place up for the international drugs market. The Soviet mafia is incredibly strong there,' he explained, pouring himself another vodka and inflicting the same punishment on us. 'People are murdered there all the time – it's incredibly dangerous. These people answer to no one and the police in Alma-Ata have neither the money nor the manpower to combat them.' He went on: 'It permeates every area of society and the only way to succeed is to have mafia connections.' He smiled, his eyes rheumy with alcohol.

Sereg had been working in the police force for fifteen years and only had another five to go until his pension. 'And then I'll be a businessman,' he announced. 'I'll make lots of money. I'm buying a Mercedes and already have a huge villa in the country that cost me a million roubles. When I retire, I'll fill it full of women – nine Kazak and one English girl.' He turned to wink at me. I laughed heartily, which seemed to please him. 'Now you can ask any question you like,' he said, leaning magnanimously back in his chair.

Turning to Buluta, I asked how many women there were in the prison. He moved to open his mouth, but Sereg butted in. 'That's a secret,' he said, with a smile.

'What's the most common crime?' I asked.

'That's a secret,' said Sereg again.

This went on for almost half an hour. Every fact that I wanted automatically became of the utmost secrecy. I began to question why Myra had got drunk with this man two days earlier. Why had we bowed and scraped to him, thanking him for his generosity, if all he wanted to do was to bring us to this cramped, airless room that smelt of disinfectant, sit us down at a table and force us to drink. Any request that we made was answered with 'no'. Can we walk around the prison? Can we talk to the prisoners? All received a negative response. I began to hate this petty bureaucrat who enjoyed throwing his weight around. But still we had to humour him, in the hope that tomorrow he would relent and honour whatever notion he had of *glasnost*.

Sereg and Buluta left and we were alone with a uniformed woman serving tea. 'Are you a prisoner?' I asked. She nodded. 'What did you do to get here?' I then ventured, as tactfully as possible. 'Murder,' she replied in a toneless voice, her lifeless eyes looking straight through me. The hairs on the back of my neck stood on end. I ignored the feeling.

Her name was Nina, she was forty-five and came from Kazakhstan. She had served five years for stabbing her lover, but the exact circumstances of the murder she would not elaborate on. She had spent three years in the zone, the central part of the prison, and another two years working in the hostel, which was a special privilege accorded only to those who behaved themselves. 'I only have two months and nineteen days to go and then I'll return to my home town,' she said with a tired smile, brushing her grey hair behind her ears.

She described her life in the zone. Waking at 6.30 a.m, 'we tidy our rooms and, always in groups of five, eat in the dining hall. The porridge is now made with water because there's a desperate shortage of milk, and we receive a daily allowance of twenty-five grams of sugar. We have bread and tea for lunch and porridge again in the evening.' Her translucent eyes turned to the floor, she shuffled from one foot to the other and furtively looked over her shoulder, watching the door. She explained that she spent the whole day packing up dresses that were made on the production line by the other inmates. These dresses were sold to keep the prison going, she explained. They have an hour for lunch and carry on sewing until 5 p.m. 'We're counted back in the evening, always in our group of five, and bed is at 10.30 p.m.,' she snorted.

The two men returned and our conversation was terminated. Nina carried on serving the tea, but never looked at me again and went about her duties with a cold air of detachment, lowering her eyes whenever she came to the table.

We went for a walk around the town, the cold air chilling our bones as we trudged through the slush. Small wooden houses lined the track, their families safe inside, the light pouring out from the windows. No one else walked the streets. The prison stood illuminated against the night sky, the searchlights around the barbed wire perimeter delineating the fifteen metres of meticulously raked sand that constituted the no-man's-land between the two sets of fencing. After about ten minutes, Sereg became bored and directed us back to the small room, where he immediately opened another bottle of vodka.

Buluta's wife came to join us, bringing a small parcel of hard curd cakes that broke up like chalk in my mouth. She was a jolly, round woman who worked with the sixty or so children in the prison. 'The women are allowed to see their children, who have more toys and games than my own. They also have better food than my own,' she said with an ironic, but not malicious, laugh. She obviously liked these children and felt a certain sympathy for them. Sereg tried to silence her. 'What d'you mean, keep quiet? There are no secrets any more,' she said angrily. 'After all, what do glasnost and perestroika mean?' Irritated by this drunken bureaucrat, she left.

Encouraged by his wife's candid behaviour, Buluta, began to talk more about himself and the prison. He had worked there for fifteen years and was on the point of retirement. He said that the prison was in the midst of a financial crisis and that they were considering a joint venture with Iran, selling the dresses they made for hard currency and technology so that they would eventually have a real business, using the women as cheap labour.

'The main problem at the moment is to establish who's responsible for the inmates. No one's prepared to acknowledge their existence, let alone help pay for them, and we are very short of resources. There are some women who have already returned to women's gaols in their own republics, but those who remain have been disowned. I don't quite know why they don't just run away – no one will ever bother to go after them. However, I hope that in six months or so the repatriation will be complete, and we'll be able to run the prison as we want.' He stood up and, clapping his hands together, wished us good night.

We were left with a drunken Sereg, who was becoming progressively more offensive. He began to repeat himself, talking about his large house and how many women he would sleep with when he left the force. I left before I became rude. I walked into the next-door room to find a short, dirty mattress on wooden slats. Pulling back the sheets, I watched as a cockroach ran across my pillow and my toes curled in horror. The only solace was that strips of the *History of the Communist Party Volume 10* had been hung on a nail on the wall as loo paper.

DAY 58

Our 6 a.m. start was a complete waste of time. We once more returned to the room that I had begun to know only too well and Sereg once more brought out two bottles of vodka. I could have cried with frustration – the last thing I wanted was more vodka, but it was impossible to refuse. One of the guards from the prison joined us for a few shots before he went to work. Sereg and the guard left in search of the deputy head, who had promised us a tour of the prison. While they were out of the room I managed to talk to Zina, who was leaning over a gas stove in her grey tunic, heating up water for our tea. She had cropped, maroon hair and, aged forty-five, was serving fifteen years for theft.

'I worked in a state shop and they kept such bad accounts that it was easy to take advantage and steal the money. I couldn't live on the wage I was being paid,' she explained, smiling naïvely.

She came to the prison in 1985, her sentence was reduced to ten years for good behaviour and five months ago she was moved to zone two. 'The main difference between the two zones is that I'm allowed to wear clothes from home underneath my tunic,' she said, flashing her red nylon cardigan that her son had brought her. Her husband had left her almost as soon as she was put behind bars and he has remarried. 'That happens to a lot of women here. Who wants a wife inside? Especially in our culture, where the women keep the families together and run and feed the house, the men just can't do that alone so they have to marry someone else.' Melancholy spread across her face. Her son visits her every six months from her home town in the south of Kazakhstan, bringing money, cigarettes and things for her to sell in the gaol. 'We're allowed a parcel weighing ten kilograms every six months,' she said.

A year ago, she was given two weeks' compassionate leave. The prison received a stamped certificate saying that her mother was dying and they trusted her to return, under her own steam, after the funeral. 'So you see,' she said imploringly, 'I've nothing to go back to. No husband, no flat and no mother. This is also a very common problem here – nothing to go back to.'

Whilst in the zone, Zina sewed dresses. 'I gave it everything I'd got,' she said proudly. 'I was never put in solitary, which is why I'm now out of the zone.' The women out of the zone are relatively free, she explained, and have contact with outsiders. But it is through this contact that drugs, alcohol and cigarettes infiltrate the prison. 'There are few hard drugs here – there's some heroin, but it's mostly grass. The women are bored and depressed, they have nothing better to do. There are a few lesbians, but they're mainly the younger women – what else are they supposed to do? We never see men here,' she laughed. Although there is fighting in the prison, Zina herself had never been touched. She had been in prison for so long that she had yet to experience the changes of *perestroika*. 'The only difference that it had made to our lives,' she said with a laugh, 'is that we can now wear watches and really see how much time we're wasting inside.'

What seemed strange to me was the discrepancy between Zina's sentence and that of the murderess. 'There are so many women in the prison who have murdered husbands, lovers or their children and some only get three or six years. I can only think that this society has little regard for human life.'

Sereg came in and Zina immediately picked up a tea towel and began to fold it. She never caught my eye again. As we left for a tour of the prison, I slipped a packet of cigarettes in the front pocket of her tunic. 'Thank you,' she whispered, squeezing my hand as I brushed past her.

Walking around the perimeter fence, we peeked through the gaps at the sandy no-man's-land. Every time we appeared to overstep the bounds of normal curiosity, Sereg would drunkenly shout, 'That's not allowed.' I spoke to the guard, who was rather enjoying the whole experience of being drunk with foreigners. He was obviously not aware of Sereg's stickling for secrecy and told me that the prison housed 600 criminals, sixty per cent of whom were murderers. 'They mostly killed their children, which is what I find strange,' he mused.

We reached the pig farm, where some prisoners worked, and were escorted between the rows. The intense smell made my eyes water. There, the women worked for eight hours a day cleaning out the pigs and feeding them. Still in their grey tunics, they wore white scarves, cloth boots and galoshes. They stopped and leant on their rakes when we approached, but none of them would talk or look at our faces. At one end of the barn, there was a small pen with two dogs and two litters of puppies. One of the prisoners became animated when we approached. Taking one of the puppies in her arms, she smiled and, kissing its taut pink tummy, said, 'This is my life here.'

As we returned to the hostel, Sereg pointed out a large villa on the side of the road. 'My villa's like that apart from the fact that it cost me a million roubles and it's much better.' We all pretended to be impressed.

We hung around, waiting for a car to take us back to Alma-Ata. It did not come, despite our booking it the day before, and we ended up hitch-hiking home. Once in the car, Sereg boasted about all his women until he eventually crashed out in the front seat. It was a relief not to have to listen to him, or be charming. We dropped him off at police headquarters. He staggered out of the car and insisted that we see him for dinner later. We said that we would phone.

Later that afternoon, we went to the Kazak film studios to meet Asia, Myra's niece. Tall and slim with long, black hair to the waist and a round, peachy face, she was the leading lady in a new Romeo and Juliet-esque film, *Kozi Korposi and Bayan Say*. At nineteen, she was studying biology at university and wanted to finish her course – she was not entirely seduced by the film industry. 'I earned 8,000 roubles for four months' work,' she said in a high voice, her lips pouting. 'It nearly killed me,' she added with a sigh. We wandered around the huge, modern complex which, like the studios in Tashkent, were more or less closed until the summer.

Asia was realistic about her chances of success. 'Although I'm pretty, my success depends on the mafia. They didn't even use my voice in the film – they said that it was too weak and dubbed it in St Petersburg.' There are so many actresses out of work and the actors' union is so strong that many films are gratuitously dubbed to keep the others in work, she explained. So she attends night school to learn English, in the hope of finding work as a translator. We sat and talked in a studio where a classical concert was being recorded, trying to ignore a fat man in a pale blue, frilly shirt, who was using his lungs to full capacity.

DAY 60

After a day's search, we managed to find a car to take us out onto the steppes. Snow tumbled out of the sky as we drove for three hours across the vast, empty wilderness to a small village at the foot of the mountains, north of Alma-Ata. Here, we met Baidjudjus, a short, sixty-year-old man who lived on the outskirts of the village.

A pure-blood Kazak, he is one of the elite, for he is a birkutchi, or eagle man. Born and brought up on the southern steppes of Kazakhstan, he has spent the whole of his life in the saddle, herding sheep on the planes. 'What can I tell you about herding sheep?' he roared. 'I sat in my saddle and moved them from pasture to pasture.'

He learnt to ride at the age of five when, after a traditional ceremony, he was placed in the saddle, his legs barely able to reach the stirrups. 'A man without a horse is useless here,' he explained. His father had given him his first eagle when he turned sixteen.

Baidjudjus could not speak Russian – he had spent his whole life out of the towns and villages, and had no need to learn it. Myra translated for us. He and his family had moved to the village on his retirement. Baidjudjus, his wife, eight children and seven grandchildren, lived in two houses next door to each other. 'Living in the village is fine but, you know, my only pleasure is hunting. I do it every two weeks or when the weather is clear and the eagle can see the fox,' he said, his dark eyes luminous with excitement.

He took me out into the yard, where I could already hear the eagle screaming. Opening the door of a small shed, the floor of which was covered with bones and lumps of flesh, he took the bird out off its stand, letting the powerful creature climb up onto his thick leather glove. He then carried the hooded bird, weighing about ten kilograms and with a wing span of three metres, to a small wooden perch in the middle of the yard. It sat angrily squawking while Baidjudjus went to fetch his saddle – high at the front and padded with wool for extra comfort – which he threw onto the horse's back. The heavy animal, covered in a dense coat, did not flinch. As Baidjudjus bent over to fasten the silver girth buckles, he ordered his son to saddle up. Dressed in felt boots to the knee, a thick, long padded coat fastened at the waist with a large silver buckle, and a red fox fur hat, Baidjudjus then led his horse around the yard to a small mound in the middle. Taking the bird in his right hand and ignoring its violent protests from beneath its leather hood, he pulled himself into the saddle with his left arm. Despite his age, he completed the mount with agility and grace. Man, horse and bird trotted off towards the plane, Baidjudjus' hand resting on a wooden fork attached to the saddle to support the weight of the bird.

Son found it harder than father to complete all the manoeuvres at such speed. His frisky horse danced in protest at the approach of the screaming bird and the boy hopped around in a circle, one foot in the stirrup. His fox hat fell off into the snow. The father was furious at such a display of inadequacy, especially in front of guests. 'Look at you,' he shouted, standing up in his stirrups, his arm outstretched, the huge bird prancing on his arm, flexing its wings. 'I keep telling you that your generation is fucked and you're now proving it. Get into the fucking saddle, you useless son of a whore.'

Myra could hardly contain herself while she translated the father's stream of obscenities and fell backwards into the snow with laughter. The son, humiliated by the exchange, hurled himself into the saddle, the eagle swinging upside down as the boy arranged himself on top of the horse. He trotted briskly after his father.

We stood on a high hill overlooking the plane, waiting for foxes. Baidjudjus is the only birkutchi in the village, but has trained all his sons in the art of capturing, training and looking after eagles, an art that nearly died out under Communism, when eagles were said to be undesirable species, to be eliminated at all costs. 'It was madness,' said Baidjudjus, spitting out some chewing tobacco. 'Eagles are the symbol of Kazakhstan – you must have heard the way we describe how large our country is? "No matter how high the eagle flies, it cannot see over its native land." What they were doing, trying to kill them off, I have no idea.

'There isn't a bird I cannot train, if I get my hands on it,' he boasted. 'I've trained over thirty birds in my lifetime. This one,' he said, tweaking its feathers, 'I've had for three years. I caught it further up in the mountains – there are thousands of them there.'

He explained that he laid a trap with a hare and supple nets. 'And then you wait for the bird to swoop into the nets. You rush out of your hiding place, bind its legs so it can't scratch you and cover its eyes with one of these little leather hats. That calms them down.' The bird is then kept hooded for a week and made part of the family. 'It sits and listens to the radio and television with us, getting used to human voices and contact,' he said, laughing. Only after a week do they feed the bird, making it take food directly from the human hand. This process is repeated each day, moving the bird slightly further and further away, until it has to fly rather than walk to collect the food. 'Then, after about two weeks if Allah wills it, and he usually does, you can take the bird flying.'

Both father and son had small pouches of meat in leather hip-bags. 'They are to reward the eagles after the kill, otherwise they'll massacre the foxes,' ventured the son, aware of his father's ear cocked critically in his direction. 'We can sell the pelts for around 600 roubles each – more if they're caught in winter, because the fur is better.' His confidence growing, he added, 'Also, it's easier to see the foxes in winter because there is less undergrowth on the steppes.'

'Normally what happens,' said the father, butting in, 'is I spot the game and we release the eagles, showing them the direction, taking off their hoods and launching them into the sky. They swoop and circle and we follow on quickly behind. The eagle breaks the fox's back: clasping the head and tails in its talons, it snaps the spine. It is at this point that we have to be there to stop it going any further. We call "Kah, kah, kah," and clap our hands, and the bird returns to us. We give it some food and whip the hood on, so that it's disorientated and forgets about the kill.' Baidjudjus bounced up and down in his saddle with excitement.

As we waited for some foolish foxes to come out onto the steppes, a heavy mist curled in from the mountains and it began to snow heavily. Baidjudjus became less than enthusiastic about the hunt. 'We can't see anything, and anyway, a fox would be fucking mad to come out in this,' he complained.

Back inside the house, we sat down to bread, jam and tea and Baidjudjus proudly pulled out a Russian encyclopaedia. Under 'eagles' he showed off his photograph. 'You see,' he laughed, 'I'm famous. I'm one of the few people who really knows how to do this.' He said that more and more Kazaks were coming to him to learn the art. 'In these lean times, they think they can earn some extra money from selling skins.'

He sat cross-legged on the floor and the whole family gathered round to listen to him. Taking off his hat to reveal a white, shaved head that contrasted with his dark, weathered face, he said grace, moving his hands downwards over his face as if he were washing it. The whole family repeated the gesture. We then tucked into home-made bread and wild strawberry jam. While we ate, he talked about hunting. 'You must always keep your first fox for at least a year to bring you good luck and only then can you sell it,' he explained. 'This is my first fox,' said one of the sons, taking off his hat. 'My mother made it up for me.' He was told to put it away, and not to interrupt. Embarrassed, he went off to make some more tea.

Baidjudjus was fascinated with hunting in England. 'It's very difficult to hunt with dogs,' he laughed. 'They have minds of their own.'

'Is the earth warm underfoot in the summer where you come from?' he asked. 'Here it stays cold most of the year round.'

'It's warm underfoot some of the year where we come from,' I replied, enchanted by the question.

'You should come and stay for the Muslim New Year,' he said, his face radiant with excitement. 'There's a special eagle-hunting competition and I always win.'

DAY 61

Larissa and Irina were dancers, but supplemented their income through prostitution. We met them as they were hanging around the hotel, drinking coffee, and invited them upstairs.

The two girls sat nervously on the bed, hugging their knees, drinking tea and lighting one cigarette from another. Their faces were painted like masks and their bleached, blonde hair lay frazzled and snapped around their shoulders. They wore cheap, marbled-denim skirts with orange tights and poor-quality boots; their thick, heavy perfume filled the room in noxious bursts each time either of them moved.

'We get our clients from a pimp who has large mafia connections,' said Larissa, who was ten years older than Irina and more comfortable with her profession. She had been a prostitute for six years, since the onset of *perestroika*, whereas Irina, who was twenty, had just started. They earned 1,000 roubles a time, but their biggest problem was actually getting paid. 'Our pimp often gives us to his friends, which makes it difficult for us to ask for money when it's all over. If they don't pay immediately then we can't ask for money – it's a kind of sweetener for our pimp.' Larissa poured herself some more tea.

They worked principally during the day, dancing in restaurants during the evening. They rarely went to hotels unless they were invited. 'It's very difficult to go to hotels. Our pimp doesn't run that patch and anyway, we'd have to compete with the hard-currency girls, who have better clothes and make-up.' Irina smoothed down her skirt, which had wrinkled up over her bottom.

Both girls were lesbians, although Larissa did have a daughter, and both gave the same reason for becoming prostitutes. 'The money's good.' They drank a pot of tea and smoked a packet of cigarettes before they left.

We went to have our farewell lunch with Myra in her small flat that she had not managed to sort out since her return from defending her dissertation in St Petersburg. With her husband out of town, she saw little need, but when the curtain rail collapsed onto the table during lunch, she vowed that she would do something about it.

Over a meal of pasta, which Myra cooked for the first time in our honour, she began to question us about mores in England, saying that this would be her one and only opportunity to find out all that she wanted to know before we disappeared. Do people shower before sex? Do girls expect money and presents from their men? Would they break up with them if they don't get presents? Did we think that all girls who dress well are prostitutes? Do people notice if you wear French perfume? All these questions said more about her perception of the female role in Kazakhstan than our replies did about England.

Myra burnt the pasta but it did not matter. She escorted us to the train, telling us to be inconspicuous, which was virtually impossible bearing in mind our bright rucksacks.

Arriving at the station, Myra immediately went up to talk to the members of Alash, who were selling illegal newspapers in the lobby. 'It makes me so angry that people are prepared to go up and buy the newspapers, but they never stand and talk because they're afraid someone is watching them. I'm not afraid anymore; I'm bored of people not fighting for what they believe in,' she said, marching towards the group of Kazaks huddled around a newspaper stand. On the balcony that ran around the roof of the station, three men in long coats were watching.

Myra hugged us goodbye. I was genuinely sad to leave her: she was a free spirit. Her zest and her ability to laugh were refreshing and rejuvenating.

Russia

· · · · · · · · · ·

DAY 63

After a night, a day and half a night on the train, travelling through the wastelands
of Kazakhstan, we finally arrived in Barnaul, Siberia. As we stepped off the train,
the cold air seized our lungs and we both choked; walking through the town,
trying to find somewhere to stay, the moisture up our noses froze.

In the dark corridors of the hotel we were confronted by a man who, reeking
of vodka and with blood pouring from his face, lay in a puddle on the floor. He
had fallen over and broken his nose and the old woman who ran the floor was
waiting for the police to take him away. She escorted us to our room and told us
not to leave. 'Everyone here is drunk and there'll be trouble,' she said as she
locked the door behind us. All through the night I heard drunken screams, banging
doors and raised voices.

After much negotiating with a shark in the lobby of the hotel, who wanted
$300 for his help, we managed to find a driver to take us to Novokuznetsk.

Valodya drove the five-hour journey through the snow-covered landscape with
the speed and expertise of someone who had spent a lifetime driving on snow.
As we left Barnaul we passed a gutted building on the side of the road. 'Racket,'
said Valodya, pointing it out. 'There's so much organized crime in this town, it's
becoming a nightmare. Gorbachev was great with foreign policy; he travelled the
world and made people like us again; but as for domestic policy, he did nothing.
There was no organized crime in this town before *perestroika*, but now it's
everywhere.'

Valodya has to pay 1,000 roubles a month protection money to the co-operative
that he works for. If he did not, then the mafia would paint his car or set it alight,
burn his flat, or beat up his wife. 'There are killings here, but they're rare – most
people usually pay before that happens. It's almost impossible to open a new

business or restaurant in the town without paying protection money,' he said. 'Actually, I'd say it's impossible.'

The shark I had argued with in the hotel would demand money from Valodya when he returned to Barnaul. 'I won't pay him. He'll try it on, but I won't pay him.'

On our route we passed a town that used to be called Comsomol Youth but was recently renamed Czarist. Built by Communist volunteers it was an Orwellian nightmare – huge high-rise flats made from pale blue blocks of concrete, and a chlorine factory that belched dark yellow smoke high into the sky and filled the car with fumes. 'Can you imagine living there?' said Valodya. 'Horrible.'

Running low on petrol, and after a few abortive trips to empty petrol stations, we found a place just outside Novokuznetsk with a queue of around twenty-five cars. Valodya ran up to the till. 'D'you have petrol?' he asked frantically. 'Yes, but we're closed for twenty minutes – we're on a break,' replied the plump woman through a slit in the glass. Valodya returned to the car, laughing. 'I'm so bored of those words,' he said. 'Shortage, break and no.' Shaking his head and muttering to himself, we drove off into Novokuznetsk. The snow was grey. 'I flew over here last summer,' said Valodya, looking around him. 'You couldn't see the town for the smog. Why on earth d'you want to come here? It's so polluted.'

DAY 64

'Hello, I'm a citizen of the former Soviet Union and member of the town Soviet. My name is Stefanisa,' said a young, fat woman with a voice that fired like a machine gun out of her pink, lipsticked mouth. She shouted facts, figures and statistics at me as we drove the ten minutes to council offices, and continued once inside. A woman dressed like a waitress arrived holding a notepad. I ordered some tea. Mortally offended, she sat down and began to organize meetings with ecological experts for me.

After a short while, Nikolai Chidg, head of ecology of the Soviet arrived. A quiet man, he was acutely concerned about what was happening to his home town. 'We have a huge social and environmental disaster on our hands,' he said.

'In the 1930s, 40s and 50s they built this town from nothing. They worked and worked, but it was all poorly made. Now, how can I put it? We live in Siberia and the snow is black.' As he spoke, he punctuated each sentence with a cough and a wipe of his nose and eyes. Everyone that I had met or seen in the town so far had a dry, continuous cough. They were used to it and no one remarked on it.

The town was plagued by heavy metal industry, Chidg explained. The three largest factories had been built as part of the massive industrialization that swept through Russia in the first half of this century and as part of Stalin's five year plans. The first steel factory was built between 1928 and 1932, the aluminium factory in 1943 and another steel factory between 1959 and 1964. 'We have three times more lung problems, skin allergies, bronchitis and asthma than anywhere else in the old Soviet Union,' he said. 'Look at me, for example. I'm coughing. I don't have asthma, but I soon will.'

The town has such a smog problem that factories have to stop working for a couple of days about forty-five times a year to let the air clear. 'During the smog, its so bad, that although it's day, it's still dark,' he said, pausing to choke. 'But what can the workers do? They're not allowed to strike.' He begged the West to do something to help.

One of the most serious problems was the contamination of the water supply. Polluted with heavy metals, it is unfit for human consumption. Thirty-six per cent of the illnesses here are due to the water. The water in the mines, for some reason unknown to the city, is radioactive, and what happens when a worker washes himself with radioactive water? Well, we don't know.

'We don't have the means to clean it. We know how to clean it, what to do, where the problem is, but we don't have the hard currency to do it.' He stared weakly at me as if I would be able to offer an immediate solution. The pollution has, of course, entered the food chain, he explained. 'We can't get clean fruit and vegetables, they're all contaminated with heavy metals.'

He saw education of the town's inhabitants as the biggest problem. As more and more people grew food in their gardens and on their balconies to combat the food shortages, and as others bought in the free market because of rationing, the problem was getting worse. They had placed numerous warnings in the local papers about the dangers of eating home-grown produce, but to no avail. 'No one believes what they read after seventy years of Communism,' he laughed. 'What can we do?' Two days ago, he had tried to get a law passed that no contaminated food should be sold in the market, that it should all first be tested for chemicals and metals. 'But it was not passed because the council was afraid of the repercussions of more food shortages and greater hardship.'

We left the Soviet and travelled through the grey town to a polyclinic to meet Dr Vyacheslav Surzhikov, Director of the Industrial Environmental Hygiene and Occupational Diseases Institute. He sat behind a desk as we entered the room. He smiled, and before I could open my mouth to ask any questions, he told me to keep quiet and listen to a few facts.

'Life expectancy in the town is fifty-four, or forty-five for a factory worker. Infant mortality is 18.6 per thousand, brought down from twenty-two per thousand two years ago. The hospitals are short of drugs as almost three-quarters of their supply, originally from Eastern Europe, has dried up. One million tonnes of heavy metals go into the atmosphere each year. Thirty-six different types of metal can be found in the dust. Thirty to forty per cent of children have bronchitis, almost five times higher than the national average. Asthma and eczema are common. Cases of TB and lung cancer are way above the national average. Seventy per cent of children have no fluoride on their teeth. Thirty-eight per cent are born deformed. Of these thirty-eight per cent, eight in a thousand have Down's syndrome, twenty-three in a thousand are physically malformed, forty in a thousand are born yellow. And in eighty per cent of these last, the yellowness is unexplained. There are increased cases of diabetes and anaemia. And there are no medicines to treat these people.

'You see, it's extremely hard to live here. You can be born here, but to live here is an entirely different matter,' he said, staring at me in the face. I had gazed at him while he was reciting the statistics, the full horror of the situation being hammered home.

'Many children die after a month of being born and it's only during the postmortem that we find that their internal organs were malformed,' he continued. 'It's not that women find it hard to get pregnant, it's just that they spontaneously abort. One woman I know, who works at the aluminium factory, has had nine spontaneous abortions in seven years. And all the babies are born small.'

Later that afternoon I went to a children's hospital. A plump woman, with a needle firmly tucked into the lapel of her white coat, showed me around. We went to room after room of deformed children, each with their own small bed. Mothers stared at us with sad, jaded eyes as the nurse reeled off the list of problems afflicting their babies. 'This one keeps having fits,' she said, picking up a small boy who had peed through his orange tights. 'Most of the children here have breathing problems, bad lungs or are deformed.'

Small coughs echoed through closed doors as we walked down long, white corridors that smelt of urine and disinfectant. We arrived at the intensive care unit, full of tiny babies stuffed with tubes. The nurse picked up a minute baby that had been born a month before, weighing seventy grams – slightly less than three packets of crisps. 'This is the smallest we've managed to save,' she said, supporting his head. 'In the West of course, you can save babies half this size, but we don't have the equipment to do that. There was one born here last week weighing sixty grams, but his eyes never opened and he died.' In this unit alone they take care of thirty underweight babies a month. 'But at the moment,' she added, 'women just aren't having children.'

The plump nurse showed us the records of the mothers who had given birth in the last month to babies in intensive care. Over half of them worked in the aluminium factory.

A thick layer of grey smoke was clearly visible against the skyline as we left the hospital. I was already beginning to cough and my eyes felt sore. We approached the large factory, built in 1923, in the centre of town. Its twenty chimneys churned out smoke into the sky. It was the end of the day shift and the 6,000 workers were pouring out into the snow-covered square to wait in long lines for the orange buses to take them home.

Sergei was seventy-two and had been working in the factory for the past forty-five years. 'Since the Great Patriotic War,' he announced proudly, his heavily wrinkled face bursting into a smile. 'I carry on because it's so interesting and I love my job,' he said, coughing into his brown handkerchief. I did not believe him.

'I carry on because I can't live on a pension of 400 roubles a month – no one can live on that. There are more than 300 pensioners who continue to work in the factory because they can't afford to stop,' said Ivan who, at the age of fifty-three had been working in the factory for the last sixteen years. 'Everyone coughs, all my friends are ill, but what can we do? There's no other work here so we keep going. We can't strike and our voices are hoarse from protesting.'

Nikolai is fifty-one but he, too, will continue working after he comes up to his pension. 'I was diagnosed as having lung cancer ten years ago, but nothing has happened, thank God, so I keep going. I have a wife and family. My daughter has bronchitis and my youngest son has blotchy skin. Look at that smoke,' he said turning towards the chimneys silhouetted in the evening sky. 'They burn dark yellow at night. This town is suffocating.'

Nikolai earns 2,500 roubles a month, but at the end of each month, since the beginning of January and price liberation, pay is renegotiated. 'There's a huge difference between people who work in the factories and mines and those who are on the state payroll. A doctor gets 1,400 roubles a month and a miner 20,000, so we do all right.'

DAY 65

In the early morning I met Inka Latkin, a sweet, bubbly girl with soft skin and a generous smile. She lived in the north of Novokuznetsk, about fifteen minutes away from the mine, Nagornaya, where her father worked and where her husband was killed. Heavily pregnant, she was expecting her baby in two weeks.

Evgeni Latkin died in the mine, at the age of twenty-five, when some unsafe timber fell and crushed him. His wife goes to the mine every day to talk to the director to try to get some form of compensation. Six months after the accident, she has yet to receive anything. 'Although they say that I might get something after the baby is born, I'll only have many more certificates and pieces of paper to get, and I'll have to queue for more people to sign them. It's terrible,' she said and giggled nervously.

She lives with her parents, her unemployed brother, his wife and their two children in a two-bedroomed flat that her father was given for twenty-five years' service in the mines. 'I sleep with my parents; my brother and his wife sleep here, which is the sitting room during the day. The two boys either sleep with me or them, or wherever. What'll happen when the baby is born is anyone's guess,' she explained, fiddling with her bracelet.

She used to live in the hostel with her husband, but after he died she could no longer afford to live there on her wages from the nursery school. '205 roubles a month,' she laughed, 'or a kilo of butter, if you can find it.' She is waiting for a flat, but does not believe that it will come. A miner has to have been working for fifteen years before he is given a flat and Evgeni had only been working in the mine for a fortnight before he was killed. She had received his wage packet for the days he had worked. '1,000 roubles for a dead man,' she said, walking over to the mantelpiece and taking down a serious black-and-white photograph from a glass cupboard. 'Look at him, he was so young.' She gazed at the thin carpet and thought for moment. Then she suddenly laughed and, turning to me gave a weak smile. 'But wives have to be brave and life goes on.'

The mine is obliged to look after Inka, but they will continue to put as much bureaucratic tape in her way as possible. Evgeni was earning 2,000 roubles a month when he died, but since inflation, miners are now earning between 15,000 and 20,000 roubles. Inka will receive sixty-five per cent of what he was being paid, or 800 roubles a month, until her child is seventeen. 'Another women I met,' she said, 'lost her husband sixteen years ago and she gets 38 roubles a month, because that is what he was earning just before he died.

While we sat and chatted, her sister-in-law and the two boys played in the room. 'I'm sorry we have to sit here,' she apologized, 'but the grandmother is ill at the moment and sleeping in the other room. We've nowhere else to go.'

We left, walking down the four flights of stone steps and feeling our way in the dark – the light bulb had long since gone. Inka finds it hard to make the trip each day to the mine. The Siberian winter has frozen the last flight into a smooth slope, but at least the cold made the smell of cat's urine in the hallway more bearable.

Quite what will happen to Inka depends on the new workers' union set up three years ago. She is entitled to three years' maternity leave, during which she will receive full pay for a year and a half and then nothing, although her job will still be there for her when she returns, she thinks.

Valeria, whose husband died in the same mine fifteen years ago, is heading the union to help those who have lost their husbands. 'Three men died in February and I've forgotten just how many in January, but I know it was more.' She said that wives find it hard to get any form of compensation. 'The directors of the mines keep forgetting who died, and when, and they hope that the wives will eventually give up fighting.

'We have rationing here, but the ration books are worthless. I have tickets up to my armpits, but the shops are empty. There are families I visit who are living on bread and tea and occasionally milk if they can be bothered to queue from about five in the morning for it.' She said that a psychologist, who had recently completed a survey among women in the town, had found that eighty per cent of them were close to suicide. 'Only those who had some form of religious belief were less depressed. You see what sort of a place we live in.'

She said that when she came from the Ukraine as a child, she had found the place so strange that she constantly asked her parents if she could go home. 'It's so depressing,' she added. 'When my five-year-old daughter paints snow, she paints it grey with black patches. I suppose she doesn't realize it should be white.'

Valeria helps the women get flats, medicine and food. She also helps them deal with the directors of the thirteen mines in the city. She took us to a mine on the outskirts of the town. As we approached, the snow turned black. One chimney in the heart of the valley ejected dense smoke into the atmosphere. This charcoal column twisted upwards and then fell on the houses around the mine. Their roofs, gardens and windows were covered in a thick layer of soot, the sky was dark, the weak sun just managed to filter through. 'People live here, can you believe it?' said Valeria, gazing through the dirty windows of the car.

We were shown around the mine, its ancient machinery in desperate need of repair. The evening shift was leaving and 6,000 men and women came up the shafts. Their faces and clothes black, their bodies tired, they went into the communal showers and dressed in a room crammed with thousands of small, metal, lock-up boxes where they kept their change of clothes. As they left to catch the buses to take them into the centre of town, I saw some had small newspaper packages tucked under their arms. 'They're fed sausage at lunch time by the mine, but many wrap it up to take it home to their families in the evening,' explained Valeria.

'Mine death is such a common occurrence here that people hardly think about it any more. I just pick up the pieces.'

DAY 66

Leaving Novokuznetsk behind, we journeyed through miles of snow-covered *tayga* passing wooden villages that the twentieth century had passed by. Horse-drawn sleds laden with straw stood outside small log houses with intricately carved windows, painted in blues and greens. The people, heavy with thick coats, wandered the single-track street that ran through the village, carrying churns of water, their feet bound in cloth and string, galoshes keeping out the snow. Small piles of wood stood neatly arranged outside each house and women transported their children, wrapped up against the elements, on the back of small sledges. Groups of older children with home-made heavy wooden skis hurled themselves down steep slopes. The pollution of Novokuznetsk was a thousand miles away for them. And even as we stopped off at a small roadside café to eat bread and thin soup, I could feel the clean air purifying my lungs and soothing my eyes.

Our driver, Misha, continued on in terrified silence, driving along the narrow, snow-packed track, his hands white as they gripped the steering wheel. We spun off the track whenever he increased his speed.

Finally, after eight hours, we arrived in Bisk, a small industrial town with one hotel. Booking in, we went to find something to eat. The restaurant was plagued with five stray cats that sprayed the faded curtains. There was nothing except potatoes and soup and we ate alone in the restaurant, the waitress dragging herself up from the table, where she had been asleep, to disturb the chef in the industrial-sized, but empty kitchen.

Gorno Altay

· · · · · · · · · · · · ·

DAY 67

We journeyed south towards Mongolia and into the Gorno Altay region, to a small village that borders the capital. After an hour driving through dense pine forest, where the sun could barely edge its way through the trees, we burst forth into a completely different region, where snow-covered rivers and powerful mountains reached for the sky. Gorno Altay is justifiably known as the Switzerland of Siberia.

Spiralling down a hill we entered the village of Maima. We had been given the address of some friends of Valeri, the beekeeper in Kiev, and drove around the town, trying to find the house. Eventually, searching among the crumbling apartment blocks, we came across a wooden house, surrounded by pine trees.

Tatyana, a small middle-aged woman with a tight perm and thick glasses, came out to meet us. She was flustered by our arrival. Her pubescent son was lounging in the sitting room, listening to hard rock music on a flash Korean tape recorder. In the kitchen, Tanya, Tatyana's husband's secretary, was cooking food for our arrival – she had spent the whole afternoon there.

We immediately sat down to an enormous supper and opened the bottle of vodka that we always had with us. 'There's nothing to buy in the shops, so everything we eat we make ourselves,' said Tatyana, toasting our arrival with an excessive slug of vodka, which she washed back with a home-made juice of plums and water. Bowls of hand-pickled carrots and cabbage packed the table, jostling with stuffed cabbage and a hot pepper sauce.

Tatyana was a vet, working in the capital, Gorno-Altaysk; her husband, the mayor of Maima, was away until tomorrow in Barnaul at a privatization conference for the whole region. The house had been entirely decorated by her husband. An enthusiastic carver, he had repanelled the walls and built an intricately designed sofa, and large pieces of strangely contorted wood lay dotted around the house.

The sitting-room walls were bedecked with icons from different centuries. Covered in gold and brass, they made an impressive collection.

We finished one bottle of vodka and opened another. As we sat at the table some of Tatyana's girlfriends began to arrive. Initially quite shy, they soon began to ask questions about the price of food in England and how we lived. 'What's hard for us,' said Tatyana, looking around the table for more alcohol, 'is that our whole lives have been turned upside down. All my life, I've been a member of the Party, working for the state farm and believing what I was told. Now, since Gorbachev, I don't know what to believe any more. Our eyes have been opened and now we see what's around us. All our lives we've been told that we live better than anyone else in the world. We have the best country and the West is capitalist and evil. Now we have nothing to eat and our children don't want to work. They want to be businessmen, although I don't know exactly what that means. My qualifications mean nothing – I earn no more than an eighteen-year-old boy who is buying shoes in one area and selling them in another for a profit.'

While we spoke, her son began to record all the tapes that we had brought with us for the journey. He was making copies to sell in the town. 'You get a lot of money for Western music,' he said, as he marked up the tapes with names of groups that he had never heard of.

After supper Yana, one of Tatyana's closest friends, began to tell our fortunes. She was reputed to be a white witch in the village, able to cure minor illness and predict the future. We sat down around a pack of cards that she laid out in various patterns of flowers, columns and pyramids. I was the first on the hot spot, desperate, of course, to know about my love life. 'You'll meet a blond knight who will sweep you off your feet and change your life,' she predicted. 'I don't actually fancy blonds,' I replied. 'This one is different,' she laughed. I had apparently met him once before, but was told he would suddenly reappear in my flat and we would run off into the sunset together.

Joth was next. He was going to get married very soon. He protested violently. 'But you'll live happily ever after,' said Yana. 'Ugh,' he said. 'I'm only twenty-six and I have the rest of the world to see.' He got up from the floor and left.

Lena, Tatyana's seventeen-year-old niece, arrived. A plump girl with hair down to her buttocks, she was studying dentistry in Gorno-Altaysk. She had left her parents behind in the mining Donbas region of the Ukraine and had been living with her aunt for the past year, while she completed her three-year course at the university.

Since the break-up of the union, however, her stay has been extended by another two years. Unable to pay for her course, she must stay and practise in the region to pay back her tuition in kind. She has not seen her parents for a year and will not see them until the course is over because she cannot afford to travel and, since her father is crippled from a mining accident, they cannot come to see her. 'Anyway,' she said, flicking her hair, 'if I leave, I can never be sure that I'll be able to return, with all the new visas and things.' It is almost impossible to telephone them, so Lena spends her evenings writing.

Today, however, Lena joined us. We had progressed to massage. Yana had both Joth and I flat out on the sofa while she rubbed our backs with her warm hands. Exhausted after our journey this was bliss. But in order to release all the tension, she carried on rubbing long after my skin had had enough. So, chapped like a nose on a frosty day, my skin throbbed pink as I lay in bed, feeling sore but beautifully relaxed.

DAY 68

When we woke, the mayor had returned. With his wife away at work he found it rather strange to have two foreigners in his house. A short, balding man with a hairy back and a sensuously curling mouth, he sat in a blue vest, smoking cigarettes in a small cubby hole off the kitchen where he carved his wood. Tatyana forbade him to pollute the rest of the house.

He talked me through his collection of icons that I had noticed the day before, telling me how they had all been taken from churches in Siberia, which were being dismantled by black marketeers. He showed me the ornate sofa in the sitting room, the panelling on the walls and the obscure sculptures around the house. 'I made them all myself,' he said proudly. 'There is nothing to buy, so anything nice that you want you must make yourself. I'm German, so I'm not afraid of hard work. If you go to any Russian's house, you won't find any of this. Their hobby is drink.' He became slightly more relaxed at our presence after the tour of the house and the right noises that I had made, so he asked us into the kitchen to toast our arrival. A few shots of vodka later and all was well. He drove us to the centre of the town to catch a bus into Gorno-Altaysk to find out about flights. We missed the bus, but caught a lift with an ambulance whose crew appeared to be on a break.

We stopped off at the main department store to buy presents for 8 March, International Women's Day and one of the main Soviet holidays. We walked past the rows of odd-sized tracksuits and faded, plastic hair slides. Dusty dresses were pinned in strangely contorted positions to the pale blue chipboard. The make-up counter was crowded. Three shades of pink lipstick protruded out of their pale grey packaging. The ambulance driver bought one for his wife and the nurse bought a bar of soap for her mother. Crumbling at the corners, it rattled loose in its package. They dropped us off at the Aeroflot office. Needless to say, after being shouted at by a fat woman from behind a glass screen, we established there were no flights, let alone tickets. We hitched back to Maima and wandered around the town.

Sitting below a crumbling block of flats, decorated with an old Communist slogan painted gigantically on the wall, praising the October Revolution and working for the Party, I met Valeri. He poked his head over the balcony. Dressed in the ubiquitous blue nylon tracksuit, he was drunk and listening to loud heavy metal music. It was midday and he invited us to finish the bottle. Walking up the decaying green stairs with peeling paint to the first floor, we entered a flat that smelt of stale cigarettes and damp. We sat in the kitchen at a small table while Valeri put on the kettle for some tea and then busied himself rummaging around in a pile of cardboard boxes that lay in the corner of the room. The damp above the stove in the opposite corner was already forming into mushrooms. He smashed a couple of objects while looking for some glasses. 'I don't normally use glasses,' he said, scratching his head and looking at the broken china. 'But with guests ...'

Three families lived in the three-bedroomed flat: Valeri, his sister and two children; his brother-in-law's family, and another couple. 'This is how a commercial director lives,' he said as he showed us one room after another, each with peeling walls and a bed, with cardboard boxes in each corner. The rusty loo was a constant stream of running water and the pipes leaked. His brother-in-law, the commercial director dealing in honey, returned home for lunch. He joined in our vodka shots, but was embarrassed and mildly irritated by our presence. He left quickly. Valeri, on the other hand, was excited and kept on saying, 'Who would have thought...'

We finished his bottle of vodka while we talked about bad living conditions and food shortages and boredom. He asked us to stay and carry on drinking and listening to heavy metal. We declined.

Later that evening we went with Volodya to judge the Miss Maima competition in the House of Culture in the centre of town. It was set up to celebrate 8 March. Volodya was fashionably late and the organizer of the competition was predictably worried that the town's most important man had not arrived. 'We've all been waiting for you,' she panicked. We walked into the hall, which was packed with mummies and daddies and children with fluffy bows in their hair. Three women sat nervously to the right of the stage, wearing their cardboard numbers. As Volodya walked into the hall the audience applauded. He bowed and took his place among the other civic dignitaries.

A woman with a grey perm introduced the three contestants. Numbers one and two were both sixteen and schoolfriends; number three was thirty and worked in the local supermarket. All of them had hair to their waists. First, the girls were asked to recite nursery rhymes, after which the civic dignitaries awarded marks out of five, holding up heart-shaped cards on sticks. Next, there was the 'name the flower' competition, which was marked for accuracy. Then came an interval. Tiny tots with oversized ribbons, in white vests and knickers and home-made tutus, danced for their mothers, who puffed with pride in the front rows.

The competition continued. 'What would you do if your husband brought you some French perfume from a commercial shop for Women's Day?' asked the grey-haired compere. The audience groaned in appreciation at the thought of such an expensive gift. 'And,' continued the compere, 'when you opened it, it turned out to be vinegar? That's to contestant number one.'

'I'd put the stopper back in and sell it to the commercial shop for more money,' she replied. This brought about rapturous applause. 'She understands *perestroika*,' shouted someone from the audience.

The tiny tots returned to perform some sort of traditional chicken dance and were followed by an adolescent pop group playing their own song. The boy in the jeans, who led the band, thoroughly enjoyed the attention and flirted with contestant number two, while the bass guitarist, strangled by his bow tie, refused to look at the audience. Next, the contestants were asked to sing. Number two refused, which I think lost her the competition. Number three, with the aid of a red-fringed scarf, got the audience clapping, and number one acquitted herself with dignity. Then followed a 'specialized subject'. Number one dressed up in a national costume and stomped and swirled for the audience; number two told an embarrassing anecdote that few could understand, and number three sang once more for our enjoyment.

The children came on again and were followed by a row of oversized women with reedy voices who sang for twice as long as was necessary. The audience began to chatter amongst themselves.

At last came the crowning of Miss Maima. She was chosen from the amount the audience clapped when her number was shown to the crowd. Number one was crowned by popular demand. Volodya was brought up on stage to hand out the bottles of shampoo for second and third place. He got to place the sash around the waist of contestant number one, kiss her on both cheeks and hand over the final bottle of shampoo.

After the ceremony, mothers left carrying jaded children covered in blue eye make-up and pink lipstick. We returned to Valodya's house, where guests had already arrived.

One of Volodya's secretaries had arrived, husband in tow. She was a frightful woman who invaded my space by constantly tugging at my arm and asking questions in a loud voice close to my ear. We sat and argued about the mafia and privatization. Volodya talked about the mayor's conference. He showed off his note book from the meeting – it was full of doodles of new designs for furniture. 'They just won't stop talking, these people,' he laughed. 'They feel that if they occupy the whole day chatting then they can ask for more money. If they talked about laws that I don't know, then I don't need to know them. I have been in this business for a long time.'

Volodya was elected mayor five years ago and will stay in the position until the people no longer want him there. A member of the Communist Party all his life, he earns 2,000 roubles a month, but seems to survive on presents people give him in order to curry his favour. 'The main problem about privatization at the moment is that no one can afford to buy any machinery.' He described the

Joseph, resettled Czech, Siberia

Victor and Maria, Gorno-Altaysk, Siberia

Gold digger, Siberia

Georgi, Christian horsebreeder, Khakassia

Jewish leader, Birobidzhan

Doctor, maternity hospital, Moscow

Circus school, Birobidzhan

Vladivostok

Sailors confined to barracks, Vladivostok

Bolshoi ballet, Moscow

OPPOSITE Strip-tease school, Moscow

Artist, Moscow

problems facing the meat factory in the town. 'There is talk of privatizing it, but no one can afford the machinery to get it going. So those who would normally take their animals to the factory to be made into sausage are keeping them for themselves. That's why there are food shortages, because everyone is holding on to the livestock. People might have the money to buy the factory, but no one can keep it going.' He said the same was happening all over the area. 'The state farms and the kolhoz are all keeping their animals. No one is sure of the future, so they hoard. Meanwhile, it's the people who buy and sell things who are making the money and, of course, the mafia.'

The argument moved on to the mafia. 'Every country must go through its mafia stage in order for it to become great,' he said. 'Look at America. The mafia made America great and it will make us great as well. We can't function without them. But their time will eventually pass.'

The loud woman had kept silent throughout the conversation, her elbow sliding further and further across the table. When her husband made a move to leave, she protested vaguely and then relented. We all toasted their exit.

DAY 69

On the way to meet Volodya's parents, we visited his daughter. She was twenty-two and had a four-year-old daughter. 'I could not stop crying when she told me that she was pregnant,' said Tatyana. 'She gave birth at eighteen, the father was only seventeen. He spent weeks knocking on the door of the state registrar, until he would let them marry.'

Their daughter was rather beautiful. She had thick, black hair that swung around her waist, huge blue eyes and the same curled mouth as her father. She lived in a badly furnished house, about ten minutes from her parents, with her husband, baby and her husband's grandmother. They were desperately saving money because her husband wanted to go into business, although quite what sort of business he had yet to decide. We collected the grandchild, along with her milk and her plastic bag of stale biscuits – she was going to stay with her great grandparents for a few days, while her mother took in some sewing to make some extra money.

The four-year-old began to sing as we drove along in the car. 'She's got used to being carried around and living with other people. We all take it in turns to look after her — it's very hard for my daughter to have to look after her all the time,' said Tatyana, as she bounced the child on her knee.

We arrived at Victor and Maria's house, a two-roomed cottage on the banks of a frozen river about forty minutes outside Maima. It was surrounded by waist-deep snow that Victor had sprinkled with ashes to help melt. They were both Germans and both born in 1925. Maria could not speak Russian until she was rounded up by Stalin's troops in June 1941. Collected in the middle of the night from a village in the Volga-Don region, she managed to grab a pair of pants before being sent on a sealed train to Kemerovo, in Siberia. Victor, who was from Krasnoyarsk, near the Aral Sea, was also rounded up and sent in a sealed train to Kemerovo. All of his family died on the journey to different parts of the old Soviet Union, except his younger sister, who left the country just before the war. She emigrated to Argentina or Brazil, he is not sure which.

They were put to work in the coal mines. 'When we arrived, there was nothing there. We had to build our own houses as well as work in the mines. They originally controlled us at gunpoint, but soon gave up when they realized that we were too weak to run and there was nowhere to run to,' said Victor, his blue-veined hands shaking as he drank his tea.

Both of them worked down the mines from the age of sixteen. Maria's hands, although gnarled now by arthritis, were deformed at an early age: she fell down the gap between two coal trucks and nearly lost a hand. 'They wanted to amputate, but I wouldn't let them,' said Maria, as she showed me the large lump on the side of her wrist that forces her hand to turn inwards at right angles. 'It all happened a few weeks before my seventeenth birthday,' she said, her face screwing up as she remembered.

They met down the mine and married. Maria gave birth to Volodya down the mine at the end of one of the shafts. 'All the other children, I managed to produce in a bed, but they could not get me up the shaft quickly enough,' she mumbled.

After the war they spent the next fifteen years in a small village near Kemerovo, where they were only allowed to move in a one-kilometre radius of the village. 'If you left the village it meant being sent to the labour camps. But of course as Germans, we worked harder than the Russians and we began to live relatively well. So they hit us with heavy taxes to punish our wealth,' said Victor, as he stood up and went to search in his dusty desk for his old tax forms. He could not find them. 'Well, we had to pay large sums of money for pigs, each tree and cattle.'

It was not until the Thaw and Khrushchev that they were allowed to move and they came to settle in this house by the river. Victor keeps bees and makes his money through selling honey, although he does have a pension of 436 roubles a month. 'My whole youth down the mines and that's all I get paid, it's terrible,' he said, flicking his pension book across the table in disgust.

They did have friends who had left recently for Germany, but they had no desire to go. 'I'm tired of living in Siberia,' said Maria, as she rolled out the dumpling mixture, her crooked hand lying useless on the rolling pin. 'But where else can we go? There's talk of a German state somewhere, but where, no one knows. I'm old now, and resigned to staying here.'

Despite their poverty they lived well. Maria looked surprisingly young for her age. She had the strength of a woman who had worked all her life and did not know how to stop. Home-made jams and bread were placed on the table and they had a whole storeroom of meat in large plastic bags that lay embedded in the snow outside. It was the things, like sugar, that they could not produce themselves that they could not afford to buy, but they made do with honey.

Victor sat down at the table. 'Gorbachev was a lovely man,' he said. 'He opened the eyes of the Soviet peoples. For the first time we can talk about the things that happened to us. But Gorbachev was weak and did not have the strength to carry out what he started.'

Their village was mostly populated with old people, with a sanitarium over the river. The house was guarded by two savage dogs that looked like a mixture of wolf and husky. The bees were asleep in boxes below the house. Victor had about thirty boxes, which he would take outside when the snows melted, he explained, in about two months.

They did not appear embittered by their experience, viewing it more like some story in history that did not really happen to them. Victor had been meticulous about cataloguing his experience, and had kept every document that had ever had his name on it. He brought some out, insisting that Joth photograph them. 'Only block out my name,' he said. 'You never know who'll be in power next.'

Returning home, Volodya went down the garden to heat up the *banya* and, after about three hours, it was ready. Running barefoot through the snow, Joth and the mayor went in first. Half an hour later, Joth came out. Puce in the face, he could hardly talk, and his heart was pounding. 'What was it like?' I asked. 'I can't tell you,' he said between gasps. 'All I can say is, I've just had my bottom spanked by the mayor of Maima.' With that he walked into the sitting room and lay flat out on the floor. I went in with Tanya and Lena.

It was a small wooden room with two wooden beds on top of each other. In one corner was a vat of cold water and in the other, a huge, wood-burning stove. The place was thick with steam that grabbed hold of my lungs. Rather bad at communal nakedness, I lunged into the corner, hiding in the steam. Tanya was having none of it and made me lie on the hot wooden bed and began to soap my bottom and back. Taking hold of a bunch of birch leaves and drenching them in hot water, she thwacked the whole of my body, her large breasts swinging from side to side with the effort. I found the whole experience heinously embarrassing and began to laugh at my own discomfort.

The whole process lasted about twenty minutes. She soaped and re-soaped, thwacked and re-thwacked, rinsing each time. Then she made me squat on the floor and, in the searing steam, she washed my hair and armpits. All the agonies of forced bathing in childhood came flooding back. I felt foolish and four. She then soaped my crotch, wiping her hands between my legs. Cringing at my very Englishness, I closed my eyes and hoped that the whole thing would be over shortly. 'Don't worry, we're all women here,' she said as she rinsed away. But I had had enough and, still covered in soap, I grabbed my towel and ran back through the snow to join Joth on the floor.

Khakassia

·················

DAY 72

We spent two days and two nights retracing our steps back through Bisk and Novokuznetsk and on to Abaza. The train to Abaza smelt of dirty clothes, stale air and damp bedding. Most of the passengers slept in their boots and no one spoke as we rattled along in the dark – the lights were broken. The silence was broken only by an argument going on at one end of the carriage. Throughout the night three women and their four children argued with one conductor, refusing to pay because the tickets were too expensive. The conductor's only revenge was to refuse them bedding. At around four in the morning, they settled down, curling up together on two plastic mattresses. One of the conductors lent me her bed, which was almost a foot too short, and I spent the night with my knees pressed against the roof of the carriage and a pillow over my face to block out the smell of pickles and the snores that emanated from the other conductor below me.

At 7.30 a.m. we arrived in Abaza, a small town in the middle of the Khakassian Autonomous Region, bordering Tuva in the heart of Siberia. Surrounded by mountains, it is a quiet town, where rows and rows of pretty wooden houses with carved window frames and small fenced gardens line the streets. We took the bus around the town and were dropped off by the driver at an address that we had been given by a friend, Peter, from Moscow. Walking up a small garden path we met Misha, a film engineer, his wife, small baby and the grandmother. His son was at school. Misha worked in Moscow but was, in his own words, 'an ecological refugee'. The polluted atmosphere of Moscow had left his son with a brain tumour and, after numerous operations, they had decided to move to the country. Misha commutes, working for months at a time in Moscow.

'This is a great town,' he said, clasping his hands over his round stomach. 'It's so politically inactive. But one evening after the putsch, some miners decided to blow up the statue of Lenin. They put dynamite in his boots and blew him off his pedestal. For a week, Lenin lay on the ground, dressed in a pair of shorts, until eventually they cleared him away. The mayor, an old diehard, has started a collection for a new statue, but so far he only has 200 roubles.' Misha roared with laughter, tears welled up in his eyes.

We sat down to breakfast in the cramped kitchen that could hardly accommodate us all. The grandmother cooked on the wood-burning stove in the corner of the room, using home-produced ingredients. 'Pollution-free eggs, pollution-free chicken and pollution-free potatoes,' said Misha, as he tucked in.

Afterwards I was placed in a delicious bed, covered in a handsewn quilt. Made of steel, it sagged in the middle, but after our journey it enveloped me in comfort. Peter, who had arranged to meet us at the house and was flying in from Moscow, had been worried because we were two days late in arriving. He rushed in and woke me up. 'My God,' he said, as he leant over me, papirossi cigarette stuck to his lower lip. 'You look terrible – almost ten years older than when I last saw you. You see what my country does to you?' he said with a laugh.

He did not look so good himself as he had stayed up all night, pacing the house thinking that something had happened to us. 'It wouldn't have surprised me if you'd been shot on the way here,' he said. 'Or mugged for your shoes, or something like that'.

Peter introduced us to Kolya, a large woolly man with a thick beard and a gentle manner. 'This is the first entrepreneur in Siberia,' he said, slapping Kolya on the back.

Kolya took us to his factory. Made entirely of wood, it was surrounded by trees on the edge of Abaza. The first stake had been hammered into the ground in June 1991. He had set up a furniture factory, making wooden chairs, tables and kitchen units with three friends, investing a total of 200,000 roubles. They now employ twenty-five carvers and carpenters, forty per cent of the profits are paid to the workers, fifty per cent in taxes and ten per cent, unofficially of course, for protection. 'We have to do that to make sure that we can operate peacefully,' said Kolya, stroking his beard. 'Although the mafia hasn't really got a hold here because everyone grew up here together and everyone knows each other. We also have our own transport system, which cuts down their ability to control us.'

The biggest problem the factory has is choosing designs for the cedar furniture. 'We have been starved of new ideas and designs for so long that we no longer have any idea what's wanted.' Kolya showed me a collection of old, cheap, East German catalogues that he was reading in the hope of inspiration. The kitchen units were selling well, going for 30,000 roubles each. They were already costing 40,000 roubles in Moscow.

Walking around the factory that still smelt of new wood, the difference between what we had seen in Samerkand was immediately evident. People were smiling, chatting and obviously enjoying what they were doing. The upper storey was incomplete and we were told to walk on particular planks so that we did not fall through, but there was an atmosphere of hope and a buzz of excitement that I had not felt before. This was one of the first truly productive offshoots of perestroika that I had seen. Kolya was creating something, employing people and using the skills and raw materials that were readily available in the area. This was not the extortionate shuffling around of Western goods that seemed to indicate success in every other area that we had been to.

Kolya then took us to his dacha at the foot of the mountains, which he had spent the last three or four years building. He had a small state flat in the centre of Abaza, but spent most of the summer in this half-completed wooden house, with no roof, no windows and no running water.

We spent the rest of the afternoon preparing for the night in the dacha, chopping wood and lighting fires. Melting snow, we made tea. Filling oil lamps and lighting candles, we settled down for the evening, cooking kebabs on the fire while Kolya heated up the banya. Joth and I only agreed to the banya experience if Kolya and Peter promised that they would not beat us. It was altogether more relaxing than the Maima experience. The steam was so hot that I could only bear sitting inside the wooden construction for a few minutes at a time, rolling outside in the snow to cool down. I washed in peace.

Piling the wood high in the fireplace, we all slept in the same bed for warmth. Almost asphyxiated by heat to begin with, I woke up in the early hours cold to the bone, the snow blowing through the windows.

DAY 73

Kolya drove us back to his flat, a hideous Stalinist construction that made the surrounding wooden houses recoil in horror. It had two rooms: one the children's bedroom, the other both sitting room and bedroom. We were introduced to Marina, who was dark with pale skin and thick glasses and just as gentle as her husband.

After breakfast we set off into the mountains. Driving along the road that leads to the Autonomous Republic of Tuva and Mongolia, we turned off onto the river. Kolya drove straight out onto the ice. Curled up in a little ball in the back of the car, I closed my eyes in terror. Kolya sensed my discomfort and smiled. 'In winter, it's the only way to travel. The roads are so bad that it's the only way to inaccessible places. In the summer, we use boats.'

'When do you know when to stop using the river?' I asked nervously. 'When someone goes through,' said Kolya, with a broad grin. He was only half joking.

After about twenty minutes a huge truck stacked with wood raced past us, crashing over the frozen bumps in the ice. I began to relax. If he can do it so can we, I thought. We came across some fishermen, lying belly down on the ice. They had bored holes through to the water, about three feet below. Georgi and Andrei had been lying there for the last four hours and intended to spend the rest of the day there, lying on their stomachs, their noses down the small hole, looking for fish.

They had come fully prepared with large sheets of felt to keep them snug while they lay on the ice; chopped egg to sprinkle down the hole to attract the fish; home-made flies; short, plastic fishing rods that looked more suitable for an eight-year-old and, of course, vodka. Both on pensions, fishing was a way of supplementing their income, passing the time and running away from their wives to drink. They had caught around eleven fish already that morning. 'That's a bad day,' explained Georgi. 'Normally I catch many more than that, but there don't seem to be many fish around at the moment.' He made me lie down next to him on the ice and I stared down the hole, my cheeks pressed against the ice. I shouted at the fish to come and take a bite. It was very restful, looking down the smooth channel into the clear water below. Dark and cold, it was extraordinary to think that animals were alive down there.

The two men began to play around. Handing me the boring device, they laughed as they watched me try to drill a hole. An exhausting business, it was like forcing a giant corkscrew into a stubborn bottle of wine: speed and force were of the essence. They applauded and laughed when I finally managed to reach the water and it shot up to the surface, splashing me in the face.

Georgi was the more extrovert of the two: he had a wicked glint in his eyes and a large smile that cracked over his chapped cheeks. Andrei kept his fur hat pushed well over his eyes and did not enjoy our intrusion. 'Things are so bad here at the moment,' said Georgi, reaching for his hip flask. 'There's nothing to eat and what there is, is so expensive, especially for someone like me. Why don't we do a swap? We'll have Thatcher and you can have Gorbachev. Let him go to England and ruin your country like he destroyed ours.' His shoulders shook with laughter. We agreed our swap and continued upriver.

We found a narrow track and followed it past empty villages of dilapidated huts. Weaving our way through the forest, we came across a gold-mining community. They had just arrived in the area a few weeks before and were still building the huts in which they would spend the next eight months. Fifty men had left their wives and children to live in the *tayga*, or forest, searching for gold in the river. They earned 100 roubles a day, working twelve-hour shifts, and only had 1 May off. They had been working that particular stretch of river for the past two years, shifting camp further and further upstream. Many of them had come from Magadan, the land of gold mines and prison camps in the far northeast of Siberia. As gold specialists, they had been shifted over here to clean out the river.

Albert, the chief foreman, explained the mining process to me as we walked along the river bank. Working the river only in the summer months, when it is not frozen, they use huge diggers to shift its course. With a machine like a large vacuum cleaner, they then suck all the mud up from the dry river bed and sift it for gold, which is immediately sold to the state – one gram of chemically pure gold goes for 50 roubles. After they have cleaned out a stretch of river, they literally put the river back and replant all the trees that they have had to rip up. 'If we did not put everything all back again,' said Albert, 'no one would let us mine here.'

A small Georgian miner, Georgi, who lived in Magadan, began to talk about the old times in the region. 'In 1966 the price of gold used to be one rouble per gram and this place was full of prospectors. But when the state stopped allowing people to collect the gold, they all gave up and the villages were left empty. 'I used to be able to collect about fifty grams of pure gold a month when I worked here in the fifties. It was quite amazing.'

This group of men have an unconventional lifestyle. For two-thirds of the year they live together as a unit, far from civilization. They do not drink alcohol and eat in a communal dining room, where they are fed three times a day, accumulating a bill that they settle at the end of their stay. 'We don't do anything at all other than work,' said Georgi. 'There aren't any cigarettes at the moment, so we seem to have given those up as well.' This is the first year that they have had women cooking for them in the kitchens – normally they do not see the opposite sex for eight months at a time. 'That's a problem,' said Georgi, with a chuckle. 'But we work so hard we forget about all that stuff after a while.'

Georgi had been a gold-miner all his life, working in eight-month stints in mines all over the country. His wife left him four years ago because she wanted to travel and, because of the supposed secrecy of his job, she was not allowed to. 'Now that she's divorced from me, she went to Poland last year,' he said with a snort. He offered us his house in Magadan. 'It's all locked up for the next eight months, so why don't you go and make yourselves at home? I'm only ever there for the winter, when it's minus fifty and dark all the time. I believe it's nice there in spring.'

Divorce and infidelity appear to be the biggest fears. 'It's hard,' said Georgi. 'You never know what your wife's been up to while you've been away.'

We sat down to lunch in the communal dining room, eating hot soup and huge hunks of bread. Afterwards, the men carried on building their small village. A group of ten were setting up the storeroom, filling an underground cavern with great blocks of ice that they had hauled through the snow on their backs. The ice would keep their food fresh well into the spring.

Driving back along the track, we stopped off to meet another Georgi. He was a statuesque man with thick, black hair, pale grey-blue eyes and a broad white smile and wore a red scarf wrapped around his head. A devout Russian Orthodox Christian, he was returning to a village deserted by the out-of-work prospectors, which he was rebuilding with a small group of Orthodox Christians. They had a collection of three or four houses that they had managed to buy at the end of last year, and they had spent the winter working in temperatures of − 40° and − 50° to make the derelict houses habitable. The place was the stuff of fairytales: surrounded by *tayga*, the houses nestled into the bend of the river, a sheer cliff dropping to the river bank on one side and flat land on the other. They had planned the perfect, pre-Revolutionary, Tolstoyan village, complete with church and school. They had begun to breed horses, having just bought a powerful, black stallion to sire their new stock, and were in the process of buying more land over the other side of the river, to build a small hotel. 'We want to take people riding to see this beautiful land that God has given us,' said Georgi, looking around him.

As we arrived, they had just finished carving up a horse. It had slipped in the snow and broken its front legs and they had had to shoot it. Its severed head lay on a wooden bench, its tongue hanging out, dripping blood into the snow. Its warm liver lay crimson against the white backdrop; its skin and hooves were stretched out on the ground. It was a macabre sight. They were not going to eat the animal themselves, but planned to give it to the miners. 'We all love horses too much,' said Georgi.

While Sasha stoked up the wood-burning stove inside one of the houses for some tea, Georgi saddled up two horses. The black stallion, frisky with sexual frustration, pawed the ground and snorted angrily while being saddled. I was given a skittish black mare that vehemently disliked the idea of a quiet ride through the forest. We trotted off together, Georgi picking my brains about Orthodox Christians in the West. 'What do they think about the current divisions in the Church at the moment?' he asked, urging his horse on in the snow. I was embarrassingly ill-equipped to answer such questions; I was also struggling to control the mare, which insisted on rubbing up against Georgi's horse.

'I'm afraid for the future of my people,' he said, turning to look at me, his blue eyes shining bright against the snow. 'Not politically or economically but, after seventy years of Communism, we're weak. Our souls have been polluted: there is no such thing as a clean and honest Christian in this country any more. What will be the strength and the future of this country is not its politics or its economic reform, but a belief in God.' He sat, dignified, astride the stallion, controlling it with the lightest of touches.

We rode through the snow along the frozen river, the horses dancing, their warm breath freezing grey in the air, their hooves making a gentle thud on the soft ground. 'It's been very hard here this winter and we've only just managed to pull through. We've had little to eat – bread, vodka and all the essential products are still rationed. But I'm still optimistic.' He sank his heels into the horse's flanks, sending it galloping ahead.

We returned to the yard. Georgi tied a charcoal-grey stallion to a lunge rein and made it prance around in circles. His back firmly straight, his left hand held high in the air, he urged the horse on, making it gallop faster and faster. Two dogs with thick heavy coats began fighting over the carcass of the dead horse and Sasha ran after them. We moved inside the only house that they had as yet made habitable and had tea. The one room was heated by a central wood-burning stove; three beds ran along three of the walls and against the other stood a table, covered with stale pieces of toast in a plastic bag. All three men had spent the winter here.

Drinking strong tea, I listened while Georgi talked. He hoped that they would have an Orthodox monk teaching at the school, although it would not be exclusively religious. 'I want religion to be taught at the school like it was before the Revolution,' he said.

Georgi had studied law at Kiev University and had then spent ten years in the police force, specializing in juvenile crime. He was a late convert to Christianity. It had been dangerous to be a Christian before *perestroika* but Siberia's vastness prevented any great persecution and surveillance. He said that more people were converting to Christianity. 'In troubled times, people turn to God.' He also added that many people were returning to the villages as the situation in the towns worsened and food became scarcer and pollution worse. We sat crunching on dry bread while he talked. His enthusiasm lit up his face. 'I want to rebuild a lost community here,' he smiled.

As we left, he blessed us, drawing a sign of the cross in the air. He thanked God for our coming. 'You will take our work to the West and people will come and see us,' he shouted as we drove away.

We drove back along the river, past the two fishermen, who were still flat out on the ice, past the deserted villages made of rotting wood, and back to Abaza, where we had supper at Kolya's. His two young sons stared at us in silence from across the table, their huge blue eyes unblinking as they studied our every move. Marina laughed. 'No one has ever met foreigners here. They'll go to school tomorrow and tell all their friends and no one will believe them.'

She fed the family with milk from her parents' cow and what they grew on the balcony. Her fridge was full of last year's crops, all pickled to preserve them. The balcony was full of meat stacked high in the snow – it had been bought before the January price rises. 'The summer is the problem here because we can't store anything, and since the rivers are not frozen, it's difficult to get produce to us,' Kolya explained. 'Marina makes jams from wild rhubarb, strawberries, cranberries and other fruits she has picked. We live off the forest in the summer and grow our own food. Other than that, things are very difficult to find and, of course, expensive.'

Kolya had invested all his money in the furniture factory but it has still to make a profit. Marina works at the local school, teaching nature studies – she studied forestry at university. She also runs a craft club in the evenings, making necklaces and other things out of small pieces of leather. 'It's really my hobby. I earn thirty-eight roubles a month running the club – that's about seven pieces of chewing gum,' she laughed.

DAY 74

Kolya took us to meet some woodcutter friends. We drove across the mountains, over frozen rivers and up a long track to an enclave in the *tayga*. There, about forty men, who spent two weeks a month trudging through the forest, were chopping down wood. They earn between 2,000 and 3,000 roubles a month, working all the daylight hours: the remainder of their time they look after small farms and drink vodka made from the sap of pines.

In 1991 this particular group of woodcutters, headed by Andrei, felled 400,000 hectares of trees and replanted 100,000 hectares. 'We're supposed to cut down in winter and replant in summer. Transport's easier in winter because we can haul the wood over the frozen river. But, of course, we never get round to replanting all that we've cut down.' Their monthly target is 5,000 trees, which they sell directly to the state. 'Although there's talk of privatizing the logging, I don't know who'll take it on,' said Andrei. They rarely meet their target of 5,000 trees a month 'because our technology is so bad,' he explained. 'But, you know, we tried

Western machinery here and it couldn't stand the wild conditions.'

Accompanying Sergei and Sasha, we went up the steep hill covered with pine pulp and broken branches. We climbed up the hill in an enormous caterpillar truck, forced back in our seats as we moved along. Sergei and Sasha, both born in the area, set off with their chainsaws, packed lunches and small cans of petrol under their arms. Within about three minutes of a loud searing noise, trees began to crash to the ground, smashing in half on the sharp rocks as they fell. It was a powerful reminder of man's command over a fragile environment. Standing at the top of the hill, all I could see for miles and miles were trees and snow. The huge caterpillar machine tore through the forest, crushing embryonic trees in its wake as it dragged those that had already been felled along the forest floor and down the hill to the works below. There, men in twos marked off the trunks in six-metre lengths for the sawmill to turn into planks.

Russian and Khakassi alike, the cutters worked in temperatures of $-40°$ throughout the winter. 'Around 19 January is the coldest. We wear three pairs of gloves to keep us warm. The temperature's about $-45°$. It's called the baptism frost because if you can work in that, then you can call yourself a woodcutter,' said Andrei with a smile.

After watching tree after tree tumble we returned to the main area, walking and slipping down the steep slope covered in pulped trees. There, a huge fire burnt all day, fuelled by fallen trees that were too short to sell. The smoke wove its way slowly into the calm sky. We walked up the hill to a small caravan, where the workmen gathered for their tea. It was their lunch break. About seven or eight had gathered in the cramped, hot room, smoking stale cigarettes and drinking strong sweet tea, while a previous Party supervisor, a slight, mad or simple man, sat telling anecdotes that the woodcutters found even less amusing than I.

'I spend my spare time fishing,' said Valeri, an old man with a weathered face and leathery handshake. 'I'm out there on the ice for up to ten hours a day when I'm not working. I enjoy being alone with nature and I love the quiet.' All the others in the room laughed when I asked them what they did when they were not working. 'We drink and sleep,' one of them finally admitted. The group varied in age: those in their early twenties were attracted by the good money; the older ones knew no other trade.

After our tea we left, driving once more through the mountains and over the solid rivers. We drove back to Abaza to have lunch with Kolya's parents and arrived at the small house on the edge of the town at the end of a wake. Kolya's grandmother had died over a month before, at the age of ninety-three. The Russian wake, or celebration feast, comes forty days after the death. There was a long table set up in the living room and we sat down to dumplings and vodka made of oxtail. The bones were still floating around at the bottom of the bottle, but it tasted pleasant enough. Most of the guests had already left. Kolya's younger sister was playing the piano for an aged aunt, while a few drunken old men sat, over-emotional, in a corner. We had to eat so quickly that I still had my mouth full as we walked out of the door and drove to the graveyard, where Kolya's grandmother was buried. He took a long, yellow, wax candle to light at her grave. 'It's hard to bury the dead without a God,' he explained. 'In this beautiful graveyard covered in snow and surrounded by trees lies a sort of frozen horror. There are many sad lives, sad stories and tragic existences frozen in this earth. I can almost hear them screaming from under the ground,' said Kolya as he approached the grave.

The Russians remember their dead through long, detailed speeches given by close friends, family and acquaintances around the grave. They are remembered also with oversized photographs placed on granite or marble stones. Many are marked with crosses that bear little or no religious significance. 'Without God we have developed other ways of remembering and coping,' said Kolya. His grand-mother's funeral had had religious overtones, but it was not an Orthodox funeral. 'We, in the time of Communism, began the glorification of the person rather than the soul. Communism denied the existence of the soul, so we had to invent something else.' As I walked among the strange stones, covered in plastic flowers or ostentatious wreaths, I came across two hard-boiled eggs, placed upon a grave. 'They are to feed the soul on its journey,' said Kolya. 'To where?' I asked. 'God knows,' he replied.

Leaving the graveyard, we drove across the steppe to a small village inhabited by the Khakassi. They are an Oriental-looking people, who stayed behind in the region when most of their forebears migrated to Kirghizstan, worn out from fighting the Mongol Tartars. They asked to join the Russian Empire in 1701 and were offered tax incentives to convert from Shamanism to Christianity. The Russians now outnumber the indigenous people ten to one and have almost completely destroyed their culture.

An old woman was on her way to collect food for her chickens from a house at the other end of the village. 'You've been sent by God,' she cried, when we asked her if she wanted a lift. 'I don't have the strength to carry the sack of food home and now you can help me.' We drove through the village, one row of wooden houses either side of the road, devoid of gardens and trees – the Khakassi do not grow fruit or vegetables. We spent ten minutes rapping on the door of the house, trying to collect her food. There was no reply. 'They're all drunk inside and won't answer,' she explained. She had paid for her chicken feed in liquid currency. 'They wouldn't accept money, only vodka as payment and they've obviously finished and are too drunk to get up.'

We drove her home to a one-roomed house that was falling down. She was born and brought up there and now she lived alone. We walked through a low door, bending double to enter in. Inside, there were two steel beds, a wood-burning stove and little else except a long table underneath the only window. She had two cows, a few chickens and a goat. Her son lived in the town and came to see her every weekend to chop wood for the stove and talk; other than that she was utterly alone. She was called Ana, but officially registered as Maria, a fact that she did not find out until she was told by her elder brother when she was sixteen.

Ana was seventy-two. Her husband died in the Second World War, but she did not receive a pension on his death, because she had not been able to understand the bureaucratic tape that she had to cut through to get it. Instead, she lived on '200 and something roubles a month'. But the bottle of vodka that she had just bought in exchange for the chicken feed had just set her back 89 roubles. She lived off her animals and still supported her son, giving him milk whenever he came to visit.

She had lived with her four brothers and sisters in the house as a young girl, all in the one room. 'One of my brothers was a deaf mute ... He and all the others are dead now,' she said. Ana left school at twelve and had spent all her life milking cows on the kolhoz.

She was a tiny woman, coming up to just below my armpits, with two thin, grey plaits snaking down her back. She was totally overcome by our arrival and began to dress up in her national costume, which she found in a trunk underneath one of the beds. She laughed and giggled as she struggled to put on the orange, embroidered dress. I tried to place the thick, silver earrings in her ears, but the holes had long since closed up, so I slipped them in her hair, just by her temples. She danced around, twirling in her clothes, showing us all her jewellery, jangling the necklace around her neck.

She then rushed around making tea, but soon forgot about it in the search for a dark blue, velvet coat, which she also tried on. She understood that we were not Russian, but she had never heard of England. 'Did you walk here?' she asked, grinning with excitement. I explained that we had come from England via Moscow. She did not know where Moscow was, although she knew that it was in Russia. I said that England was a small island in the middle of the ocean. 'How lovely,' she replied. 'You must all be fishermen there.' I did not have the heart to disagree. 'Are all the people tall in your country?' she asked. 'About the same as me,' I replied. 'How wonderful,' she exclaimed. 'They must all be good workers.'

She made us all sit down on the bed and gave us all slippers to keep our feet warm. She then stocked up the fire. 'What was life like under Stalin?' I asked. She looked at me with a piece of wood in her hand and a puzzled expression on her face. 'Stalin? No, I don't think he ever came to our village.' She put the wood on the fire. 'What was it like here after the war, then?' I asked. 'After the war? There was starvation here. That was extremely hard. I couldn't feed my children and people died and disappeared. What a terrible time it was, almost as bad as now, but then life has always been hard here,' she said, as she placed a loose strand of grey hair behind her ear.

She sat and showed us a pile of browning black-and-white photographs of her grandchildren and began to talk about the house, saying that the kolhoz would be giving her a new one. 'The rain and the frost come in. They have promised to give me a new one by the summer, and as I know one of the leaders of the kolhoz, I believe them. Then I'll be warm and won't have rain in my bed,' she announced proudly.

As we left, we offered to take her to collect her chicken feed. 'I'll collect it tomorrow. They won't be drunk then and I'll manage to get it home somehow. Don't worry about me,' she said with a laugh. As she squeezed me goodbye, she muttered, 'Foreigners in my house, no one will believe me tomorrow when I tell them. They'll think that I've gone mad, but I know that it's true and that's all that matters,' she giggled.

As we drove away, I turned and watched, waving from the window. I felt a deep sadness about leaving her alone. I also felt that we had somehow defiled her with our presence, tipping up in her house and disturbing her routine. It left me with a foul taste in my mouth.

We returned to Kolya's, where Marina had been cooking all day for Alyosha's, the youngest son's, birthday. All the relatives, each with watery blue eyes and thick black lashes, sat down for supper. I had met most of them earlier that day at the wake. Alyosha was not given many presents: almost everyone gave him money. 'There's nothing to buy in the shops,' explained Marina. 'So everyone has given money this year.' Alyosha had been given two toy cars from a friend from school. The paint was jaded and chipped, but he did not seem to notice. His grandparents gave him a slide projector. He had no slides, but enjoyed shining the light against the wall. An uncle had given him 100 roubles. 'What will you buy with that?' I asked. 'Chewing gum,' he replied with a happy grin.

Tuva
· · · · · ·

DAY 75

Setting off early, we drove through awesome scenery. The densely forested mountains gave way to snow-covered slopes as we drove higher and higher above the tree line. On the border between Khakassia and Tuva, we stopped at the summit of the 100-kilometre mountains, so-called because of their distance from the nearest village. From the summit, Tuva lay before us, miles and miles of snowscape with no trace of civilization. It was the most extraordinary feeling, standing on the frozen snow. I felt remarkably small and insignificant.

We drove through the mountains into Tuva. The countryside was wild and completely untouched by man. This was the only route to Mongolia, but we did not see another car for hours at a time. About three hours inside the border, we came across two *yurtas* nestling in the frozen bend of a river. 'At last,' said Kolya. 'I don't understand it. There used to be hundreds of *yurtas* and yaks along this road. It's very strange, I wonder what's happening.'

Outside the huts, a Tuvinian family were sitting on the ground, watching an older man mend a chainsaw. Dressed in traditional, hand-embroidered clothes, the grandmother squatted on the floor, her lined, Mongolian face furrowed in concentration as she smoked a crumbling cigarette. Her grey hair plaited up, she had a white turban swathed around her head. The settlement of two *yurtas* – round buildings constructed around a central wooden pillar with an umbrella-shaped slatted roof covered in felt and waterproofing – were the winter residence of one family: a grandmother, two sons, one daughter, two wives and one grandson. Only one of the sons could speak Russian; the others spoke Tuvinian.

Valerka was twenty-three and had lived with his family, herding yaks on a state farm, all his life. He moved with his family every summer and every winter to various different parts of Tuva. In the summer, they moved deep into the *tayga*; in the winter, they moved closer to the rivers and the roads. His wife had given birth to a son the day before we arrived. It was his first child, but he had not yet seen him because the bus to the village where his wife was, only came twice a week and was not due until tomorrow.

We sat inside the *yurta*, drinking salted tea and eating a flat, pancake-type bread. The stove in the centre of the hut gave off so much heat that the roof of the hut was open. Brightly coloured mats covered the floor and all around the edge, jolly, painted, carved furniture contained their possessions. Just to the right of the low entrance was a small pen crammed with tiny, woolly goats. 'Why are they inside?' I asked. 'All our animals are ill and dying,' explained Valerka, running his hand through his thick, black hair. 'We're trying to keep these ones alive.'

Valerka's yaks were dying at the rate of seven or eight a day. His herd of 300 had dwindled to seventy since January. No one seems to know why, but the animals grow weak and die within two or three days. 'Every morning I come to the herd and I collect corpses, and in the evening I collect still more,' he said, curling the rubbery bread around his thick fingers. The situation was the same all over the region, he maintained. 'Before, this valley was full of yaks and *yurtas* and now, no one is here.' Most of the families had either fled to the town to get food or had gone deep into the *tayga*, where fewer yaks were dying. It appeared that near the road, they were dying more quickly. Valerka was expecting a government commission, who were coming to look into the problem. Meanwhile, their whole existence was threatened: yaks are the Tuvinians' main source of food. Valerka earns only 500 roubles a month, working on the state farm and his family are feeling the winter incredibly hard as most of their animals have already died. 'I've no idea what'll happen to us in the next few months, but we're already hungry.'

They do not eat the meat of the dead animals, but take it to the meat processing factory. 'The old people will not let us eat the meat,' he said. 'They tell us to burn the animals and kill the whole herd. It happened before here, many years ago, and that's how they stopped the disease.' He explained that he had no idea what happened to the meat of the sick animals. 'Maybe they sell it to the Russians,' he said, with a mischievous laugh. 'We won't eat it.'

While we talked, his sister hovered at the entrance, curious to know who we were. She poked her smooth face round the door of the hut and giggled into the back of her hand. Neither of them knew where we had come from. They thought that England was another part of the Soviet Union.

After another two hours driving through this wild country, passing herdsmen on horses, bells jingling on their harnesses as they led sheep across huge plains, we came to Teeli. Wandering through the main square, we met Vasili. Well dressed in a smart blue coat, he had studied Tuvinian language and literature at university. He told us that about ten kilometres outside Teeli, the first Buddhist temple was under construction. Since he spoke both Russian and Tuvinian, he offered to act as our guide.

As we drove to the temple, Vasili explained that his father had been a Lama and had died from a weak heart after twenty years in a prison camp during the years of the Soviet repression. 'Buddhism is undergoing a revival in Tuva, although there is no Lama at the moment. The last one died about two years ago. But there are four studying: one in Mongolia, one in Tibet and two in Ulan-Ude,' he said enthusiastically, his elbow propped on the back of the front seat.

We arrived at the temple. Its carved roof, painted in green and red and curled up at the corners, contrasted greatly with the small, flat buildings that surrounded it. Inside, there were rows of dragon heads rigorously copied from a head taken from a museum two months before. All the painting, building and sculpture had been inspired and brought about by Saaya Kogel. A small man with neatly shaved hair, he seemed to inspire the respect of all the workers around him, who remained still while he spoke. He could not speak Russian, so Vasili translated for me.

In 1989, at the age of sixty, Saaya had managed to persuade the Ministry of Culture that he wanted to build an artist's studio. As soon as he got the money and the go-ahead, he announced to the people of the area that he was going to build a temple. Money and offers of help came pouring in. He, with the help of thirty artists in the village, built the temple with their own hands. Saaya is a respected sculptor and artist in Tuva and one of its leading spokesmen and exponents of traditional art. From the age of five or six, he had connections with the Lamas of Tibet. He suffered years of persecution for his religion, but eventually, through his fame as an artist, he managed to rebuild the religion. Under *perestroika*, there was a greater freedom to worship the 'golden religion'; the temple was started in June 1989 and they expect to have finished it by the end of 1992. He showed us the half-completed dragon sculptures that would decorate the roof. Upstairs, there was a golden altar in a room, painstakingly painted in traditional colours and patterns; gold, red, pink and green swirled over the walls, thick clouds of incense hung low in the air. 'When people come here to worship from all over Tuva and the rest of the Soviet Union, they say they have never seen such beauty,' said Saaya, with a gentle smile. To my eyes, jaded by the joylessness of Russian streets and architecture, I felt that I had been allowed to peep through the keyhole of a secret garden.

Opposite the temple live Sergei Kocha, a master of softstone carving. Some of his work was already in the museum in Kizil, the capital of Tuva. He was trying to set up his own carving school to pass on his art to the younger generation, but he said that they were not interested. 'Since perestroika, all people want to do is take a small piece of softstone and carve a simple animal and sell it for too much money. No one is interested in art any more, just making money. What I do takes too much time and no one has the patience.' He showed me some beautiful, intricate carvings in a pink and pale-yellow softstone. 'What's strange about this country, after perestroika, is that the Communists have just moved villages and taken positions elsewhere, or they have just turned their coats and said that they are now democrats. All the people are interested in doing now is making money.'

As we left his two-roomed house, two relations arrived to see him. They had come to shop in the town from the country. The first, in a thick golden coat, snaked in embroidery, a silver buckle clasping his waist, came on his red motorcycle. The other arrived on his horse, its dense coat damp and steaming with sweat after the ride. They came once a month to buy supplies that they needed and then returned to the tayga.

As we drove out of Teeli we came to another collection of yurta, owned by an old man, Chermek. He used to be a manager of a state farm, but has owned his own farm for the past three years. 'I have a whole wealth of experience which I can now use for myself,' he said with a chuckle. After standing outside in his cotton shirt in the intense cold, he eventually invited us in. Once more, we drank salted tea while he explained his theory as to why the yaks were dying. The winter had been particularly hard this year and there was a layer of ice between the snow and the earth, which meant that the yaks could not get at the grass. 'They are weak, thin and so they die,' he said. I had heard this theory in Teeli, but had dismissed it. 'Don't you think it's strange that all the state animals are dying and the private ones are not?' he asked. 'I've only lost two or three yaks, but everywhere around here they are dying. I'm not afraid of hunger because I can feed myself.'

He had six children, all of them daughters. They had all left the *yurta* to go and live in Kizil, but one of them returned a month ago and another two were planning to return in the next few weeks. 'Life is so bad in the town, the people are starving. A few years ago, all the young were leaving the countryside for the town, but now they're coming back,' he explained, pouring himself some more tea into a thin-lipped china bowl. He rents his farm from the state for a small amount of money. 'How much for?' I asked. 'I don't know,' he replied. 'I mean, what's the use of money? I have everything I want. I feed myself and that's all that matters.'

Chermek helped build the Buddhist temple in Teeli. He was not devoutly religious, but he firmly held on to the Buddhist traditions. 'The young must respect the old. That is the only way our society will remain civilized. The Soviets destroyed our culture but we are slowly getting it back.' He said his daughters were becoming more interested in religion. 'Those who think, think that Buddhism should come back; those who do not think that, don't think at all.'

The sun was setting as we drove back down the road to Khakassia. Kolya would not stay in Tuva. He was frightened that the people would steal parts from his new Niva car or that someone would siphon his petrol. We had carried enough with us to get us home. He also cited many cases of Russians being murdered and chopped up at the roadside. 'The Tuvinians are wild people. They hate the Russians and there are many stories of people driving here and not coming back.' He said that we had been lucky to find someone to show us the area. 'Normally, no one will speak to you unless you're with another Tuvinian.' Throughout the day, Peter and Kolya had been ignored. All questions and comments had been addressed to us.

We drove through the night, skidding along the narrow mountain tracks, arriving back in Abaza in the early hours. Kolya preferred the long drive through the snow than a night spent in Tuva. I found such fear difficult to comprehend, but then I'm not Russian.

Russia

· · · · · · · · · ·

DAY 76

We spent the morning as animals in a zoo. *Perestroika* had caught on with Kolya's two sons, who had invited all their friends over to view the foreigners. Charged a rouble a go, they queued up outside the flat to come and check us out. Sniggering and giggling, the small group of six- and seven-year-olds begged us to speak English and collapsed into fits of laughter when we obliged. The two boys had become instantly popular, having told all their friends at school that we were staying with them.

Kolya drove us to the airport in Abakan. On the four-hour journey through the mountains we passed numerous Khakassian graves, strange pieces of rock that stuck out of the snow at odd angles. They were interspersed with Christian crosses, marking the turning point in the history of the Khakassi when they rejected Shamanism and turned to Christianity.

Arriving at the small, provincial airport, Joth and I were nervous. We did not have a visa for Irkutsk or Abakan and after the numerous brushes with authority that we had had, we were wary of bureaucrats. The whole process went off smoothly, we managed to find some tickets and were ushered through to the deluxe departure lounge reserved for foreigners. We sat drinking our tea until our midnight flight.

The plane was minute and the cabin lacked any pressure. My ears screamed throughout the flight. We tried to move to the back of the plane to sleep, but a surly stewardess warned that our weight would make us fall out of the sky, so we returned to our seat over the engines.

We arrived in Irkutsk at four the following morning. It was − 20° as we walked off the plane. The cold enveloped us, biting our cheeks and noses, contracting our lungs so that we could hardly breathe. We drove through the town, eventually finding a hotel. Exhausted and disorientated, we spent the day either asleep or pondering our next move. We had arrived in Irkutsk, on the shores of Lake Baykal, without any friend or contact and little idea of what we would find here.

DAY 78

The day was a bureaucratic nightmare. We had decided to try and reach a small island, Olkhon Island, in the middle of Lake Baykal. Car, bus or train were simply not an option since the one road through the *tayga* was blocked with snow, and no trains ran north to the coast. The lake, which contains a fifth of the world's fresh water, was frozen ten metres thick, so no boat would be launched until well into the spring.

Finally, we met Sergei, a short Siberian with thick blond hair and sharp blue eyes, who spoke at speed, as if he were frightened of interruptions. He used to work for the Communist Party, but had left three years ago. 'I was one of the first of my friends to leave the Party,' he spluttered. 'Many people I know, who used to work for the Party, are now unemployed or doing jobs they're over-qualified for. The thing is, no one wants to employ an ex-Communist, and particularly someone who was a Party official like I was. But I got out early and re-trained myself – the others I know, they only have administration skills, which are useless now, really, in these commercial times. What you need now is business sense, and they just don't have it.'

Sergei had re-trained himself as a photographer and film maker. He now runs a company, very much in its early stages, filming the lake and photographing the landscape and selling the slides. He hopes eventually to produce a book about the lake. 'It's one of the most beautiful places on earth, the largest freshwater lake on this planet. It's full of rare and wonderful animals that live nowhere else in the world and no one really knows anything about it,' he said with a glint in his eyes. He obviously loved his lake with a passion and was obsessed with its nature and the environment that surrounded it. He arranged that we should fly to the island by army helicopter.

DAY 79

Sergei came to collect us early in the morning and drove us to the airfield, half an hour out of Irkutsk. Rows of Soviet army helicopters lay like fat beetles, stranded in the snow. The sky was dark grey and large flakes fell in intricate patterns, obscuring our view and putting our journey in jeopardy.

As the sky cleared we soared up into the air. We flew over the immense *tayga*, the pine forest stretching out as far as the eye could see. Small patches were bare, chopped down by the woodcutters. From the air, it was easy to see how they had torn into the forest, ripped it apart, robbed it of its riches and left it bare and naked. Some areas had been replanted, but they were few and far between.

We flew above damaged *yurta*, which were hibernating, waiting for their summer residents to spruce them up and settle in. Then, nestling on the banks of the lake, we spotted a small settlement. We taxied round, flying over a small, wooden house. Surrounded by red rock, it hugged the slope that descended gently towards the lake. Below, a large flock of sheep scattered in all directions, running from the noise of the helicopter, but the three cows and two horses tethered to the barn could not move. A new house was under construction next to the old one. As we landed, a large Byrat family came out to meet us. (The Byrat resemble the Tuvinians, with flat, Mongoloid features, and were the original inhabitants of Lake Baykal before the Russians conquered Siberia.)

The family of seven adults had been living in the house for the past four years. They worked on the *kolhoz* and all their animals belonged to the state, as did their house. They were nomadic in the sense that they worked where the state told them to go. They would stay on this particular farm until the grandmother, who had been given this patch of land, stopped work – then another family would be given the area to farm and these people would have to move on.

The two roomed-house was crammed with people and possessions. The state was in the process of building them another house. 'You see, there are too many of us in this house,' said the grandmother as she crouched by a low table, chopping onions. 'It should be ready by the summer, but in times like these, no one really knows.' The three sons lived in the house with their three wives. Platon's wife had just given birth to a baby, who lay fast asleep in his cot. 'It's impossible to find any nappies or baby food for him,' she said, looking over the cot. 'So I continue to breast feed him and he pisses in his tights. And he's only got two pairs of those because they're 40 roubles a pair.'

The other children were away at school: the bus collects them on Monday morning and they sleep with relations in the main town, returning home at weekends. There is only one bus a week, and the family have a three-hour walk to catch it. It is their only contact with the outside world. They speak a mixture of Byrat and Russian at home and are Buddhists, unlike some of the Byrat, who are Shamanists.

'Life is hard here at the moment,' said Sergei, one of the sons. 'We feed ourselves with what we produce, but things that we don't produce are extremely expensive and hard to come by. We have not had sugar for months and, of course, after these new price rises on 1 April, we won't be able to afford anything.'

As we left the grandmother shoved a jam jar full of cream and a plastic bag of curd cheese into my hands. 'It's bad enough here,' she said with a smile. 'But it's worse for you in the towns, you don't have anything.' Sergei siphoned off some petrol from the helicopter to power their chainsaw. They had not been able to use it for two months due to a shortage of petrol.

We set off over Lake Baykal, the ice unfolding for miles below us. Waves were frozen and ice had shifted into huge, square slabs which, pointing skywards, glistened in the sun. These massive natural ice sculptures extended for miles towards the island. We flew over the barren rocky island, where small forest-less hills gave way to empty valleys. One red mud track ran the length of the island like an artery, with a few narrow tributaries branching off to small villages.

Landing near a hamlet, we walked to a house that overlooked the frozen bay. The muddy courtyard was surrounded by a wooden fence. Inside the stone house I met Fenya. She was seventy-three and rather plump, with thinning, red-grey hair. She was sitting down to lunch with two postal workers who came to have lunch with her twice a week after they had finished their eight-kilometre post round. They were the only people she saw. She had six children, four of whom had died through illness and accident; the remaining two lived in the town and rarely came to see her. Her husband had died in the Second World War, so she lived entirely alone. The postman's visit was the highlight of her week and she was in good spirits.

Fenya was born and brought up on the island and had lived there all her life. 'All the young people have left the island,' she said as she tucked into her boiled fish and potatoes. 'But I think that they'll all start to return because the situation is so bad in the towns.' She lives on a pension of 500 roubles a month. A fisherman all her life, she continues to supplement her income out on the ice. As we sat around the table in her one-roomed house, the postmistress handed out an extra 300 roubles, a form of compensation for the January price rises. 'Whether they'll do the same after the rises on 1 April is anyone's guess,' said the overweight postmistress. Fenya had never seen the crisp, 100-rouble notes before and held them up to the light. She did not believe that they were real money.

They all carried on eating their fish and potatoes, along with a potent garlic and onion dip. Fenya did not stop for about half an hour: no sooner had she finished one mouthful than she grabbed some more. 'I'm old and haven't got much longer to live, so I'll eat as much as I want,' she laughed, displaying the contents of her mouth. 'Although at the moment, that's quite hard to do.'

This comment brought about an argument concerning Yeltsin and Gorbachev. 'Gorbachev is useless,' muttered Fenya, between mouthfuls. 'We lived much better under Brezhnev. If I did not have my four cows and pigs, then I wouldn't be able to feed myself. And when my children come to visit me, they also expect me to feed them.' The postmistress was more pro-Gorbachev. 'Neither you nor I have met foreigners before,' she said. 'And now we are eating with some. That is due to Gorbachev.'

The spotty boy who drove the post van, kept silent and, after bolting his food, left the table to go and sit in the van. I think Fenya had been at the home-made vodka that morning because when she finally got round to offering us some tea, she made a protracted song and dance about the whole process. Rocking backwards and forwards, she stocked up the stove and removed some rings which regulated the heat and rattled around unco-ordinatedly in a cupboard, searching for a mug. Eventually, she poured me out an uncomfortably large cup and ostentatiously poured in the milk. 'From my own cow,' she smiled. 'There's no sugar of course – haven't had any for months. I've forgotten what it tastes like.'

As we left, she pointed out a large barrel of potatoes tipped over on its side in the yard. They had kept her alive through most of the winter. She would have to wait until next season before she would have any more. She escorted us to the edge of her garden, dressed in her grey, woollen shawl, brown dress and ginger stockings. She hobbled as she walked. 'Go with God,' she smiled, opening her toothless mouth.

On the way back to the helicopter, I met Galya, a Byrat on the way to the capital of the island. Dressed in her long fur coat and fur boots she was making the two-hour walk to buy some food and then she would walk home again. 'I make the journey every day,' she said, as we linked arms, 'either to work or shop.' She had three small children all below the age of four and had just moved to the village away from the town. 'It's much better for our children,' she said. But there was no school on the island, so she envisaged problems when her children were older.

Back in the helicopter, Sergei handed us a plateful of cold spaghetti that he had brought in a thermos. It landed in a lump on the plate. At the bottom of the thermos, strips of corned beef floated around in a thin jelly. 'Humanitarian aid,' he said, as he chopped up some thick, white fat and placed it on pieces of bread. We washed it all down with cold, strong tea that I could feel stain my teeth.

While we ate, I spoke to the pilot, Andrei. He had studied flying at a school in Kiev – the state had paid for his lessons, giving him free tuition for three years. He had flown in the army but was now making a fortune, working for anyone who would pay him. As we flew away, he enjoyed showing off, circling around above the rows of fishermen lying on their stomachs on the ice, and swooping down in the path of cars as they drove across the ice towards the island.

We landed on the ice in a bay, at the shore of the capital of the island, Khazhir. Children were skating on the ice, which was so thick that heavily laden lorries did not disturb them as they drove by. They ran away from the helicopter as we landed, screaming and tumbling over each other in their skates. Standing on the ice, it was so clear that I could see straight through to the blue water below. The children had set up their own obstacle courses and ice-hockey pitch. An ice-bound ship in the bay was covered in cascading icicles that poured overboard, spewing over the edge of the deck and dripping onto the ice, as if one large wave had hit the boat moments before the big freeze. The rocks around the bay were also decorated with huge crystals, like fat diamonds, shining in the sun.

We flew back over the ice as we had done before. I was enchanted by it and desperately wanted to leap out and touch it, feeling the cold, smooth surface of the vertical slabs. It was not of this world. We crossed back over the *tayga*, small rivers curling their way to the lake like locks of wayward hair. This was a truly magical place.

DAY 80

It was still dark and the temperature was $-20°$ when Sergei came to collect us, bringing with him a young girl, Marina, who was nineteen with a long plait down to her bottom. She was studying English and German at the university and had asked to come along because she had never met foreigners and was desperate to practise her English. Her family lived in the Ukraine, but she had moved to Irkutsk because she could not get into Kiev University. It was easier to get a place at Irkutsk and, as her grandmother lived in the city, she was entitled to go there. She had a grant of 300 roubles a month, which she could not afford to live on. 'How do you survive?' I asked. 'My grandmother helps,' she replied. She, like everyone I had spoken to there, was terrified about the new price rises on 1 April. 'People are storing at the moment. There is nothing to buy because everyone is buying in bulk and hoarding,' she explained.

On our way out of town, Sergei pulled in and joined the petrol queue. He calmly said that we were in for a long wait as there had not been a drop of petrol anywhere in the city for the last three days. 'We're very lucky to have found this place,' he muttered, as he lay back in the car, making himself comfortable. We sat in the queue for an hour, crawling slowly forward as car after car filled up and the owners brought out any container that they could lay their hands on. Glass jars that were usually reserved for tomatoes were being filled to the brim with petrol. 'Rumour has it that the price will go up twenty times on the first,' said Sergei. 'I already have litres stored at home, but I can't buy any more because I have nowhere else to put it.'

Eventually we set off to the south of Baykal, driving off into the forest. We drove into a small village which is cut off from the outside world all of the summer months, its only connection being a frozen river. We were one of the last cars to cross this winter – the ice was already beginning to crack up and the river was covered in slush.

There was a queue outside the bread shop in the main square. Women in thick coats were stamping their feet in the snow. Beside them, sledges with empty bags or boxes lay, waiting to transport their goods home. Bread shop number 31 was about to open. The general store next door was already selling its pickled cucumbers in cloudy jars; its rusty tubes of tomato paste and its few plastic bags of broken biscuits. Opposite, was a low, flat building littered with hammers and sickles and a few slogans calling the workers to battle on. It was the main union for the woodcutters in the area. One woman, bursting out of the bread shop, her arms crammed full of loaves, announced that the shop was ready for business. She threw the eighteen loaves onto the sledge. 'They're for the hospital,' she explained and walked off into the distance, pulling her load behind her. Others joined the queue. One woman, with a hairy mole on the side of her face, had her daughter's ration book with her as well as her own. 'She can't queue for bread so I do it for her,' she said. Others were buying in bulk before the prices rose. One old woman was buying three loaves: two to eat now and the third to dry and toast so that it could be eaten later.

'How are you living at the moment?' I asked. 'Off our land,' said the woman with the mole. 'We grow all we want. It's only bread and sugar that we buy. If we did not have our gardens then we would starve, but as it is, we live better than those in the towns – they all want to come back here.' This brought about a murmur of agreement from the crowd. 'All the old Party members are buying dachas here, and settling down on their pensions, hoping that people will forget who they are,' she continued. 'Why don't they just go away, the bastards,' said someone in the crowd.

They all pushed into the shop as the door opened, frightened of losing their place in the queue. There was no love lost between them. One woman, losing her balance, fell into the snow. Swearing loudly, she was forced to the back.

We continued further into the *tayga*, coming to a hamlet where half the houses were empty, their wooden structures decaying, their windows broken and their roofs falling in. We went up to a house at the end of the street. Its neat structure was in a good state of repair, its white windows newly painted. Sergei set up lunch in the driveway. Bringing out a table and deck chairs, he began to serve up the bread and fat. As we sat in the sun, he said, 'This is a small village. The man who owns this house will soon be back when he sees us here – he'll run home for fear that we plan to rob him.' The man never came, much to Sergei's surprise. 'He can't be here,' was the explanation.

Returning to the centre of the village, we knocked on the door of the house nearest the well and opposite the remains of a bakery. An old man in a grey cap came to the gate. His little wooden house was somewhat decrepit. His greying dog barked loudly at our arrival, but soon became bored. The old man blocked the way into his house and would only talk to us over the garden gate, which swung loose on its hinges. His name was Joseph and, at the age of seventy-seven, he had lived in the village for the past twenty-five years. He was Czech and had made his way into Russia through the Gulag, or prison camp system. Arrested near the Polish border in 1942, he had spent the war in a prison camp in the far north of Siberia. 'There weren't that many foreigners: just me and a few Poles,' he muttered. 'But I had been a woodcutter all my life, so that's what they made me do there. I became quite a master and ended up teaching all the young lads who came in, showing them where and when to cut down the trees.'

Joseph had not spoken Russian until he was in the Gulag and his accent was thick and hard to understand. He said that he was arrested for being in the wrong place at the wrong time and for being the wrong nationality. He has a Soviet passport but no citizenship, which means that he cannot leave the village, although he does receive a pension. 'After all, I chopped wood for this country for the past thirty-five years or more,' he said, his eyes narrowing. He lives separated from his wife, Ana, who also lives in the village. I met her quite by chance as I was leaving. A chatty woman with no teeth and a scarf tightly wrapped around her head, she had tattoos on both her wrists, which were to identify her body if she had been shot during the war. 'All the nurses had them,' she said with a loud squeal. She worked in the military hospitals during the war, along the border with the Ukraine and Poland. It was there that she met Joseph. 'He was such a fool. He said, let's move further towards the border because the wood is better there. He went out one day and never came back. I eventually found him in north Siberia.'

They were married for thirty-five years and have been separated for three. Quite why, she would not tell me, other than he was impossible to live with. They had three children, all of whom lived in Irkutsk. 'All the young have left the village,' she said. 'There was a large exodus of Lithuanians about fourteen years ago – I think they all went on to Germany. There are only forty families here now, with about eight children, five of whom are of school age,' she explained, while she leant on her stick in the snow. A car comes to collect them at 8.30 every morning to take them the twenty kilometres to the nearest school, bringing them back in the evening. 'There are few young people in the village. Why?' she shouted. 'Because they are afraid of hard work, of getting their hands dirty. Who is going to feed them? Not me, that's all I know. They expect us to work and feed them – no wonder there's nothing to eat in the towns.'

There were some people returning to the village, she said. A small house at the end of the road was being done up, but those who were coming to the villages were unpopular. They brought in nothing and wanted to make the house into a dacha, so taking property but doing nothing at all for the community. 'If they want to come to the village, please do. But come to live here, not to have a rest,' she said.

The shop in the village sold very little except poor-quality goods left over from the town. The bread was no longer made here but brought in from the town, as was all the fat – the only other thing on offer.

That evening we returned to Irkutsk, crossing the melting river once more, crashing around over the ice and slush. On the way back, we dropped in on a taxi company where a friend of Sergei's worked. Yuri used to be in the Party with Sergei. He used to be head of the Transport Division for Central Irkutsk, making sure that the trams worked properly and that if anyone was late for work, they had a reason. But he had unfortunately only left the Party in the summer after the putsch, after it was disbanded. He is also a people's deputy, a job for which he does not get paid, sorting out the housing or financial problems of anyone who needs his advice. He is currently in charge of personnel at the taxi company, but has not been able to find another full-time job since leaving the Party.

'I'm not qualified for anything and people do not want to employ ex-party members,' he said. He has many friends, particularly the older ex-Party members, who have been unable to find work and have taken early retirement. He described working for the Party as a complete waste of time. 'You could work until about 8.30 p.m. Your work would be finished at six, but it was like a competition to see who could put in the longest hours to impress the boss. We used to come in on Saturday as well. A complete waste of time – we never did anything. We just had to be there if one form or another needed stamping.' I got the impression that he was slightly in awe or jealous of Sergei, who had managed to get out before him. He was a tired man who was struggling with a system that was unfamiliar to him.

'What I find funny,' he said with a jaded snigger, 'is that the Communists are still in power, but now they call themselves democrats. I don't know whether it's because nothing has changed or because they are the only ones who know the system and the young, real democrats haven't been given the chance or have not risen through the ranks yet.'

I left Yuri's brown office and watched him put on his brown coat and brown hat. We went downstairs to book a taxi to take us to the airport. He insisted that if he booked it, it would definitely come at 4 a.m. Eventually Sergei dropped him off at the government building. 'I want to pop in and see some old friends,' he said.

Yevreyskaya Oblast

DAY 82

After flying to Khabarovsk, on the border with northeast China, in the early hours, and spending the night there in a ridiculously expensive hotel, we left in the morning for Birobidzhan, the capital of the Jewish State, Yevreyskaya Oblast. We managed to persuade a young adventurer called Constantin to drive us across the Amur river.

The track carved across the ice had been officially closed a month ago, but the lack of any other link between Khabarovsk and Birobidzhan meant that we had no option. Since Vladivostok was a closed town, all air traffic passes through Khabarovsk: it is the main crossroads in the Siberian far east. I found it extraordinary that no one had built a bridge across the Amur. During the autumn and spring, when the ice is not thick enough to drive on and the ferry cannot sail on the semi-frozen river, it is impossible to drive to Birobidzhan.

Fortunately it had been cold for the last couple of days and a fresh fall of snow had frozen hard on the ice. We drove at speed across the wide river, cheering when we reached the other side safely.

As we drove the three hours along the Chinese border towards the Jewish State, Constantin explained that he had been born in Moscow but that, around seven years ago, he had gone to live in the far northeast of Siberia, next to Alaska and the Bering Straits. 'Why on earth did you go there?' I asked, amazed.

'We have the largest country in the world and probably the most beautiful and I wanted to see it. The pioneers forged from west to east and I wanted to do the same, to go to places that people would never normally go,' he replied, laughing. Constantin had thick black hair and wild blue eyes and drove like a man possessed. He had lived with Eskimos for five years as a fisherman and miner. 'There's only gold and fish up there,' he said. He loved the Eskimos. 'It's great. Whenever you go to dinner, they make you stay and give you a woman for the night. They make love in a different way from white people, you know, it's very exciting.' He laughed.

Birobidzhan was smaller than I expected. It had one main street and one square, yet there was an atmosphere in the town that made it appear more alive than most other Russian cities we had been to. We went straight to the synagogue. I was shocked to find a small, wooden building that looked like a country dacha, surrounded by high flats. It was maintained by a ginger-haired dwarf with short, gnarled hands and a long red beard. Boris was Jewish but was a practising Sabbath Christian. 'We are like Christians, except that we come together on Saturday and not Sunday,' he explained. It was Friday afternoon and he said that some Jews would come and worship later, when the sun went down. 'There's always one woman who comes. She's very dedicated,' he said with a smile.

The official statistics state that only five per cent of the population of the Jewish State are, in fact, Jewish, but it seemed untrue, because as we wandered through the town, a large proportion of the citizens looked Jewish. We came across a door with a plaque written in both Hebrew and Russian, and walked in. Sitting behind a desk was Semen Hondrash, a large man with a mass of uncontrolled, greying hair, large dark eyes and a big smile. He was chairman of a computer software company, employing programmers and distributing programmes. It was a private firm set up two years ago when Semen left the Party.

'Why do so many people in this town look Jewish?' I asked. 'Because they are,' he replied, pouring me out some tea. 'But people lie on their passports, so the statistics are wrong. People of mixed race, with, for example, a Jewish mother and a Russian father, will say on their passports that they're Russian – it makes life easier. But having said that, people are doing that less because they're now proud to be Jewish and it's less of a problem than it was a few years ago.' He estimated that about thirty per cent of the population is Jewish, although it may be less now, because so many have left for Israel.

Semen had set up the company with a friend, Vladimir Goldberg, in an attempt to stop talented Jews emigrating. 'The only reason why so many people were leaving here for Israel is that there was nothing here for them. We decided that if we could show people that things could be done here, then fewer people would leave and we could make a go of it.'

The company is doing well. 'All our employees are Jewish,' he said. 'But that's not through discrimination: they're just the best people for the job.'

He introduced us to Alec, a programmer. His parents had left for Israel two years ago and his brother, a doctor, left last month, leaving his wife behind. 'My brother is working for free at the moment: he is on a three-month trial to see if he can get a permanent job out there. He keeps asking me why his wife does not contact him in Israel and I don't know what to say to him – the situation is very difficult.'

'My son is desperate for us to move out there,' said Semen. 'But I wouldn't fit in there. I'm Jewish, but we have none of that culture here. I can't speak Yiddish or Hebrew. This is my home and I must make it so.'

The Jewish State was set up in 1934, he explained. It was settled with returning Jews from the US, Argentina and other countries that the Jews had fled to after the Revolution. 'Many young and naïve people came to build this state. There was a big decision to be made in the early 1930s. Do we go to Palestine or Birobidzhan? They chose this shitty, swampy place because there were few people living here and they thought they could minimize the anti-Semitic backlash. In 1937, after only three years of tranquillity, the whole thing fell apart. The rest of the world forgot about us when the purges began. Jews were killed right up until Stalin's death,' said Semen, while he fiddled with a pencil, deep in thought.

'I don't want a Jewish republic set up,' he said. 'There's no need for that, although if we did have a republic, it would mean that we did not have to go through Moscow for everything and a transition to a free-market zone would be easier.' Most of the trade in the state is between Japan, South Korea and China. 'We are Eastern-looking. We don't need Moscow.' There is a movement to make the Jewish State into a free economic zone, although Semen does not expect that to happen for another couple of years.

We returned to the synagogue for the Sabbath service. Inside, a middle-aged woman, a young girl and the ginger-haired dwarf sat around a wooden table covered in candles. The middle-aged woman led the service, reading aloud in Hebrew, while Boris phonetically transcribed a Hebrew text for the young girl to read aloud. We joined in, eating the bread and wine. After passing around the cup, everyone decided that the wine was rather delicious, so we tucked in and finished the bottle.

After the service, the young girl took us to the youth service in the town hall in the main square. There were about forty young people gathered in one small room, surrounded by Israeli flags, maps of Israel and the Star of David. They were discussing their faith and traditions and what it meant to be Jewish. At the end of the meeting, they talked about an exchange programme that they were trying to set up with young people in Israel. Hebrew is only taught at night school in the town and they were hoping that, if the exchange programme worked, they would be taught the Jewish traditions as well as the language.

DAY 83

I went to meet Michail Weinman, who runs the Israeli-Jewish society at the town hall in the same room where I had been the night before. He was reading a copy of *Birobidzhan Stern*, the local newspaper written in both Russian and Yiddish. Only about five people in the state speak Hebrew – most of the old people speak Yiddish – although ten youngsters have learnt it for the local television station.

Michail sorts out the applications for those wanting to go to Israel and helps people keep in touch with their relatives once they are there. There is no direct telephone line between Israel and Birobidzhan: all calls must go through Moscow. 'Most of the people left two years ago. The exodus is diminishing,' he said. 'When they come into my office and say they want to leave, I point to the centre of the map of Israel, and say, "Look at this desert. If you're prepared to forge your own life out there in the dust like the Israelis did then, go. If not then, stay." '

Some 12,500 Jews have already left Birobidzhan in the last two years, although there were only forty-five applications in January, and twenty-five Jews returned last month. 'It's very hard to move from a Communist country and arrive in a capitalist and democratic one. They find it hard to work for themselves. It's also hard to find work and houses. Those who want to be real Jews have already left for Israel,' he explained.

He said that many of the traditions have been lost. 'We don't know what it means to be Jewish here.' Michail's grandmother died at the age of 104, so many of the traditions were passed on to him through her. Others have not been so fortunate. Two months ago, a group of twenty Israelis came to Birobidzhan to try to teach some of the customs and ceremonies. Just before we arrived, there was the Purim festival. 'Half the people did not know what to do,' said Michail. 'It's so embarrassing when people down the sacrament in one and ask for a refill.' He looked forward to a time when all the customs would be known and respected by everyone. 'After generations of repression, when no one could worship and to be Jewish was almost a crime, when people denied their roots and traditions, it is amazing that the young want to know how to be Jewish. There is a large number of them asking about their culture, wanting to learn the language and many are becoming religious.'

The lack of a substantial synagogue in the town is a problem, but they had no money and no finance was forthcoming from Israel. There is also no rabbi in the state. They have, however, sent two boys off to Moscow for two years to study. They will then spend a short time in Israel. Michail expects there to be a rabbi in the state within two years.

That morning a government minister arrived from Moscow. He was touring the state to try to establish the specific needs of the people, in order to help rebuild their lost culture. 'I'm Jewish but I don't want a Jewish republic,' said Michail. 'It would be a stupid political decision. Look what's happened to Moldavia and Nagorno-Karabakh – there's war there. We don't want any of that here. The most important thing is that we remain Jewish and conduct ourselves as Jews.'

There is little anti-Semitism in Birobidzhan. 'Of course, there are people who shout words like Jew at you,' he said. 'But then, is that an insult?' Michail perceived the returning Jews from Israel as an ideal opportunity for those who had not gone to learn more about the homeland and the language.

Above the Jewish Society on the second floor of the town hall was a circus school. A group of about fifteen children between the ages of twelve and seventeen were being taught how to tumble, juggle, tightrope walk and fly on the trapeze. The school was run by Volva and Sasha, both former acrobats. For 20 roubles a month the children came to train almost every evening. The school had been going for the last twenty years and could boast of having trained at least one performer for the famous Moscow State Circus, but most of the others had gone on to smaller circuses in Samerkand, Khabarovsk and Comsomol, the largest nearby town.

Volva, an old man dressed in a well-worn tracksuit, had built all the equipment himself. He had also decorated the room to look like the Big Top. Clowns and jugglers were painted all over the walls, giant multicoloured balloons flew towards the ceiling and rearing unicorns and elephants greeted you at the door. The room was awash with reds and golds. The tightrope was strung up in one corner, the trapeze hung in the middle of the room: a long rope dangled to the floor and various unicycles and juggling clubs lay in heaps.

First, the children warmed up, running around the room, hopping and twisting in the air. Then followed the stretching exercises. Little girls in vests and pants did split after split, dividing their bodies in half. They then tumbled. One after the other, they threw themselves in the air, turning somersaults and flick-flacks. Lena, in red knickers, was wonderfully supple and highly competent. After the tumbling, they all moved on to their own particular speciality or piece of apparatus. Lena curled herself around a ring hanging from the ceiling. Natasha, who was slightly older, worked on the trapeze. A rather gawky girl in too much make-up who was obviously in love with twenty-two-year-old Sasha, stood lamely juggling in the corner and occasionally mounted one of the unicycles. When Sasha tumbled down the centre of the room, she stopped to watch and ran over to tuck his vest back into his tracksuit bottoms at the end of the routine. He enjoyed the attention.

Most of the children started when they were about six or seven. 'When do they leave the school?' I asked Sasha. 'When they're good enough to get a place in the circus,' he replied. 'Otherwise, they could go on for ever.' All the children desperately wanted to work in the circus and their faces lit up at the suggestion. 'I dream of going to Moscow,' said Lena, sitting cross-legged on the floor, her hair falling out of her pony tail. 'Not all of us want to work in the circus,' said the gawky girl. 'Some of us just come here to keep fit.' The others looked at her with a puzzled expression on their dedicated faces. Most of the girls had been at the school for seven years. The two boys were less talkative. They concentrated on their routine on the tightrope, juggling balls and jumping up in the air. Auditions would start soon for the summer season. They were preparing for Khabarovsk or Comsomol. 'You can make money in the circus,' said Sasha. 'But not that much. It's all about art, not profit.'

We spent the evening in the restaurant of the small hotel. It was obviously the nightspot in town and was packed out with drunk people. Girls in gaudy clothes and garish make-up strutted around in pairs. Dancing together, they protected themselves from the hoards of Azerbaijanis and Armenians, who were in Biro-bidzhan on business and looking for a good time. The band knew three songs, which they played loudly and in the same order, but no one seemed to notice. Everyone sang along, checking each other out. Swarms of prostitutes circled the dance floor, taking up provocative stances in the shadows. Two rather drunk students were home for the weekend and were out, trying to supplement their grants. 'We do this every weekend,' admitted one of the girls. 'They give us a couple of hundred roubles for sex and it keeps us alive for the week. How d'you think I could afford to buy these boots?'

I sat down to watch the dance floor and was soon lost in a world of my own. Someone threw a bottle at my face. It just missed and smashed at my feet. I was completely taken aback and presumed that it was an accident, until another flew towards me, hitting my shoulder and smashing behind me. I looked up to see a large, drunk man with sweat pouring off his face. 'Get out of my chair, whore,' he shouted, losing his balance as he reached for another bottle. It was time to leave.

Russia

· · · · · · · · · ·

DAY 84

We managed to persuade an even more daring taxi driver to take us back across the Amur river to Khabarovsk. The snow had more or less melted during the warm couple of days that we had spent in Birobidzhan, but we managed to persuade a man in a blue car, with flowers moulded into the top of his gear stick, to make the journey. He loudly barged to the front of the petrol queue, shouting that he had foreigners in the car and he was about to make a very important journey. The queue gave way.

As we approached the semi-frozen river, the cars in the opposite direction were few and far between and our fear began to mount. There was a truck to the left of us and he and our driver began to play a sort of chicken, both advancing forward slowly in the hope that the other would go first. The truck driver suddenly went for it. Slamming his foot on the accelerator, he lurched forward, smashing onto the ice. He sped off in front of us, bouncing on the cracking ice and splashing water and slush in his wake. Still on the bank, we watched to see if he would go through. When he was halfway across, our driver put his foot down. I was holding my passport and note books and had crammed my pockets with money. Joth and I had formulated a plan: if we went through, we would throw ourselves out of the window and lie flat on our stomachs on the ice, saving what we could and hoping for the best.

We bounced onto the ice. I could hear it cracking around me and moaning under our weight. My hand, white with tension, gripped the door handle. I did not know whether to open or close my eyes, but elected to keep them open, thinking that my imagination was probably worse than the reality. The slush on the ice fanned high in the air as we careered on. We reached an island in the middle of the river — a moment's respite when the blood rushed back to my knuckles — but back onto the ice we went. Bounding from side to side on the uneven surface and swerving to avoid the puddles, we eventually made it to the other side.

A relieved silence swept the car. Then in as matter-of-fact a voice as I could muster, I said: 'Have you ever gone through?' He replied nonchalantly, 'I've lost two cars in my life. But we Russians are fatalists: if we're meant to cross, then we cross. If we aren't, then we go through.'

He dropped us off at the bus station where we met Alyosha. He was twenty-four and told us he was on a 'pension'. 'I left the army three years ago without a kopeck to my name and now I own half a Mercedes,' he said with a laugh, slapping the dashboard of his Lada. Alyosha dealt in second-hand cars from Japan – Toyotas, Hondas – and occasionally the odd BMW or Mercedes. They are brought in to Russia through Vladivostok and driven to Khabarovsk. Here, the rouble millionaires who trade with Japan and China, and the mafia with dealings in the Southern States, buy them from Alyosha, while he takes a cut.

As we drove to the hotel, we passed the dull façade of the new, and only, sex shop in eastern Siberia. 'There was a riot there last week,' he said, sniggering. 'The shipment of French vibrators ran out too quickly and all the frustrated women who had been queuing outside got out of control and started hitting each other. All very funny.' With this extraordinary anecdote, he dropped us off at the hotel. We sat down to supper surrounded by prostitutes. In their short skirts and painted faces, they circled the room, looking for a lonely businessman.

DAY 85

We caught the early morning flight to Sakhalin, an island just north of Japan, where Chekhov sat in prison; where thousands of Koreans worked as slaves for the Japanese and where Fyodorov, tired of Moscow's dallying, had gone to set up a free economic zone. We arrived in South Sakhalin, the capital of the island, and drove to the centre. We passed rows of decaying apartment blocks, crumbling dull shops and grey streets. The only difference between here and the rest of the country was the number of Japanese cars on the roads.

We went to see Fyodorov, only to find that he was talking with Yeltsin in Moscow. Instead I spoke to Yuri Mishuta, Vice-Governor of the Sakhalin region.

Sakhalin he said, was on the verge of economic prosperity. Large American companies were awaiting oil contracts; Shell, Exxon and Mobil were all taking an interest in Sakhalin's huge oil reserves. They have a good barter trade going with South Korea, Japan and China, exchanging fish, the island's main export, for butter. They have new tax incentives for private companies, which number around 600 already. This extra money will help them buy the new technology that is becoming increasingly expensive. There are three foreign-investment joint ventures already on the island: two American and one Japanese. 'Of course, these countries are closer to us than Europe, which is why they're in here first,' said Yuri. 'I just hope that the foreign investment will continue.

'We hope that we'll be able to rebuild or repair some of the buildings on the island,' he said. 'It was all built so quickly under Stalin that most of the houses are falling down. But there is a desperate shortage of building materials, so no work can get under way just yet.'

Moscow's influence is not welcome on the island. 'We desperately need a stable rouble in order to do business and Moscow keeps playing around,' he said as he sat behind his wooden desk in a peachy room with peeling paint. Sakhalin is only allowed to keep thirty per cent of what it produces: the remainder has to be sold to Russia. 'At the moment, Russia takes and gives us nothing in return. We haven't had any milk here for months,' he said, running his hands through his lank grey hair. The island tries to ignore Moscow. 'We had no reaction to the putsch, all we want is for them to stop hyper-inflation and to stabilize the economic mechanism. We aren't dying of hunger, but things are very hard here.'

The South Korean community, left behind after the Second World War, has proved to be a huge asset to the island. There is little nationalism, there are Koreans in the government, and their ties with South Korea and Japan are proving to be highly profitable. 'Many of them are doing much better than the Russians,' said Yuri with a smile. But he explained that the infrastructure of the island, which prevented many of the South Koreans in the villages from moving to the town, is beginning to cause problems, although as yet there have been no national problems. 'Touch wood,' he laughed, slapping the top of his desk.

Walking through the streets in the driving snow, it was easy to see the difference between the South Koreans and the Russians. The Koreans drove flashy cars; played loud, Western music on their stereos, and parked where they liked. The Russians, on the other hand, were frantically queuing for soft cucumbers outside a large lorry parked on the side of the road. They were served by Koreans. The market, usually the centre of activity in every town, was deserted except for an industrious row of old Korean women selling the pickled contents of their allotments to Russians who had not quite got round to doing it. A few Russians had set up stalls selling rusty tins of condensed milk and pairs of nylon tights.

'The Japanese used us and left us behind,' said Olya, a seventy-two-year-old Korean woman selling shredded pickled carrot in the market. She came over to Sakhalin with the Japanese before the Second World War. 'The Russians don't work,' she said, as she put her red, chaffed hands under her shawl for warmth. 'They are a lazy people. They used to hate our industriousness, but if it weren't for us, then there would be no food in the market, so now they appreciate us.'

She went on to talk about her children. They could not speak her language, they could only talk Russian. 'They don't know our customs or our culture; they could probably never go back home – they would never fit in,' she muttered, leaning over to sell a small bag of carrots to a large woman in a thin coat. All the Korean schools on the island were closed in 1961, so a whole generation of young Koreans has become completely divorced from its roots. However, two years ago, a group of Koreans came over to the island and started up a small school that teaches language and culture. 'So things are finally getting better. We will be able to teach our children what they should have known all their lives,' she said. Many of the Koreans, she said, wanted to return home. Some had made the trip to see relatives, while others were too frightened to see what they were missing, knowing that they could not stay.

Her neighbour joined the conversation. 'Do you know how the Russians are trying to control us?' she asked, poking her head out from under her shawl. 'Through starvation. Rice, which is our main source of food, is rationed, whereas bread, their staple diet, is not. We have a small bowl for the whole family, which just isn't enough. This whole place is a disaster.'

We spent the evening with two Americans who had been on the island waiting for an oil contract to come through. The contract was due to be signed in October of last year but, because of Moscow's meddling, they had been living in the hotel for over six months. They were among the first foreigners we had met. They gave us oranges and whisky, which were like manna from heaven. They had their own office set up in the hotel, with regular supplies sent over from the US. 'What do you think is going to happen here?' I asked one of them. 'We don't talk politics in this room,' he replied, pointing to a rather gaudy lamp that hung in the centre of the room. 'You're joking!' I said. 'Absolutely not,' he replied. 'We keep having engineers come into the room to mend faults that don't exist.'

DAY 86

We flew to Vladivostok and took a taxi to Nakhodka. We drove for miles along the coast, twisting up and down hills and coves, passing through one hideous, purpose-built town after another. The streets were crowded with the long black coats of the marines. We eventually arrived in Nakhodka, grabbing some greasy food in a small cooperative café at the bus station before travelling on to Vostochny Port. We crossed a wide bridge spanning a frozen river that was littered with fishermen lying on their bellies on the ice. 'The fish are delicious,' said the taxi driver. 'They taste just like lemons.' He had come to Nakhodka as a pioneer or explorer, leaving Moscow behind. 'Our country is so large and I wanted to see it before I died,' he said. He drove us to a monstrous collection of turquoise, prefabricated flats. Each block was about nine stories high and stood like giant wafer biscuits, facing the beautiful bay. Seeing the shock on my face as we hauled ourselves out of the car, the taxi driver squeezed my hand. 'Don't worry. They're probably better inside,' he said. He drove off, leaving Joth and I surrounded by our luggage and row upon row of these grim faceless flats, wondering exactly how to find Galya, whose address we had been given by Kolya in Abaza.

We were soon surrounded by children. They had been playing in the mud when we arrived and they all gathered around, begging cigarettes. I walked up to two women who were gossiping on a bench.

'Do you know where flat fifty-seven is?' I asked.

'We know,' replied one woman, turning her shoulder towards me.

'Will you tell me?' I asked, irritated and tired.

'Who wants to know?' she said.

'I do,' I said, putting my hands aggressively on my hips.

'Who are you then?' she asked, standing up from the bench.

The mood of apathetic disinterest changed suddenly into a panicked frenzy of friendliness as soon as I explained. We were ushered up to her flat and made to sit on the bed; her son was told to turn off the television and made to run to the kindergarten to find Galya. 'She can't have got the telegram,' said the woman, tucking her dyed, blond hair behind her ears. 'I would know, you see, if she was expecting guests. She would have told me. We all know everything here.'

I was offered tea, and, after a dramatic pause, 'coffee.' We leapt at the chance for some coffee, something we had not drunk for a long time. It was rationed out in small teaspoons. We half closed our eyes in pleasure as we drank.

After a short while, full of long gauche silences, Galya burst through the door. A large woman with heavy thighs and long, dark hair, she was puce in the face from running. She apologized profusely, saying that no one had told her that we were coming. She directed us up the damp stairs, feeling her way in the dark, and showed us into the flat. It was small, dark and damp and looked out onto the building sight. Down below, a lone cow wandered among the rubbish.

Galya had a dog and a cat that she loved with the passion of a woman who had no children. She taught at the kindergarten down the road, which was built and maintained, like the whole quarter of the town that we were in, for the workers at the port. The port workers paid 200 roubles a month for the school, whereas other workers in other parts of town had to pay 2,000 roubles a month. 'Prices are becoming a huge problem,' said Galya, as she tickled her cat's stomach. 'What it means is that many children are now not going to school because their parents cannot afford it. This whole town is falling apart. The ration system can't work. It's all very well to say to some one, you can have a kilo of sausage a month, but what happens if you can't afford one? It's terrible. The children here are having the worst time of course. They are either fat, because their mothers feed them badly, or they are so thin because they don't get enough food. Every one has bad teeth – you can't buy brushes or toothpaste. The other day, a friend of my husband brought a lemon back from Japan. I took it into school and none of the children knew what it was. Imagine children who have never seen a lemon before. I am so tired of *perestroika*. We all are. No one knows what's happening or what will happen. Sometimes that can be exciting, but then it becomes exhausting.'

Galya had nothing in her larder, which she found extremely embarrassing. 'If only I had known that you were coming, I could have made an effort. As it is, I have nothing to give,' she kept on saying as she searched among her empty shelves.

We had to wait until after eight before we could wash. Just as in Turkmenia, the water was rationed, not because of a water shortage but because there was not enough fuel to power the plant. Her husband, Andrei, came home. A stocky man, he was unattractive and rather aggressive. He offered to take us for a drive in his new Japanese car. A docker for six years, he left to join the police force. Like Alyosha, he was a middle-man in Japanese car deals. 'I hang around the port and deal with the men who organize the shipments. Each mafia group controls one shipment. I organize buyers to come to the port to collect the cars,' he said as he jangled the car keys.

We drove up the hill to a small watchtower on the edge of the bay. The sun was setting on the calm sea; the lights in the port reflected in the water. From the top of the hill I could see the fringes of the immense forest that surrounded the town. It highlighted the ugliness. 'A Siberian tiger strayed in from the forest last year,' said Galya as she looked out to sea. 'It ran madly through the housing estate and was eventually chased out of town.'

We drove to another part of the town, built by the steel factory. Each major employer in the town was responsible for housing and providing services for its workers. We passed a prison on the way. It used to be a top security prison but has since become a juvenile detention centre. 'The whole town protested about the prison,' said Galya. 'But no one listened, of course.'

All along the side of the road in these built-up areas, children were playing in the earth. They had lit camp fires and stood around in small groups, smoking cigarettes in the cold. 'Why are they all out on the streets?' I asked. 'They have nowhere else,' said Galya. 'Ever since Comsomol Youth and the Pioneers were disbanded after the putsch, they roam the streets. They have nowhere to go, and nothing to do, so they take drugs and smoke cigarettes. Drugs have become a huge problem in this town. We are a port, so they're easy to get hold of and all the young are bored. What else are they supposed to do? They can't stay at home – the flats are too small and there are no youth clubs anymore, so they meet and play in the streets, the older children corrupting the younger ones.'

We drove up to the other side of the bay, passing a group of drunken sailors on their way back to base. Andrei took us to the police station, to introduce us to his friends. They would not let us in. They had just detained a man on drugs charges and were questioning him in the cell. 'We can't let foreigners see us in action,' said the officer in charge.

After this mini-tour, we returned home. Galya and Andrei shared their supper with us, while Andrei poured more and more vodka down our throats. Galya was quiet and intelligent. She had shelves of books reaching to the ceiling, Pushkin and Bulgakov were among her favourite writers. Andrei showed us photos of himself in the army, drunken men hugging each other with guns. I could not understand why they were together. Andrei forced Joth to go on a drunken drive through the housing estate with him, while I stayed behind to smoke cigarettes with Galya. She had given up years ago, but viewed such an occasion as special enough to warrant breaking her fast.

She talked about her desire to leave the town. 'I hate it here. It's miserable and depressing. But we can't leave: we're registered here and that makes it final.' She desperately wanted to go to Vladivostok or a larger town, where people lived better. 'The problems here are acute, with crime, drugs and poor services. When Vladivostok was closed, we lived better here: but now the trade goes through there, we've been left behind.'

DAY 87

We awoke unreasonably early and went to work with Galya. Walking through the housing estate, we came to a small low building with bright red railings. Wandering along the diminutive corridors, we arrived at the headmistress's office. She was a gentle-faced woman with a quiet voice, who welcomed us with open arms and showered us in presents. She was desperate to give us a guided tour of the school.

Just outside her office was a small hall enclosed in glass, where the children had planted small trees and flowers. They were also growing tomatoes to feed the school. In the middle of the room, in a large brass cage, six guinea pigs lay fast asleep, snuggled on top of one another. The classrooms were bright and cheery;

the children all stood up as we walked in, and were ordered to greet us in English. They all bounced around in excitement, their hands shooting up into the air as they all pleaded to say their name.

We walked into the gym, where running races were in progress. Next door there was a small swimming pool with frogs and flowers painted all over the walls. Moving on, we were shown a sauna, with a medical centre attached. Lying stretched out on a short bed was a skinny girl in a pair of large grey pants. She was being massaged by the doctor. 'There are so many small, weak children that we have to have a full-time masseuse to help them get their circulation going and build up their strength,' explained the headmistress. 'This little girl has to come every day.' The child cringed with humiliation as we all stood and stared. The screams from the gym echoed down the hall, but she was not allowed to join in.

Andrei came to collect us in his new car and drove us to the edge of town. A barrier marked the end of the town and the beginning of the open road. It was guarded by the police. Andrei went to talk to his friends and one of them showed off his new trainers, dancing up and down on the tarmac. They stopped every car that passed, checking the documents of drivers. Joth and I stood on the side of the road, our bags at our feet. Andrei was arranging for us to have a lift into Nakhodka, as the bus would not leave for another six hours. Eventually, after the police had flagged down every car and asked them to take us, a mini-bus agreed. We waved goodbye, leaving Andrei and Galya standing in the middle of the road, surrounded by police.

The mini-bus dropped us off in Nakhodka and we eventually found a man who would drive us to Vladivostok. Everyone else whom we had spoken to protested that it was too far. We returned along the route by which we had just come, passing the morbid towns with their drains and cables and inner workings on display like large factories.

Finally we arrived in Vladivostok, our last port of call before returning to Moscow. The relief was incredible. Joth and I went out to supper in the restaurant in the hotel. The food, for the first time in the whole journey, was delicious – gently fried fish and noodles that melted in our mouths. We sat and toasted our arrival. We toasted that we would not have to stay any more with people we did not know; that we would not have to drink vodka if we did not want to; that we would not have to be jolly and fun ever again. We got drunk!

DAY 88

There was something of a buzz about Vladivostok. As we walked the streets in the early morning, there was a tangible feeling of agitation, a feeling of new prosperity and of commerce. Russia's window on the East, officially closed to foreigners until 1 January 1992, has remained beautiful in its isolation. Early twentieth-century architecture graces the rolling hills that look out onto the Pacific. The harbour, home of the Russian Pacific Fleet, dominates the city, as do the sailors who, hunting in packs, roam the streets in their long dark coats.

The roads are congested with Japanese cars. Korean and Japanese restaurants do a brisk trade, and the people are better dressed than anywhere else outside Moscow. On every street corner, someone was selling something. As we walked down the road to the harbour, a consignment of bikini briefs from China were causing a stir. Groups of men were elbowing each other out of the way, tearing at the packaging. Rows of young men were standing, holding up marbled jeans from South Korea. Next to them, old women hunched over baskets of home-made spirit.

Walking along the harbour, we met three sailors from the Crimea. Dressed in their black uniforms, they were eating ice creams. All three were professional sailors and, after five years in the navy, were about to become officers. Despite the argument between the Ukraine and Russia over the Black Sea Fleet, none of them intended to join the Ukrainian Fleet. 'They can't afford us,' said Maxim, who was twenty-one, with thick dark hair and dark eyes. 'We get 143 coupons a month to live on. It's pathetic – it's about enough for one bottle of vodka. And the navy wonder why the sailors sell their uniforms or anything else they can lay their hands on.'

Fortunately Dima, who was also twenty-one and married four months ago, had relations in Moscow who sent him roubles, otherwise none of them would have been able to afford the ice creams they were eating. 'All we get are Ukrainian coupons, which you can't spend outside the Ukraine. What are we supposed to do in Vladivostok?' said Dima, crunching the last of his ice cream.

They hoped that they would be able to stay in the Russian navy and all three of them hoped to be posted to St Petersburg.

We walked further along the harbour, passing the huge, grey, steel vessels of the Pacific Fleet, covered in weapons and still flying the Soviet flag. A group of sailors, who were confined to their ship, stuck their heads out from between the white railings and asked for cigarettes. I could not see their whole faces, so I passed through the cigarettes and talked to a pair of blue eyes called Alexei. He was leaving to join the Black Sea Fleet. He had no choice: he had received his call-up papers last week and would join on 1 May. He was furious. 'They're going to pay me 150 coupons a month. What can I do with that? Nothing!' he snorted. While we were talking, his commanding officer stole up behind and, grabbing him by the scruff of the neck, hauled him away from the fence. 'Stop chatting up girls,' he shouted. 'Get away from the barrier all of you! Get back inside.'

We move on to a smaller boat manned by boys on their National Service. They were surrounded by young girls who, hanging over the railings, talked from the edge of the harbour. They invited us aboard and began to show us round the boat. 'We had no choice about going into the navy,' said one boy from Moscow. 'I have a friend who pretended that he was mad to avoid National Service; but now he is officially not allowed to have children because he is certified as insane. So I thought I would do my stint and then I'd be able to start my life.'

One blond boy did not enjoy our illegal trip around the boat and started to shout at his contemporaries. But as soon as he realized that we were foreign, he whipped downstairs and reappeared with an officer's coat, complete with epaulets and medals. He sold it to us for dollars. 'That's how we survive on 90 roubles a month,' said the boy from Moscow.

DAY 89

We were summoned by the visa office. They had heard of our arrival from the hotel, and since Vladivostok had only just opened up to foreigners, they thought it highly irregular that we had just turned up without prior warning or clearance from the authorities. We had no visa for the town, but we were not going to admit it. Joth and I had more or less developed a routine for dealing with people who stamp and write out documents: big smiles, a few lies, never hand over the passport and keep talking.

We were highly nervous when we arrived at the office: we had avoided the summons the day before by pretending not to understand the woman shouting at us from the hotel reception. But the patter worked a treat and they ended up fighting over who would stamp our papers.

We wandered once more around the city and ended up talking to Sasha, a young, thin man who was selling ginseng capsules and powder from deer's antlers. 'The mafia basically run this town,' he said. 'They deal in cars, champagne, drugs and weapons. It's no coincidence that, a couple of weeks ago, something like 5,000 kalashnikovs were stolen from a warehouse out of the city and next week, 100,000 bottles of Georgian champagne are coming to the city. Where's the civil war and who has the best champagne? It's logical: weapons for champagne. They divide up the cars themselves, each group taking a shipment. It is too late for anyone else to get in on the act because they should have been doing it about two years ago. No one could bring champagne to Vladivostok now except the mafia, because they just wouldn't have the contacts, the supplies or the transport system.'

He explained that the city was divided up into families, who did not seem to be getting on very well at the moment. Vakhov, one of the leaders of a big family, had been decapitated – his head had been found in a train station in Moscow. 'They haven't found the body,' he said, flicking some dust off his coat. 'Another, Koval, was gunned down in the street last week and is currently in intensive care.'

'This is a strange town,' said Sasha, as he rearranged his ginseng, which he was selling for 200 roubles a packet. 'The town is empty at the weekends because everyone goes to cultivate their allotments in order to feed themselves. The only people who are here during the weekend are from the countryside – they come to buy bread in Vladivostok because it's not rationed. There is a 400-gram limit everywhere else. Sugar and vodka are, of course, but bread isn't. But things like butter are very expensive. That's 300 roubles a kilo.

'Haven't you noticed that there are no men in this town?' He asked. I had not. 'There are 30,000 more women than men here, because all the men go to sea, earn hard currency, become rich and leave for Moscow or St Petersburg. That's also why there are so many foreign cars here – there are a lot of rich people. The city is divided in half: those who earn hard currency and those who don't.'

We returned to the hotel to feast in the same restaurant that we had done the night before. Waking early, we made the ten-hour flight, crossing seven time zones, to Moscow. As I sat on the plane, I contemplated the strangeness of flying ten hours and landing in the same country.

MOSCOW

Kolya and Peter collected us from the airport in our own private bus that they had acquired from Intourist. I collapsed on arrival. Somehow it felt like it was almost over. Kolya took us home, fed us and made us drunk. It was wonderful to see him. We could now relax. I don't think he quite knew how much we wanted him to look after us, but he rose to the occasion, making our beds up and washing our clothes.

Moscow had changed dramatically since we had been away. I had a strange feeling of fear and inadequacy as I walked through the streets. They had been almost deserted when we left, but the whole place had since metamorphosed into one, throbbing market. The whole of the centre of Moscow was a flea market. Rows and rows of people stood next to each other, their arms outstretched, tempting you with their wares. There was no room to set up a stall, so they stood with one item in their hand – a tea cup, a pair of knickers, a spoon, a packet of cigarettes. It was a strange sight as the swarms of people threaded their way around the KGB building, the Lybianka and poured into Derzinsky Square, its statue-less column a reminder of the events the previous August.

Running between the sellers was a single-file queue of buyers. Once in the queue, it was impossible to escape. Hemmed in on both sides, I was forced by the crowd pushing behind me to move forward. I could not stop and buy anything without incurring the wrath of those behind.

At the end of January, Yeltsin had authorized trade in the streets, and this was the result. People who had no money queued in the state shops at dawn, buying two sausages instead of one. They would then sell the extra in the street that afternoon to those who could afford not to wake up. Others raided their freezers or houses, selling everything they could – huge slabs of meat that had been in store for months were now on sale in the street. Old women were selling their tea-sets that had been in the family for generations. There were reports of outbreaks of salmonella all over Moscow. The city was desperate for money and was selling anything.

Sasha understood the concept of the new commercialism. He had given up his job as a chemical engineer two weeks ago to sell beer on the street. He lived half an hour outside Moscow and came in every morning on the train with cases of beer. He bought them for 10 roubles a bottle in his home town and sold them for 15 roubles on the pavement. He was doing a brisk trade. 'I make much more money this way than I did before,' he said with a smile. 'And I don't work as hard.'

The woman next to him was selling jackets that she had bought on a trip to China. She was selling them for 3,000 roubles each so that she could finance another journey to China to buy more. She was also selling a few pots of coffee. 'I wouldn't buy that,' she whispered as I picked it up. 'I've had it in my cupboard for two years: it's probably stale.'

The first sex shop had opened up since we had been away. Down a side street in the ground floor of some apartments, it was hard to find. I had to ignore the sniggers of every commercial shop storekeeper as I asked directions.

When we arrived, there was a queue of men outside. Their heads down, they were all waiting to get inside the main shop. In the hall, there was a counter with two young women dressed in white coats selling sexual gadgetry. Kolya and Joth joined the queue of men; I went up to the counter.

'Can I have a clitoral stimulator please?' I asked the girl, biting my cheeks to stop myself from laughing.

'Certainly,' she smiled. 'What size is your husband's penis?'

'Oh,' I said. 'The smallest one you have.'

She looked at me with a puzzled expression. 'The smallest?'

'Yes, yes the smallest,' I replied. I could not keep a straight face any longer. I started to laugh and she, too, cracked up. With tears rolling down her face, she cut a small pink rubbery thing from a strip of stimulators. They came from a state-run factory.

We paid our 20 roubles and filed in with the rest of the queue into the shop. It was remarkably bare, with only a shelf of various vibrators, a shelf of porn mags, and one large inflatable woman in an armchair in the middle of the room. Kolya laughed so much at the plastic woman lying there, her legs apart and her mouth wide open, that he was asked to leave.

A middle-aged woman in a white coat ran the shop. Dr Tatyana Agassova was chief of the Department of Sexology. She gave me her card. The shop had opened a month ago, sponsored by the state and one private sponsor. 'There are many couples who have sexual problems and we hope that this shop will be part of their marriage counselling.' She did not find our juvenile behaviour amusing. She gave me a tour of the vibrators, talking me through their advantages, switching them on and off, and added that upstairs there was an adult education department for sexual therapy. She was worried that so many man came into the shop to snigger and gape at the equipment, and so few women ever bothered to turn up.

Anka and I spent two days at the striptease school that had just opened in Moscow. The first was spent watching the beginners; the second surveying the professionals.

The school was in a small community centre just out of the centre of Moscow. It had been set up two years ago, but had been illegal; now it was official. The first class we saw had little to differentiate it from an aerobics class, except the girls wore high heels instead of trainers. The plump, heavily made-up girls in their vests and pants were being taught how to move by an ex-choreographer from the Bolshoi. He made them snake their way to the front of the stage and thrust their hips from side to side. Most of the girls were overweight and lacked co-ordination. They had just started the two-month course. For a fee of 1,200 roubles, they had three classes a week for two hours – one hour of striptease and the other of movement.

Sergei, the skinny instructor, stamped on the floor in frustration as one girl, who looked more like a librarian than a stripper, messed up the routine for the fifth time. 'Look and feel sexy,' he shouted. 'You're supposed to turn people on, not make them feel sick.' One blonde was rather good. She strutted around in her pink heels, her pants shoved up her bottom, thrusting her crotch towards the audience. 'Better, better,' said Sergei, clapping in delight. Her friend in the class tried to follow her example but her stiletto slipped on the stage and she lost her balance. Distraught with frustration, Sergei shouted, 'You do all realize that you'll have to pass an exam at the end of the month to see if any of you are good enough to carry on. You'll have to lose weight and tone up, otherwise you're all out.' With that, he stormed off.

The next day we returned to see the last students to graduate and were greeted by the woman who owned the school. Ala had long, dyed, black hair, turquoise eyelids, dark red lips, and a bosom that was trussed up in the air like two small apples. She had a minute waist and a long black skirt to the floor. She looked like a French *Madame*. Either side of her, were two, large, dark-haired brothers. 'They look after the financial side of the business,' she said.

We told her that we had seen the beginners' class the day before. 'Not those girls,' she snorted. 'They have to lose ten kilos each and if their tits don't sag afterwards, then they may become strippers. Now, the girls that you are about to see – they are really good. Some of them might make it abroad, which is, of course, what they all want to do.'

She wafted into the next-door room and ushered out a group of girls all dressed in elaborate but extremely revealing costumes, which had been provided by the school. The first to dance was Sveta. With long, blonde hair and a taut body, she was dressed in a red G-string and red transparent shirt. She began to take her clothes off. It was a surreal sight; the mirrored ballet studio of the community hall, the daylight pouring through the window and the music playing on a small tape recorder in the corner. Bored by the whole display, the two brothers did not even watch.

Ala sidled up to me. 'Sveta is one of the best we have,' she said. 'She came third in the striptease championships last month.' Sveta danced with herself in the mirror, throwing her head back and grinding her pelvis. As soon as the tape finished she stopped and picked up her shirt. Getting dressed, she went to the back of the hall to chat to her friend and smoke cigarettes.

Natasha was next onto the floor. She had long dark hair to the waist and a pretty face. She stripped off to her pants and danced in her high shoes. 'Natasha has a problem,' whispered Ala. 'You must be a bit of a prostitute to do this job and she won't fuck people after her performances. I think that she has a psychological problem. She only enjoys taking her clothes off and showing off her body: she won't have sex.'

Most of the girls work in clubs and the hard-currency, mafia-run restaurants in Moscow in the evening. They also work the Ismailova Hotel on the outskirts of Moscow. I went into the room and talked to them while they changed into their normal clothes. They were aged between eighteen and twenty-two and had all given up jobs to become strippers. 'It's the money, you see,' said Sveta, as she pulled on an expensive pair of boots. I looked around and noticed that they all had the same boots. '3,000 roubles a pair,' said Ana, watching me looking at them. The girls earn anything between $150 a night, when they work in the hard currency bars, or around 6,500 roubles a month when they work the hotels. They work two shifts: 7 to 10 p.m. and 3 to 5 a.m. They are collected from wherever they are working and are driven home by the two brothers. 'Why did you learn striptease?' I asked Natasha. 'So that I can leave this horrible place and go and work somewhere like Germany. That's what we all want to do, go and work in Berlin.'

We spent days in Moscow trying to get in touch with the mafia. We made numerous telephone calls and arranged numerous meetings. We arranged to meet some of the Arbat Mafia, the team that runs the famous commercial street and artistic area in the heart of Moscow, in the banya. They were going to gather the group together, but for some reason they dropped out at the last minute.

We finally agreed to meet with Alexei, a young man who dealt with the mafia but who was not part of it. We arrived at his apartment in the outskirts of Moscow. He had a steel front door set in a steel frame. 'That's for protection,' he said, as he saw my surprise. His flat was beautifully decorated with new furniture. He had a microwave, stereo and cupboards crammed with hard-currency convenience food. He ran an import-export business, dealing with computers. His dealings with the mafia came about when he opened up two shops to launder the money that he was earning because the bank would no longer give him access to his cash. 'I had the money in the bank, but there weren't enough notes in the bank to give them to me,' he explained as he poured us a glass of whisky.

He paid the mafia protection money so that neither they nor a different group would attack his shops. 'I'm protected from them and if any group comes to give me problems, I call on my own mafia to sort the others out.' The money he pays increases with the profitability of the shops. 'They're not stupid. They don't want me to go bust. That's not in their interest. So the amount you pay is carefully worked out.'

He traced the history of the mafia back to Lenin's New Economic Policy in the 1920s. He explained that heads of ministries always had the KGB to look after them and that the mafia had been a result of the pilferings of the second in command. 'If you are a head of a ministry, for example the coal ministry, you can take as much coal as you want, sell it for hard currency and put the money in your Swiss bank account. But if you are number two, you also want to make extra money.' He illustrated the whole process using T-shirts. 'You make the man at the T-shirt factory make twenty extra T-shirts above his quota; you get the woman behind the counter in the state shop to sell the extra and to give you the money. The problem occurs when you need to keep them all quiet. That's where the mafia comes in. All ex-criminals, they kept the others quiet. And so it began. It is, of course, much more sophisticated now.'

The whole process only worked, said Alexei, as long as the populace remained ignorant, carried on doing their boring job for a low wage and knew nothing of the outside world. 'So you see, the Cold War was necessary to keep the people stupid, while the clever ones creamed off the country's resources, getting rich and living well.' He said that the stories of special shops for Party members were a myth propagated by the members themselves. 'They didn't pay for these luxury goods, they just took them. They told their secretaries that they had bought them Belgian chocolates for Christmas, but it was only to make them feel better.'

The modern mafia, he said, permeated every layer of society. 'People say even Andrei Voykov, chief administrator for law in Yeltsin's government, is involved with the mafia.' He explained that the areas of Moscow were divided up between the groups, and each group deals with the shops, prostitutes, cars sold and bars in their area. 'There are some who deal with drugs, but I know that the Arbat don't.'

Alexei was one of the new rich. He employed a personal bodyguard and chauffeur and his flat exuded a wealth that I had never previously seen. His driver drove us home in the early hours of the morning. Alexei paid him $35 a month. He was twenty years Alexei's senior.

*   *   *

Early one morning, Anka took us to the hospital where she had given birth to her son, Koka. She had gone to hospital number 28, on the other side of Moscow, because she was friendly with a doctor there and could pay money to ensure that she would have anaesthetic during labour if she needed it. Her doctor friend was leaving for Israel the next day but he organized that we should be allowed into the hospital.

Vladimir Shanin had a long beard and moustache that flowed down his face and hid his mouth completely from view. He was the head doctor of the hospital. He explained the situation in the hospitals in Moscow had reached crisis point. They were desperately short of drugs – they used replacement drugs in some cases, but they rarely worked. 'We have much less than a year ago,' he said, shaking his head. 'We have more money but it buys less. We do have food but it's of very poor quality.' He said that the new price rises had seriously affected the old. 'There are people officially dying of hunger in Moscow. Many of the hospitals are full of old people who are starving. If they live with their family, then they are usually all right, it's the old who live alone who can't afford to feed themselves – they're the ones who are dying or knocking on the hospital doors.'

He said that maternity hospitals all over Moscow were closing down because women were not having babies. 'The intelligent women are not giving birth because they know that they can't afford to look after the children. The average is one child, maximum two. The remainder of the pregnancies, we abort.'

Hospital number 28 performs between 12,000 and 15,000 abortions a year. It costs 300 roubles to have the operation done privately. 'Although,' said Vladimir, 'it doesn't make that much difference. Maybe you'll be out in a day, but it does mean that, if there is anaesthetic, then you'll receive it if you pay.' He explained the main reason behind so many unwanted pregnancies was not only the lack of contraception, but also lack of education. 'Few women understand their bodies and few understand how to use contraceptives,' he sighed. 'We get so many young kids in here who have no idea what's happening to them.'

As we walked around the hospital, the head doctor explained that it would cost 5,000 roubles for a normal delivery and 7,000 for a caesarean. He introduced us to the sister and returned to his office. We walked into one room where four women were lying on small beds with a stained glass window separating them from another room. I asked the sister to remain outside. Olga was twenty-one and expecting her first baby. Her pregnancy was a mistake but she said that she was too frightened to have an abortion. 'They don't use anaesthetic and they make you sterile,' she said. Lena already had three children and did not want a fourth. 'My husband will not let me have an abortion. God knows how we'll be able to look after this one,' she said, pushing her thin, red hair behind her ears. Tamara was forty and three months' pregnant. She would stay in the hospital throughout her pregnancy because the doctors thought that she was too old to be having children. All the women agreed that if there was any possibility of complications, then they would pay immediately. 'You can try and have the baby free, but then if anything goes wrong, no one will help unless you bribe them. That's what is known as free health care.'

None of the women were given any fruit or vegetables at the hospital. They relied on their husbands and families to bring them what they needed. The hospital could not afford to feed them.

We went into another room. This time the sister followed us in. Sitting on the bed was a young girl covered in heavy make-up. She was about to leave hospital with her five-day-old son. She had given birth under anaesthetic. 'Did you pay for that?' I asked. There was a pause, she looked up at the sister standing next to her. 'Say no.' said the sister. 'You didn't pay, did you?' The girl looked at me and then at the floor. 'No, I didn't pay,' she mumbled. 'There, you see,' said the sister. 'We have free drugs here.'

Walking downstairs to the delivery room, Anka began to shake. 'I remember all this so well,' she said, grabbing hold of my arm. The delivery room was small with two short beds; metal syringes lay in bowls of water, waiting to be used again. The equipment looked out of date. 'Oh look,' whispered Anka. 'I lay on that bed. That's where I had Koka. He was so small. I can remember when I first heard his scream. I don't think that I can stay here much longer. Can we leave?'

On our last night in Moscow we went to the Bolshoi. Settling down in the beautiful golden theatre, we watched *Swan Lake*. The music was wonderful, the sets incredible but the dancing itself, disappointing. I had seen the Bolshoi before and had been carried away by the lightness and precision of the dancers, yet this time there was something missing. The corps de ballet was as unified as ever, but the principal dancers did not fly as they had done before: they lacked emotion.

After the performance we went backstage to meet a dancer, who had bought us the tickets for that night's performance. She refused to let me use her name. She was frail and beautiful and whispered in the wings at the back of the stage. 'We read about *perestroika* and *glasnost* in the newspapers but there is still Communism in the Bolshoi. It's a law unto itself.' She denied that there were any huge financial problems in the theatre. 'Well, no more than the rest of the country. Of course, we can't afford things.' She said the decline in standards was due to the two directors. 'The two directors can't make a decision about what day it is. One will not decide without the other. They also employ their friends and relations, placing them in the principal roles. Did you not notice how many Nikonovs there were on the programme? They're all related to Nikonov, the director.'

She said that many of the best dancers were leaving the company because they still could not dance the modern ballets that they wanted. She added that other dancers had to dance in different theatres, like the Tchaikovsky Concert Hall, to perform the roles that they were not allowed to do at the Bolshoi. 'There's no art, no culture left at the Bolshoi,' she whispered. Someone walked past and she rushed back into her changing room. 'I really can't talk any more, it's far too dangerous. I'll never dance again if they find out I told you this. Things have not changed at all here.'

On the morning of our departure there was a fight outside the shop opposite Kolya's apartment. People had been quietly queuing for vodka all morning. There was a crowd of about fifty standing around the small vodka stall, waiting for it to open. Suddenly there was shouting and elbowing at the front of the queue as a large man in a leather jacket barged to the front. This soon developed into a brawl and one man fell to the ground while three men repeatedly kicked him in the head, stomach and kidneys. The police arrived and grabbed one man from the crowd. Kicking and hitting him on the head, they threw him into the back of the van, locking the metal grill behind him. The rest of the crowd watched, shouting and arguing among themselves. 'That's the petty vodka mafia, arguing over the patch,' said Kolya, as he stood with forehead pressed against the window.

On the way to the airport, we stopped off at the Irish House hard-currency shop.

We were going to buy Anka a birthday present. I stood at the toiletries counter, looking at the beautifully packaged soaps and creams, trying to work out what she would like. Priced in dollars, they were beyond the reach of almost everyone we had met on our trip. The choice was large – four brand names.

Three American students were standing next to me. 'Has anyone ever heard of Palmolive shampoo?' shouted a girl in a nasal drawl. 'I can't possibly wash my hair with Palmolive shampoo. It doesn't even sound like shampoo. Don't they make hand cream? I can't *believe* they don't have anything else. I just can't wash my hair with that.'

I was suddenly angry. 'Then just bloody well wash it without,' I snapped.

Epilogue
. . . .

It is hard to sum up an experience that has so profoundly affected you, as this journey affected me. There was something tragic about the people I encountered, and yet at the same time something proud and strong. They have survived extreme adversity and come out the other side with their souls intact. The whole society is permeated by a fatalist philosophy — what is meant to happen, will — backed up by vodka and a fundamental belief that man is essentially good. It was this belief that allowed us into the homes and lives of the people we met. No questions were necessary.

As I left Kiev, I remember Iliya saying: 'You'll come back. I know you will. This country has your soul. It takes it away without you realizing and then you have to come back.'

I think he was right.